MARVIN D. DUNNETTE
University of Minnesota

WAYNE K. KIRCHNER
Minnesota Mining &
Manufacturing Company

Psychology Applied
to Industry

New York

APPLETON-CENTURY-CROFTS
Division of Meredith Publishing Company

To the ladies in our lives:

Jean, Bonnie,

Nancy, Peggy, and Sheri

PREFACE

This book might best be viewed as a collection of brief essays about the present accomplishments of psychologists in industry. As such, the book is short. It is simply an overview; some might even claim that it is not much more than an outline. If so, we hope, at least, that it is a *good* outline of what industrial psychologists are up to, for we have tried above all to capture and to describe the excitement and exhilaration provided by opportunities to study and to solve problems of human behavior in the *real world* of industry. We may be entirely foolhardy, but we are even so presumptuous as to hope that this short volume might serve as a recruiting manual to stimulate the interest and enthusiasm of beginning psychology students and to "seduce" the brighter and more pragmatic ones into this field which is growing more rapidly, probably, than any other in psychology. Our purpose may be overly ambitious, but it does, at least, help to define our intended audience and to explain some of the reasons for things the book does or does not include. First, since the book is directed toward the beginning student, it should serve well as a supplementary text in general psychology courses. This is what we wrote it for, and we hope it is utilized in this way. Second, it should find use as a text in undergraduate courses offered to nonpsychology majors—engineers, business students, teachers, etc.—who can profit from knowing something about psychology applied to industry because they will likely be running into industrial psychologists at one time or another in their subsequent careers. We do not envision the book as a primary text for advanced students in Industrial Psychology. It is probably too sketchy and has too many gaps for this. However, if it is viewed strictly as an outline, a good instructor might still use it for such courses by assigning and discussing the suggested additional readings at the end of each chapter.

What are some of the features we feel proud of and where are some of the gaps? First, we believe we've covered a good deal of ground in a rather short space. Diversity and breadth is emphasized, probably at some expense to the depth of coverage. We would plead guilty to the charge of clothing Industrial Psychology rather scantily, but we hope, at least, that the raiment we have chosen fits the wearer well and that it does not unduly change his appearance.

Second, we have tried to avoid technical terminology and detail. Statistics are almost nonexistent. Certainly no prior knowledge of statistics is presumed. At various points, however, simple statistical methods are "slipped in the back door," presented in the context of their usefulness for coping with particular problems rather than as ends in themselves. Thus, statistical inference is not mentioned except in passing, but cross-validation and its importance is given heavy emphasis in our discussion of Selection. Sampling methods and simple scaling techniques are described in the Survey Research chapter. And a simple Analysis of Variance problem is given in the context of discussing errors and their allocation in the chapter on Engineering Psychology. After completing the book, the student should appreciate the usefulness of statistics for solving problems. We will guarantee that he will *not* feel burdened with much knowledge of statistical *techniques*. In fact, most students will very nearly escape without knowing what a correlation coefficient is, although, if eager, they will find it dealt with briefly in Chapter 2.

Third, and most important, we have tried to present an accurate and current picture of the achievements of psychologists in industry, their methods of approaching and solving problems, and some of the major unanswered research questions. In each chapter the reader will find a discussion of current practices and basic principles followed by a rather detailed account of at least one study chosen to illustrate the practices and principles discussed previously. Industrial Psychology is presented, therefore, as a framework of problems, principles, and methodology rather than as a lengthy listing of studies. This explains, but cannot necessarily exonerate us from, our decision to exclude rather large numbers of the studies reported in the research literature.

We hope this book serves the purposes we intend for it. The demands for industrial psychologists are great and growing, and if we can stimulate just a few additional students to look toward industry as the site for applying their psychology, we will feel well rewarded.

M. D. D.
W. K. K.

CONTENTS

1

INTRODUCTION AND OVERVIEW

INDUSTRY: A PLACE TO STUDY HUMAN BEHAVIOR

We shall define *industry* as comprising all organizations established to create goods and services. Such institutions as government agencies, hospitals and clinics, educational institutions, hotels, theaters, and research institutes as well as manufacturing organizations, advertising agencies, banks, and insurance companies all fall within this definition. Adopting this broad point of view makes apparent the vast theater of human behavior which is available for systematic observation and study in industry. Psychology, as one of the major sciences dealing with human behavior, is well equipped to make observations and to conduct studies on the problems and issues arising out of human behavior in industry. Opportunities for human behavior research in industry have not gone unheeded by psychologists. Over the last forty years the application of psychological methods, principles, and resulting personnel techniques has become widespread in the industrial setting. If present demands by industry for the methods and services of psychologists are indicative of the future, we may expect an impressive burgeoning of applications of psychology in industry in the years ahead.

With this in mind, let us take a brief look at the science of psychology.

1

PSYCHOLOGY: THE SCIENCE
OF HUMAN BEHAVIOR

Psychology is usually defined as the science of human and animal behavior. For our purposes we may exclude animal behavior from the definition. Industry is not particularly concerned about animal behavior, and it would be an extremely uncommon event for any industrial psychologist to be asked to give attention to the behavior of animals. This is not to say that principles derived from the study of animals may not be useful in industry. In fact, they have been, and we note later some of the interesting instances of such applications in industrial settings.

Thus we are left with the disarmingly simple statement that psychology (in industry) is the *science of human behavior.* Simple as it seems, this definition contains elements deserving of careful thought. The important words are *science* and *behavior.* Since psychology is a science and since it deals with behavior, we gain immediate implications concerning its stance, its methods, and its subject matter. As a science psychology seeks to discover or to develop explanatory concepts. Explanation demands the identification, description, and observation of variables. The observation should be of a special sort. At the very least it needs to be planned and systematic; ideally, it should be experimental, that is, certain variables should be controlled (either actually or by statistical techniques) while others are systematically varied and their effects studied. Most important perhaps, the observations and experiments of science are specified or spelled out ahead of time. Observations of science are subject to confirmation or invalidation by any other scientist who wishes to repeat any particular observation. Opinions, whims, argumentation, pet notions, or theories do *not,* therefore, constitute an appropriate source for scientific conclusions. Facts, developed by specified observational and experimental procedures, *do* constitute the appropriate basis for scientific conclusions. The prime contribution that psychology can make in industry is to introduce the scientific method as *the* basis for deriving decisions involving and bearing on human behavior. In fact, Skinner (1953) has suggested that science (and therefore, psychology) consists of a set of attitudes which direct us to accept facts even though they may run counter to our expectations, hopes, or desires. Psychology does not work in the realm of wishful thinking about human behavior; instead, it works with facts and with *all* the facts. Some years ago, a psychologist, working in industry, developed a promising new diagnostic test for potential use in the selection of employees. Performing further research, he discovered, to his consternation, that responses on the test could not be depended upon to be consistent nor even honest self-appraisals of examinees. To his credit, he immediately published these facts against his test and refused to sell further copies of it. Such is the stance of intellectual integrity demanded of a person who would call himself a scientist or a psychologist.

HUMAN BEHAVIOR RANGES FAR AND WIDE

As suggested, the subject matter of psychology in industry is human behavior. Behavior refers, simply, to what a person or persons may be doing. Psychologists study behavior in all its forms—ranging from the very simple to the extremely complex, from the involuntary blinking of an eyelid to the intricate configuration of actions and reactions which may be demonstrated by a team of astronauts charged with controlling and directing a mooncraft. The range of human behaviors studied by psychologists in industry is fully as great as that studied by other psychologists. For example, human factors psychologists are intent on assuring that the design of equipment takes account of the special abilities or limitations of the human beings who may be assigned to operate it. A human factors specialist is, therefore, concerned with human sensory and motor behavior, and his research will often involve the study of seemingly simple forms of human behavior such as sensory discrimination and motor response characteristics. At the other end of the continuum, the industrial social psychologist or the organizational psychologist is intent on learning about human behavior as it is evidenced in group situations. Such specialists are concerned with the total behavior of groups and organizations and with the interactions between individuals as they affect the total group or organizational effort. Between these two extremes the differential psychologist is most concerned with the behavior of individuals in an effort to predict their behavior in different industrial circumstances. To be sure, these different levels of complexity never occur alone; the psychologist working in industry must be broadly trained and able to cope with the entire range of human behavior whether it be simple or complex. He must avoid tendencies toward provincialism in his enthusiasm for his specialty. The human factors specialist, intent as he is on designing equipment for *all* human beings, must be careful not to ignore differences among humans which may dictate significant design modifications in certain equipment. The differential psychologist, intent as he is on relating individual abilities to different forms of industrial behavior, must nevertheless remain constantly aware of the important potential influence of social factors—human interactions and group and organizational characteristics—on the nature and magnitude of the relationships he is studying.

STANDARDS OF SCIENCE MUST BE APPLIED TO PSYCHOLOGY IN INDUSTRY

Our discussion of psychology as a science of human behavior makes apparent our orientation as we consider *applications* of psychology in industry. It is unfortunately true that current psychological practice in industry is far from uniform, and in a distressingly large number of instances, it has departed rather far from the standards set by scientific rules of evidence. Some observations have been poorly planned and inappropriately conducted; occasionally, experiments have lacked proper controls thereby resulting in conclusions which may not flow necessarily from the data presented; studies have been conducted which do not meet the necessary standards of replicability, and occasionally, it has seemed that certain individuals have been more intent on proving a pet theory than on developing valid explanatory concepts. It can be argued that the lack of uniformity and the varying degrees of excellence merely reflect the growing pains that may be expected as a science moves from the laboratory into the real world. The standards of science must not, however, be forgotten or mislaid. In this small volume we have attempted to examine examples of psychology applied to industry from the scientist's point of view. We hope the reader will thereby gain an awareness not only of applications but also of misapplications of psychology in industry. Such awareness, if it becomes widespread, should insure in the years ahead that standards of scientific excellence will come to be more broadly and more uniformly applied to the practice of psychology in industry, with a resulting decline in the number of bad examples that may be cited.

PSYCHOLOGY APPLIED TO INDUSTRY IS DIFFICULT BUT EXCITING

It is to be hoped that such standards of excellence may prevail, for industry does afford a magnificent opportunity for studying human behavior. Gainfully employed men and women spend nearly half their waking hours in the world of work; the nonemployed members of our society have an obvious stake too in what goes on in industry. Thus, industry, as a setting in which to study behavior, is exciting simply because behavior there has such great relevance to the continued well-being of our society. A psychologist working on industrial behavior is concerned most broadly with creating optimum circumstances for the utilization of human resources in industry. He is concerned with enormously complex problems of human productivity and work performance, of human learning and the acquisition of skills, of human motivation and the effects of various incentives and environmental circumstances on the utilization of human capabilities, of physical safety and of mental health, and of the interaction between industry's needs or goals and individual employees' needs for the full development and actualization of their personalities. These are exciting problems; they also are eminently practical problems. The student who is pragmatic, who values opportunities to see the day-to-day results of his efforts, but who also seeks and enjoys studying complex problems involving human beings will be deeply gratified by the study of psychology applied to industry.

AN OUTLINE FOR THE STUDY OF HUMAN BEHAVIOR IN INDUSTRY

We have said that a major aim of psychology in industry is to introduce the scientific method as the basis for decisions involving human behavior or the utilization of human resources. Let us consider the various kinds of decisions which involve different aspects of human behavior. The following outline summarizes areas of decision and the corresponding psychological research activities implied by each of them:

I. Decisions based on institutional requirements.

Such decisions assume that certain aspects of industry or of the organization are constant. The problem becomes one of selecting people whose job behaviors conform to the requirements of the institution.

A. Personnel selection.

A careful study of job requirements will suggest the necessary human qualities for performing a job successfully. Scientific selection demands that these inferences be tested empirically by showing that the assessment methods developed for measuring the appropriate human qualities actually are related to successful job performance. The typical industrial firm has many jobs of various types to be filled and must assess the characteristics of applicants in an effort to assign them to the jobs so as to maximize the total organizational efficiency. Decisions bearing on such assignments are the ones involved in any program of personnel selection.

B. Personnel training and development.

A second method of assuring efficient performance on a job is to teach or to train employees in the skills or knowledges required by the job. The psychologist's role in training includes determining what things need to be learned, setting up procedures for teaching employees, and, most important, designing and carrying out experiments to determine whether or not the training programs have achieved their desired aims. The areas of personnel selection and personnel training are inextricably intertwined. Persons must be selected who are capable of being trained, and the design of training programs must take into account the individual qualities of the persons to be trained. In some instances the psychologist will need to develop several training procedures in order to take into account the varying levels of ability, experience, and present knowledge of the individuals who are to be trained.

C. Personnel counseling.

The counseling relationship affords the most individualized and most intimate learning situation in industry. Institutional requirements may occasionally come into conflict with an individual's capabilities and aspirations. In such instances personal guidance from a psychologist may be helpful. Such counseling may simply take the form of determining discrepancies between an individual's qualities and the demands of his job in which case placement on a more appropriate job or a learning program to help the individual develop new skills, attitudes, or knowledges (to fit the demands of his job) would be the usual outcome. Or, counseling may go deeper into situations or personal problems which affect the individual's total life experience. It is difficult to assess how far a firm should go in bearing responsibility for the personal and emotional well-being of its employees. The area of personnel counseling in industry is in sad need of careful research. Unfortunately, nearly none is being performed.

II. Decisions based on or modified by individual characteristics. The assumption here is that institutional requirements or characteristics may need to be modified because of the so-called human element, that is, the special characteristics, capabilities, and limitations of human beings. One possible implication of such an assumption is that individual differences among humans may be relatively unimportant. Such an inference would seriously weaken the net effectiveness of psychological research in industry, and it should be strenuously avoided. Thus, research questions become far more complex than is the case if individual differences are ignored. Instead of asking how industry must be modified to take account of the abilities of *man,* we must ask in how many ways must industry be modified in order to take account of the varying capabilities (and modifiabilities) of *men.*

A. Engineering psychology.

World War II witnessed the emergence of teamwork between engineers and psychologists necessitated by several instances in which it was obvious that equipment had been designed and produced without giving sufficient attention to limitations of the human being who would be required to operate it. Many accidents and near accidents in aircraft were traced directly to inadequacies in equipment design characteristics (Fitts & Jones, 1947; Fitts & Jones, 1961). Broadly speaking, the engineering psychologist studies the characteristics of human operators in order to learn how equipment should be designed or how a complex production system consisting of men, materials, and machines should be put together so as to insure optimum efficiency of operation. The purpose, then, is to learn how the mechanical components of an industrial system need to be arranged or modified in order to utilize most efficiently the capabilities of the human elements of the system.

B. Human motivation.

Among the most important of the decisions made in industry are those involving human motivation. Even when care has been used in the selection, training, and placement of employees, there is no assurance that they will show the intensity of effort in the industrial setting of which they may be capable and which they do demonstrate in other settings (e.g., in pursuing their hobbies and leisure time activities). There is no shortage of theories concerning human motivation in industry; there is an unfortunate shortage of experimental evidence bearing on it. The task for industrial psychologists is to discover the kinds of conditions within the industrial milieu which do result in high employee motivation. Again, individual differences must not be ignored; different persons probably are differentially motivated by different circumstances. It is up to the psychologist in industry to discover principles of human motivation which may form the basis for recommendations concerning modifications necessary for maximizing employee motivation.

C. Organizational psychology.

Only within the last decade has widespread attention been given to the possible effects on human efficiency of different organizational structures. In the early 1950's, Sears Roebuck and Co. moved from a vertical organization with many levels of management to a flat or horizontal structure. This resulted in greater responsibility and autonomy for persons at lower levels in the firm; authority was decentralized and decision making became diffused among many persons throughout the organization. It was argued that this change was made because the new structure gave employees a greater sense of importance and more opportunties for self-fulfillment than the old structure. It is not certain that this contention can be sustained, but the Sears reorganization is an important illustration of the impact of organizational psychology. This is the broadest and most complex area of psychology applied to industry. The organizational psychologist is intent on developing a better understanding of total organizations and the human interactions which comprise them. His discipline represents a merging of differential, experimental, and social psychology and is, perhaps, the most concerted effort so far undertaken in the effort to understand human behavior in industry.

III. Decisions based on group perceptions and group influences. Many industrial decisions grow out of the need to evaluate and act upon the opinions or perceptions of groups. Often this may require the resolution of group conflict. The desire to belong seems to be an elemental human characteristic; humans of like interests and needs form groups, and when they do, their goals become defined and intensified. Every employee in industry belongs to many groups ranging from his own work group to his union or professional society and to religious, political, or community groups outside the premises of his firm. Decisions in industry often require information about the attitudes and desires of such groups. The psychologist can help to gain such information.

A. Industrial communications and union-management relations.

Industrial activity—the creation of goods and services—cannot proceed without communication between people and between groups. One of the major barriers to accuracy in communication is engendered by the differing perceptions people have. A sincere request by a manager for help on a difficult assignment might be viewed by an insecure employee as a deliberate effort to show him up. A more secure and confident employee might more accurately view such a request as an opportunity to show his true merit. Accuracy in communications implies not only the faithful transmission of the mechanical components of a message but also the faithful transmisison of the purposes and meanings intended by the sender. The wisdom of personnel decisions in industry depends, therefore, on the fidelity of processes for gathering information relevant to the decisions. In turn, the implementation of decisions demands accurate transmission to persons and groups in the organization. Psychological research on communications is directed at identifying and eliminating the important barriers to accurate communication in industry with the desirable result that the frequency of individual and group conflicts based on misunderstanding will be significantly decreased. One of the major sources of potential group conflict in industry comes from the differing perceptions and goals of labor and management. Both groups would probably agree that their broad goal is to insure the efficient and humane utilization of human resources, but they often differ on the definitions and relative emphases to be placed on such terms as "efficient," "humane," and "utilization." They most certainly encounter differences in defining the employment conditions which may lead to such a goal. Katzell identifies a number of psychological issues generated by the potential conflict between union and management, "including the degree to which their identification with the union may either facilitate or interfere with employees' loyalty to their employer, the circumstances contributing to union-management conflict or cooperation, the factors leading to employees' satisfaction or dissatisfaction with their union, and the characteristics of successful and unsuccessful negotiating sessions between labor and management representatives" (Katzell, 1961, p. 198). Psychologists have thus far performed only a limited amount of research in the area of union-management relations, but it does represent an extremely important and rich field for future psychological research in industry.

B. Consumer psychology and survey research.

The consuming public obviously constitutes an important group for industrial decision making. The opinions of the public concerning a firm's products or services can mean the difference between success and failure for the firm. Thus, more and more firms check consumer reactions to new products before they are released en masse on the market. Similarly, marketing decisions demand information about the most effective techniques for telling the public about the firm's product or service (advertising) and a careful evaluation of the public's reaction to the various products and services. Psychologist experts in the sampling and measurement of public opinion have become active in these important areas. By developing and perfecting methods of survey research, psychologists are able to provide information about various groups of consumers. In turn, this information aids in making marketing decisions and in developing marketing strategies, product modifications, and improved company services.

PLAN OF THE BOOK

The above outline provides a convenient classification for presenting examples of the contributions made by psychology to personnel decisions in industry. Subsequent chapters present industrial applications of psychology in each of the eight problem areas discussed above. It is important to emphasize that this outline, though convenient for identifying major problem areas, does *not* give an accurate classification of psychologists who are working on industrial problems. The human problems of industry demand psychologists who are widely trained and who possess broad perspective. They must be equipped methodologically and substantively to tackle any and all of the major problem areas outlined above. It is true that early industrial psychologists invested most of their efforts in the measurement of individual differences, and later, many psychologists became impressed by and preferred to emphasize social factors in industry to the near exclusion of individual differences. Provincialism of this kind resulted in a sort of technique-bound industrial psychology characterized by a narrow focus and only a limited attack on many of the problem areas discussed above. Today, however, industrial psychology, by adopting a broader and less provincial point of view, is doing a much better job of applying all the knowledge and all the methods of psychology to the solution of human behavior problems in industry. In the chapters ahead, then, the reader finds described a number of actual industrial experiments or applications of psychology illustrative of the way in which broad psychological knowledge and careful scientific methodology have been combined and utilized in the industrial setting. We believe that the illustrations are examples of effective and carefully thought through procedures in industry; they have been carefully chosen in order to illustrate the planning, design, conduct, and methods of data treatment and interpretation characteristic of *good* psychological research and practice in the industrial setting.

Suggested Additional Reading

Division 14, American Psychological Association. *The psychologist in industry*. New York: Research Institute of America, 1959.

Haire, M. Psychology and the study of business: joint behavioral sciences. In Dahl, R. A., Haire, M., and Lazarsfeld, P. E., *Social Science research on business: product and potential*. New York: Columbia, 1959.

Katzell, R. A. Psychologists in industry. In Webb, W. B. (Ed.), *The profession of psychology*. New York: Holt, Rinehart and Winston. 1962. Pp. 180-211.

2

PERSONNEL SELECTION

THE STAFFING PROBLEM

Imagine you are an industrial foreman responsible for the job activities of fifty production employees. Along with many other responsibilities such as inventory control, production scheduling, equipment maintenance, quality and cost control, and shipping, you also must see to it that you have the right people in the right jobs at the right times. To do this you need to establish and maintain a personnel organization. Consider how you might go about this task of selecting and placing employees on jobs in your small organization. What difficulties would you encounter? What factors would you need to consider to assure an efficient allocation of men, materials, and machines?

As the supervisor you would have a broad knowledge of the human duties demanded by your production system, and you would have formed impressions about the varying personalities of people already working for you; you would have noted that some are friendlier than others, that some work easily with others and others do not. Somehow you would have to translate this knowledge of job requirements and the social characteristics of your present people into descriptions of the qualities desired in any additional persons to be hired. Ideally, you would want new employees with the necessary skills to do the required tasks and with the social and personal characteristics that would fit in with the rest of your group. Your only remaining problem, then, would be to develop methods for judging these skills and personal characteristics in people; you would apply these methods to applicants and select the ones which appear to possess the proper traits.

At first you might feel confident of your ability to size up your manpower requirements and to select the proper persons for your group; however, you would soon learn of the many pitfalls present in the seemingly straightforward and simple set of procedures outlined above. Estimating the relative importance of various job duties, translating them into human requirements, and then assessing these human requirements are tasks which are far too complex to be handled by human judgment alone. Many years ago, Hollingworth (1929) reported what happened when he asked sales managers to interview 57 applicants for a job in selling and to rank them in order of their apparent capabilities for the job. The interviewers showed an amazing lack of agreement in their rankings. One interviewee was rated 1st by one manager and 57th by another. Other discrepancies were equally startling and demonstrated clearly the differing standards used by these managers in their efforts to carry out a staffing assignment. The managers differed from one another for a number of reasons. Most important, they did not know the human qualities necessary to successful selling, and were forced to depend on opinions or hunches. Each brought his own point of view and his own experience to the situation. None of them was aware of how to test the validity of his assumptions about sales success, nor did they know how to assess the presence or absence of these qualities in another person. Human judgment, fallible as it is, is not an adequate basis for making staffing decisions.

In your imagined assignment of staffing a small production group, you probably would have the same difficulties as Hollingworth's managers did. You would soon discover that selection and placement demand greater precision than is usually afforded by the judgments of any single individual.

The earliest applications of psychology in industry involved staffing problems. They were a natural outgrowth of the development, during the early 1900's, of methods for measuring individual differences in aptitudes among people. These methods were combined with systematic procedures of job analysis and the assessment of employee job performance to help increase the accuracy of selection decisions. Before we outline how psychology helps in the selection process, we need to discuss several basic contributions which made scientific selection possible. These are job measurement, performance measurement, and man measurement.

STUDYING THE JOB

Job measurement or job analysis is important for many reasons. Knowledge of the important duties of a job is fundamental not only to employee selection but also to many of the other problem areas discussed in Chapter 1. Development of training programs, compensation policies, safety standards, and the design of production systems all hinge on knowledge gained from job analyses.

Job analysis is often viewed simply as the discovery of the duties of the job, but this is too limited in scope and does not, in fact, take account of the major goals of job analysis mentioned above. A better definition is: *job analysis is the discovery of employee behaviors necessary for successful job performance.* Measurement of job characteristics is not complete if it stops with a simple description of job duties; it must also take the next step of focusing on significant behaviors making the difference between success and failure on the job. A listing of such behaviors provides the base from which to tailor selection, training, compensation, and design specifications.

These then are the crucial questions: How can one develop such job standards? How may one be assured of the validity of his observations and judgments concerning the critical behaviors in a job? Possible answers to these questions are considered below.

The problem is: how can we describe a job in a manner useful for other personnel procedures? As a start, the usual methods of job analysis such as observing the job, interviewing employees, and using written questionnaires are helpful preliminary steps. Careful observations, possibly with the aid of a checklist, can provide a detailed account of the duties of the job, the materials and tools used by the employee, the actions and decisions required, and the relation of any given job to other jobs. From such a description we might infer the necessary abilities for doing the job.

USES procedures

One way of inferring human abilities is to ask a number of experts such as vocational counselors or trained job analysts to read job descriptions and to estimate the worker requirements implied by them. This has been done for 4000 different jobs by the United States Employment Service (USES) (Fine, 1958; Fine and Heinz, 1957). Trained raters, working independently, agreed well with one another in their ratings of the following six worker requirements: Training Time, Aptitudes, Temperament, Interests, Physical Capacities, and Special Requirements Necessitated by Unusual Working Conditions. The USES provides job analyses and rating manuals based on this system, which are valuable aids for directing a thorough and systematic analysis of job and employee requirements. Still, they are based on inferences concerning expected requirements, and although different raters do agree in their inferences, there is no independent estimate of their accuracy. This would involve placing people with the indicated skills on the job to see how they do. Their job performance could then be used to make necessary changes in the specifications for hiring subsequent applicants.

Psychological job analysis

A less time consuming but also less desirable approach would be to conduct a "psychological job analysis" (Link, 1920) by administering psychological tests to employees already on the job and to set hiring specifications on the basis of their scores. However, this method suffers a number of serious limitations. First, it assumes that employees already on a job are ideally suited to it, a fact which, if true, would negate the need for any other selection procedure than had been used in the past. Secondly, the method would not succeed in specifying minimum selection standards; presumably many job incumbents would be overqualified for the job, and they would possess abilities, temperamental characteristics, or interests beyond those necessary for successful job performance. Finally, the results would be dependent on the limited number of persons available for study and on any biasing factors introduced by our particular selection of tests to be employed in the study. These limitations are serious, but the method does, at least, suggest the direction we want to take.

Critical incidents

Flanagan's (Flanagan, 1954) Method of Critical Incidents is an excellent way of connecting job behavior with actual employee requirements. The method asks supervisors, employees, and others familiar with the job to record critical incidents of job behavior. These incidents are just what the name implies—actual occurrences of either outstandingly successful or unsuccessful job behavior. In applying the technique critical incidents are recorded in the form of stories or anecdotes, and from these, a composite picture of job behavior is built up. The final job description, abstracted from these incidents, does not involve routine activities but rather those essentials of job behavior making the difference between success and failure. These descriptions can suggest the human qualities necessary for performing the jobs successfully; thus, guesswork concerning necessary job requirements is substantially reduced.

Ideally, then, a complete job analysis includes both a systematic description of the job being performed, using guides such as the USES manuals and a detailed collection and analysis of critical job behaviors. The resulting job description is a complete account of both routine and critical job behaviors which are strongly suggestive of the qualities necessary in persons to be placed on the job.

Changing job patterns

So far, our discussion of job analysis has implied that the job is fixed—that the duties and activities are the same regardless of who may be assigned to it. This may be true for some jobs, particularly those at the lower levels of the occupational hierarchy, but the assumption is far from realistic for many jobs in present day industry because they are defined to a significant degree by the persons assigned to them. Many employees are proud that they can make of their jobs what they will; they are assigned rather broad goals, and, within this loose framework they conduct their job activities as they see fit. Jobs such as selling, teaching, research, managing, and engineering are of this type. In such instances, observational and interviewing techniques yield only confusing and unreliable information. The Critical Incidents Method is useful, but it is complicated by the necessity of determining whether critical job behaviors are a part of the job requirements or simply a function of the particular behavior patterns of certain individuals. What is needed for such jobs is an empirical classification taking account not only of different job demands but also of the different approaches to jobs by different people.

One good example of such a classification is afforded by Hemphill's research (Hemphill, 1960). He asked executives from three managerial levels in five companies to indicate the relative importance in their jobs of each of 575 management activities. He then identified ten groupings of executives where the men in each group were highly similar to one another in what they said was most important to their jobs; yet, they differed from the men in all the other groups. Hemphill succeeded in identifying ten dimensions of executive work which can now be used to describe objectively the patterns of behavior involved in any executive position. The important part of Hemphill's research is that these complex jobs were analyzed not only in terms of the static demands of different jobs but also in terms of what different executives brought to their jobs. These descriptions may now be used in conjunction with critical incidents and the measurement of personal characteristics to develop information about the personal qualities necessary for the successful performance of different executive jobs. Similar methods of empirical job classification have been applied to jobs in engineering (Dunnette and England, 1957), selling (Dunnette and Kirchner, 1959), clerical jobs, and for various Air Force jobs (Thorndike, Hagen, Orr, and Rosner, 1957).

Obviously job measurement is not a simple procedure. We cannot be satisfied with a superficial description of job duties; we must try to secure information which has a good chance of being accurately translated into specifications concerning desired employee qualities. While job measurement is obviously the important first step toward developing such specifications, it must be supplemented by information about differences in the performance of different employees. Let us turn then to a discussion of performance measurement.

STUDYING JOB PERFORMANCE

Measuring the quality of performance on the job demands careful logical analysis of job behavior. For adequate measurement we must define the goals and purposes of our organization and determine the kinds of job behavior leading to the achievement of these goals. Admittedly, such an ideal can only rarely be perfectly accomplished; however, careful rational analysis does help to define the many facets of successful job performance and offers some basis for measuring it.

Successful sales performance

For example, consider how one might define the qualities of successful selling. Some time ago Kirchner and Dunnette (1957) asked a number of sales managers to outline the critical factors in successful salesmanship. Their replies yielded the following categories of factors in successful selling:

1. Following up
   a. on customer complaints
   b. on special requests
   c. on orders
   d. on leads for new business
2. Planning ahead
3. Communicating important information to sales managers
4. Being truthful with customers and managers
5. Carrying out promises
6. Persisting with "tough customers"
7. Telling customers about other useful company products
8. Keeping up with new sales techniques and methods
9. Initiating new sales approaches
10. Learning customer requirements and trying to fulfill them
11. Defending the company's policies
12. Calling on all accounts
13. Showing a nonpassive attitude

Note that none of the above factors includes actually bringing in business or signing the order. Instead the critical factors describe behaviors, which, it is presumed, will result in high sales volume. The major conclusion apparent from the above is that selling is a broad job including many facets of potentially successful or unsuccessful behavior. It is unrealistic to seek any single measure of successful performance; success is multidimensional and must be accepted as such. In turn, equally successful people may achieve their success by different avenues or different patterns of job behavior; several modes of successful performance must be identified rather than only one.

Requirements of performance measures

What we have said raises a number of problems concerning performance measurement. They may be highlighted by outlining the requirements of measures of job success:

1. *Measures should be stable.* In using a performance measure to assign success scores to different jobholders, we need to be confident that the measure represents a stable quality in the behavior of persons. We might assess a measure's stability by applying it at two different times and comparing the two results. If they show little or no agreement, we would feel uneasy about using the measure as a stable indicator of job success.

2. *Measures should possess content representativeness.* This is perhaps the most important quality for measures of job success. It demands that we fully define the entire domain of job success and that we develop measures to tap *all* aspects of it. A common problem in performance measurement is that measures are deficient; that is, they fail to include all aspects of job success. In the listing of critical sales job factors illustrated earlier, any series of measures which failed to include all the critical factors involved in selling would be deficient.

A second common problem in performance measurement is that measures may be contaminated; that is, they include elements which go beyond the definition of job success. In selling, a measure such as sales volume is usually contaminated by such factors as the differing potentials of territories to which salesmen are assigned, differential effectiveness of various advertising campaigns, differing amounts of competition from other companies in different territories, etc. During World War II, psychologists, investigating bombing accuracy as a possible measure of the skill of bombardiers, found that the measure was contaminated by such factors as air turbulence, condition and calibration of the bombsight, condition of the bomb (relative freedom from dents and bent fins), altitude, and length of the bombing run; the measure of bombing accuracy was more affected by these factors than by the skill of the bombardier.

Content representativeness implies, then, that the measure must be relevant to what the individual himself does to be successful or unsuccessful on the job. Performance measures must continually be examined to detect the influence of biasing factors acting to reduce the relevance of the measure as an index of individual success.

3. *Measures should reflect temporal changes in job success.* Job success for experienced persons often depends on factors different from those defining job success for less experienced persons. For example, Fleishman and Fruchter (1960) showed that different abilities were required during the early stages of learning Morse code from those involved in the later stages of learning. Ghiselli and Haire (1960) collected productivity data (dollar volume of fares collected) for 54 cab drivers during each of the first 18 weeks of their employment. As might be expected, average productivity increased sharply during the 18 week period. Of greater interest, however, is the fact that a productivity ranking of the drivers at the end of the first week showed practically *no* relationship to their productivity ranking at the end of the eighteenth week. Furthermore, various psychological tests showed widely fluctuating relationships with the productivity index, depending on the length of time the drivers had been employed at the time productivity was measured. Apparently, then, there were important changes in the elements of behavior comprising job success during the time when the cab drivers were gaining experience on the job. These two studies point to the importance of investigating the nature and extent of temporal changes in the structure of job success

whenever one sets out to develop performance measures of job behavior.

4. *Measures should reflect different patterns of job success.* As already noted, a variety of behaviors may result in equally successful job performance. If the entire domain of job success for any given job has been adequately sampled, we should end up with *many* measures of successful job behavior rather than any single one or any composite of different ones. Our selection task becomes one of ascertaining the personal qualities which are associated with the many different facets of job success and formulating recommendations about selection based on the expected patterns of job behavior from various applicants.

Possible measures

It is no easy task to establish adequate measures of job success. Many are usually available for examination, but they should always be judged against the standards which have been outlined above. The range of possibilities is suggested by the following list which has been modified from one given by Wherry (1950):

1. Measures involving volume of output, such as
   a. Units produced
   b. Items sold or commission earnings
   c. Items filed
   d. Words typed
2. Measures of quality, such as
   a. Number of items rejected
   b. Cost of spoiled work
   c. Coding, filing, or typing errors
   d. Dissatisfied persons (customers, subordinates, colleagues, the public)
3. Measures involving lost time, such as
   a. Days present on the job
   b. Times tardy
   c. Length and frequency of unauthorized pauses
   d. Efficiency of time utilization
4. Measures involving personnel turnover, such as
   a. Length of service
   b. Quits
   c. Discharges

d. Transfers due to unsatisfactory performance
5. Measures involving training time and promotion rate, such as
   a. Training time to reach performance standard
   b. Rate of salary increase
   c. Rate of advancement (number of promotions for given time period)
   d. Level in organization
6. Ratings of job performance, such as
   a. Ratings of personal traits or qualities
   b. Ratings of critical job behaviors

Most of the above measures would not often meet all the requirements of an adequate job performance measure. However, each of them does deserve careful study in order to develop a complete and broad sampling of job performance.

Measures based on critical incidents

The Critical Incident Method, in addition to being an excellent basis for job analysis, also provides good information for developing measures of job performance. Critical incidents can be translated rather easily into statements descriptive of different job behaviors. Examples of such statements, drawn from the listing of critical sales behaviors given previously, are the following:

- Gossips about customer's confidential information
- Follows up quickly on requests from customers
- Shows lackadaisical attitude
- Promises too much to customers
- Is familiar with competitive products and sales methods
- Writes poor sales reports
- Assists fellow salesmen with displays when needed

Such statements may be used by raters (employees' supervisors, coworkers, or subordinates) to describe the characteristic job behavior for any given individual. Since each of the statements has been drawn from an incident associated with either successful or unsuccessful job behavior, a ratee's overall level of job success may be estimated from the ratings. It is also appropriate, of course, to use the descriptions to estimate areas of strength and weakness in the ratee's job performance, thereby affording guidelines for the selection of future applicants. For example, ratings on such a listing of statements might identify a group of salesmen with strengths in the critical areas of following-up and effective customer contact with accompanying weaknesses in the critical areas of planning and attitude (or enthusiasm). Other information available on the group (e.g., test scores, interview data, biographical information) could be studied in order to identify personal characteristics associated with this particular pattern of job performance. The information could also be used as a basis for a training program designed to develop improved habits of planning and to encourage increased enthusiasm. The great advantage of performance ratings based on critical incidents stems from their basis in actual job behavior. All that is required of the rater is a systematic recording of his observations of an employee's behavior rather than the far more difficult assignment of estimating the employee's status relative to some quality (e.g. dependability or integrity) which often is poorly defined and which either does not include or goes far beyond the relevant aspects of the job behavior being rated.

The procedures of Job Analysis and Performance Measurement are obviously crucial in developing informed selection decisions; however, they are not sufficient in themselves. Actual recommendations about the selection of applicants rest necessarily on the discovery of measurable individual characteristics related to effective job performance; the final step in formulating hiring specifications must involve Man Measurement.

STUDYING AND MEASURING HUMAN QUALITIES

Measuring intelligence

Measuring differences among people has a short but exciting history. No other development in all of psychology can match the contribution made by psychological testing to both the understanding and the prediction of human behavior. In less than a century psychologists have mapped the major dimensions of human abilities. These achievements can be summarized in the creative genius and research activities of a few great men: Sir Francis

Galton of England, Hermann Ebbinghaus of Germany, Alfred
Binet of France, and Lewis Terman and L. L. Thurstone of this
country.

In his book, *Hereditary Genius,* published in 1869, Sir Francis
Galton presented a classification scheme for the different levels of
human ability. He was impressed by the great differences among
persons in contributing to society through business, the arts, and
the sciences. In order to express the relative standing of any
person on the normal curve distribution of human ability, he invented the concept of the standard score. Today, we express Galton's standard score as follows:

$$\text{standard score} = z = \frac{X - M}{SD},$$ where: $X =$ the score of any given individual on a measure
$M =$ the mean score of all individuals on the measure
$SD =$ the standard deviation of
the scores of all individuals
on the measure

Galton, by creating this useful statistic, gave great impetus to the
idea of measuring human abilities and of expressing differences
among people in terms of a single index based on the scores of all
other persons in the comparison group. This development represented a massive logical leap forward. Prior to Galton, only limited
thought had been given to the possibility of measuring individu-
ality; in fact, deviations from the average were widely viewed as
indications of "nature's error" in striving for the so-called ideal
represented by the average human being. Galton thereby founded
the study and measurement of individual differences by emphasizing their significance and by providing the first appropriate
statistical tools for their measurement.

At about the same time Hermann Ebbinghaus noted the failure
of his contemporaries to study complex mental activities such as
thought and memory and did something about it. At a time when
most psychological experimentation was being devoted to the
study of sensory acuity and human reaction time, Ebbinghaus
conducted an exhaustive series of studies on human memory. He
did not emphasize individual differences because he performed

most of his experiments on only one person (himself). However, he was a strong force in promoting the desirability of studying *complex* rather than *simple* mental functions. In this, he advocated studying human mental processes as they occurred in real life rather than trying to break mental processes down into their most elemental sensory and motor components, as was characteristic of most other research of the time. His point of view strongly impressed and influenced the direction taken by the father of intelligence testing, Alfred Binet.

In an important paper, published in 1895, Binet and Henri discussed the principles of their *individual psychology*. Severely criticizing the current practices of sensory testing, they argued that the whole individual must be studied, and they emphasized the importance of measuring the higher faculties such as memory, imagery, imagination, attention, comprehension, and persistence. During the next decade Binet experimented with a number of short tasks designed to measure such faculties. He carefully analyzed the mental processes necessary for learning in school, and he asked teachers to nominate bright and dull pupils so that he might study and contrast their particular characteristics. In other words he carried out a careful job analysis of learning behavior, and he asked teachers to measure the performance of their pupils so that he could compare it with the pupils' performance on his testing materials. Using this empirical approach, Binet successfully developed tests that separated bright children from the dull children, and he suggested that these were the measures of the higher faculties which he had been seeking. The first Binet test, published in 1905, consisted of thirty tasks ranging from the very simple to the rather difficult. Examples of some of the tasks are the following:

• Follow a lighted match with the eye
• Define the words: spoon, house, mama, and dog
• Put the words parrot, bank, and fortune into a meaningful sentence
• Define the difference between esteem and friendship or remorse and chagrin

Binet's work set off a world wide response. Investigators tried his tests and learned that they yielded accurate estimates of children's mental status and good prediction of learning ability. In this country, Lewis Terman of Stanford University undertook a thorough revision and extension of the Binet tests. He added many new tests, and he carefully standardized them on the basis of his work with 2300 school children. His revision, published in 1916, included ninety tasks arranged in order of increasing difficulty. The score on this Stanford-Binet Test was expressed as an intelligence quotient (IQ), the ratio between an individual's "mental age" (calculated from the tasks he successfully completes) and his chronological age. With this test the measurement of individual differences came of age gaining added impetus from the widespread testing and screening of nearly two million army recruits during World War I.

Understanding intelligence

With the widespread use of intelligence tests came a concerted effort to understand the nature of intelligence. It was known, of course, that persons scoring high on such tests usually learned more quickly, advanced further in school, and were able to handle jobs encompassing highly abstract and complex problem situations. However, a great deal of controversy arose over whether intelligence was a single unidimensional trait or whether it might be made up of many more basic aptitude factors. You will remember that Binet originally set out to measure the *several* faculties comprising intelligence, and it is clear that Terman never believed in a unidimensional concept of intelligence even though his use of a single score (the IQ) seemed to imply that he did. However, British psychologists, led by Charles Spearman, argued forcefully for considering intelligence as a broad general ability cutting across all other aptitude or skill areas. It was the monumental work of L. L. Thurstone of the University of Chicago which finally settled the issue. He developed and used the technique of Multiple Factor Analysis [1] to study the patterns of relationships among scores of human abilities. Thurstone's research

[1] Multiple Factor Analysis is a complex statistical procedure enabling an investigator to identify the number of variables or factors which underlie the interrelationships among a much larger number of test behaviors.

led him to the conclusion that human aptitudes consist of the following seven basic and nearly independent factors:

Verbal Comprehension: consisting of vocabulary knowledge, success with verbal analogies, and reading comprehension

Word Fluency: consisting of fluency in naming words (e.g., making many words from one larger one or playing anagrams)

Number Aptitude: consisting of speed and accuracy in making simple arithmetic calculations

Induction: consisting of the ability to discover an underlying rule or principle (as in a series of numbers or words)

Memory: consisting of rote memory for items (such as paired words, number lists, etc.)

Spatial Aptitude: consisting of the perception of fixed geometric relations and their manipulation through visualization in space

Perceptual Speed: consisting of the quick and accurate perception of visual details

Thurstone's listing of the so-called primary mental abilities should not be regarded as fixed or unchanging; other investigators, notably J. P. Guilford, have identified additional human abilities, suggesting that the list may include many more than the seven mentioned above. The great contribution of Thurstone is that he forced a recognition of the several dimensions of human ability beyond and within the general ability of intelligence.

Today, psychologists are equipped with appropriate psychological tests to measure the many dimensions of human skills and to relate such measures to information gained from job analyses and performance measurements. Although central to the process of man measurement, aptitude measurement does not give the whole picture. It is necessary to know something about other human behavioral tendencies, particularly those involving vocational interest and personality characteristics.

Measuring interests

The measurement of vocational interests constituted the life work of Edward K. Strong, Jr. During the early 1920's, he reasoned that the likes and dislikes of men in different occupations should differ. He set out to determine how much they might differ, how stable such differences might be, and what the predictive significance of the differences were. He developed an inventory listing 400 occupations, school subjects, amusements, activities, and different kinds of people and asked men in each of over 40 occupations (physicians, architects, lawyers, salesmen, etc.) to express their liking or disliking for each of the items. Over many years of research, he learned that differing interests are stable individual qualities, that they do show substantial differences from occupation to occupation and that scores on the inventory (Strong Vocational Interest Blank) do provide accurate evidence of a person's motivation to enter an occupation and to stick with it (Strong, 1943; Strong, 1955). Thus, measures of vocational interest are a necessary part of any program of "man measurement." They give us a picture of the vocational direction that we might expect a man to follow and to be satisfied with.

Factor analyses have also aided in the effort to define the basic dimensions of vocational interests. Super and Crites (1962) have summarized the results of all these studies and suggest that the following factors comprise the major dimensions of vocational motivation (interest):

• Scientific Activities
• Social Welfare Activities (a nurturant interest in people)
• Literary, Linguistic, Verbal Activities (e.g. journalism and law)
• Manipulation of Materials (such as carpentry)
• Systematic Activities (such as clerical and business detail jobs)
• Personal Contact (manipulative interest in people, e.g., selling)
• Aesthetic Expression (the performing arts)
• Aesthetic Appreciation

Measuring personality

By far the least advanced part of man measurement is the area of personality assessment. Psychologists do not agree on a definition for the term "personality," but for our purposes, it is helpful to regard personality simply as a *reflection of the manner in which a person adjusts to the interpersonal and situational demands of his environment*. The key word in our definition, therefore, is *adjustment*. Psychiatrists and clinical psychologists work mostly with manifestations of poor adjustment. In diagnosing emotional illness and in conducting therapy, they try to tap all aspects of the individual personality including not only stable traits but also qualities which are dynamic and changing from day to day such as anxiety or depression. In contrast, the industrial use of personality measurement is not directed toward psychiatric diagnosis or therapy but is instead directed toward measuring the relatively stable modes of behavior reflected in normal patterns of adjustment. In other words we desire rather simple measures of the major dimensions of manifest behavior rather than complex measures designed to plumb the deep recesses and underlying dynamics of the human psyche.

Such measures may reasonably be obtained by observing and describing or rating the behavior of people in normal everyday intercourse with one another. Many such studies have been conducted, and Tupes and Christal (1961) have recently summarized the results from eight of them. The subjects in the various studies ranged from airmen with only high school education to male and female college students and first year graduate students. The observers supplying the ratings ranged from psychologically naïve persons (e.g., the airmen) to clinical psychologists and psychiatrists with years of experience in observing human behavior. In spite of these wide differences among subjects and among raters, the same five major dimensions of personality were shown in all the studies. These were:

Surgency: the tendency to be assertive, talkative, outgoing, and cheerful as opposed to being meek, mild, and reserved
Agreeableness: the tendency to be good natured, cooperative, emotionally mature, and attentive to people
Dependability: the tendency to be orderly, responsible, conscientious, and persevering
Emotional Stability: the tendency to be poised, calm, and self-sufficient
Culture: the tendency to be imaginative, cultured, socially polished, and independent minded

The above five dimensions should not be viewed as the only fundamental personality factors. However, they do yield a stable and useful classification for the different modes of adjustment to people and situations in industrial settings.

Other methods of man measurement

Figure 2.1 summarizes some of the human qualities which may be measured by psychological tests. Of course, tests are not the only means of gaining information about people. In industrial selection, two other methods, used by almost everyone, are the

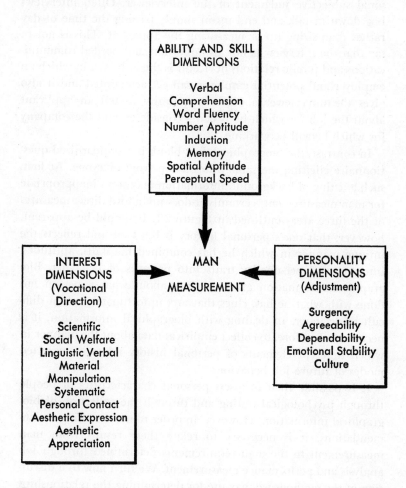

ABILITY AND SKILL
DIMENSIONS

Verbal
Comprehension
Word Fluency
Number Aptitude
Induction
Memory
Spatial Aptitude
Perceptual Speed

INTEREST
DIMENSIONS
(Vocational
Direction)

Scientific
Social Welfare
Linguistic Verbal
Material
Manipulation
Systematic
Personal Contact
Aesthetic Expression
Aesthetic
Appreciation

MAN
MEASUREMENT

PERSONALITY
DIMENSIONS
(Adjustment)

Surgency
Agreeability
Dependability
Emotional Stability
Culture

Fig. 2.1. The Major Areas of Man Measurement and Illustrative Dimensions within Each Area.

personal interview and the biographical data blank (e.g., an application blank). Both methods seek to estimate the nature of a person's past accomplishments as reflected in such aspects of his personal life as employment, educational, and family histories. Of the two methods the interview is the least desirable. It is poorly standardized and difficult to apply; too much is left to the personal subjective judgment of the interviewer. Often interviews bog down in talk and end up in simply passing the time of day rather than sizing up or measuring the applicant. This is not to say that the interview is not an important and needed communications and public relations device; it is the only way in which an employer and potential employee can get acquainted and it also gives the interviewer a good opportunity to tell an applicant about the job for which he is being considered and the company for which he will be working.

In contrast, the biographical data blank is a standardized questionnaire eliciting the same information from everyone. At first, such a listing of background information may seem inappropriate for man measurement; certainly it does not afford direct measures of the three areas outlined in Figure 2.1. It should be apparent, however, that one's personal history is built on and reflects the unique manner in which he has combined his skills, aptitudes, interests, and personality traits into patterns of behaving. Biographical information gives us clues about what a person has done with what he has, clues that are, unfortunately, often difficult to decipher. In dealing with biographical information, it is necessary, therefore, to collect empirical data about the manner in which different elements of personal history relate to expected modes of future job behavior.

It is possible then to assess personal characteristics of people through psychological testing and through the collection of biographical information. However, in order to make staffing recommendations, it is necessary to relate these results from man measurement to the man requirements determined through job analysis and performance measurement. We turn now to a discussion of the methods we may use for determining the relationships among these measures.

VALIDITY AND MEANING

The model for Selection Research shown in Figure 2.2 summarizes our discussion thus far. Job Measurement undergirds selection research providing a base both for defining desired behaviors on the job and for developing inferences about the kinds of measures we will want to try out in a selection research program. Assuming these important steps have been taken, we may turn our attention to a most important link in the Selection Model, the estimation of how well the measures predict different aspects of job behavior. These relationships—the degrees of predictability between man measures and performance measures—are functions of the tests' "validities." Most broadly, the validity of a measure refers to the *meaning* that may be attached to different levels of performance on the measure. In using a test we desire as complete knowledge of the interpretability or meaning of test scores as possible. It is apparent then that a test's validity cannot be expressed as a single index or in terms of any single element of information. Since the validity or interpretability of different levels of performance on a test is *not* an either-or, all-or-none concept, the process of test validation is never ending. It is not a one shot affair. Instead, validation goes on indefinitely; the interpretability and meaning of a particular test is based on the total accumulation of research information available on the test at any given time. It is this total amount of information which is most useful when we decide which measures to try in a specific selection research project; it enables us to choose tests about which we know a good deal and about which the accumulated body of evidence suggests validity for measuring the desired man requirements and job behaviors.

It is still necessary, however, to check whether or not the measures we have chosen actually are useful predictors in the particular situation and for predicting the job behaviors we have specified and measured. After we have done this, we will know better which measures are the most useful for selecting future applicants. Moreover, the evidence from this study can be added to the accumulating body of research information about the tests we

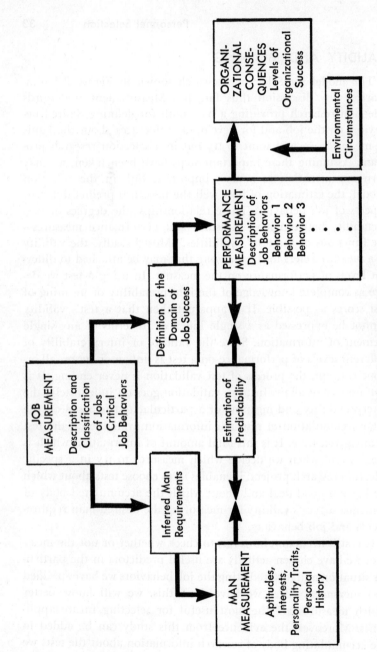

Fig. 2.2. A Model for Selection Research.

are using, and our knowledge about the meaning, interpretability, and potential uses of the tests for future selection problems will be extended.

ACCURACY OF PREDICTION

Estimating predictability involves a number of decisions which are reflected in the following questions: How can we estimate the predictability of man and performance measures? What statistics are useful for expressing the accuracy of prediction? How shall we determine the practical importance of the degree of accuracy obtained? How can we judge the stability of the predictability estimate; that is, how certain can we be that our obtained level of predictability will be about the same for future applicants, and what safeguards should be employed to assure that it is?

DESIGNS FOR SELECTION RESEARCH

Experimental designs for selection research are disarmingly simple. The essential idea is to compare the test scores of persons who show different patterns of behavior on the same or very similar jobs. A straight comparison between successful and unsuccessful persons is far too coarse. Several quite different behaviors may result in success and several others may lead to failure. For example, it has been shown, in selling life insurance that plodding, persistent hard work and planning is usually as successful (in volume of sales) as behavior involving assertiveness, sociability, a winning way, and a so-called sales approach toward potential buyers. Yet these two patterns of behavior—both successful—would be related to quite different scores on any battery of man measures. The purpose in selection research is to predict actual job behavior rather than to predict organizational consequences directly. If future job behaviors can be estimated with accuracy, applicants may be chosen who will be expected to show certain desirable (successful) behaviors and not to show certain undesirable (unsuccessful) behaviors. The definition of so-called desirable and undesirable job behaviors will normally be the prerogative of top managers in a firm; usually, of course, the nature of successful and unsuccessful behaviors will have been discovered and studied during the job and performance measurement phases of the research program.

An ideal design for studying predictive accuracy would follow the sequence in Figure 2.3. For a period of time, all appli-

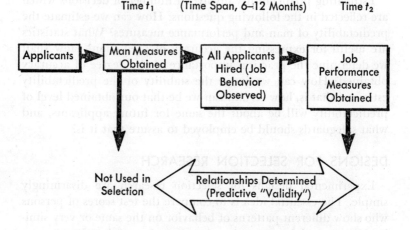

Fig. 2.3. Research Design for Determining Predictive Accuracy of Man Measures.

cants would be hired without regard to their showing on the selection tests; the results would be put away until a later time (six months or a year) when job performance measures would be collected and related to the measures used at the time of hiring. Such a design is a true *predictive* study in that a span of time intervenes between man measurement and performance measurement. As such, the results should be directly useful for the selection of future job applicants. Unfortunately, this approach involves a substantial time delay before results become available. A second disadvantage stems from the possibly detrimental organizational consequences accompanying the selection of all applicants without regard to their measured capabilities. It can be argued that placing any large number of poorly qualified persons on a job is too great a price to pay for the sake of conducting an ideally designed predictive study.

The alternative is to carry out a concurrent study on present employees as shown in Figure 2.4. This design assumes that results will give evidence of predictive accuracy even though the man measures and the performance measures are not separated in

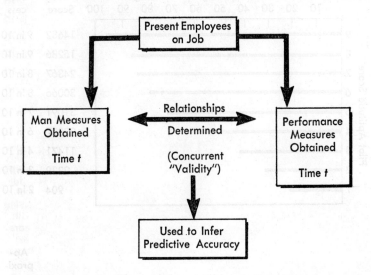

Fig. 2.4. Research Design for Determining Concurrent Accuracy of Man Measures.

time. Usually this is not an unrealistic assumption, but sometimes skills required to do a job change over time. As mentioned previously, Ghiselli and Haire (1960) found marked changes in the qualities related to success in cab driving at various times during the first eighteen weeks of employment. Since concurrent studies are typically conducted on experienced employees, they should not be used to infer the accuracy of measures for predicting shorter-run job behaviors.

Concurrent studies may underestimate the degree of accuracy to be expected in actual use. The range of job behavior shown by present employees will usually be less than the range shown by employees followed up in a predictive design. In the concurrent study the sample does not include those who have failed and left the firm; since they are unavailable for testing, the accuracy of the tests for pinpointing the patterns of really poor job behavior will not be determinable.

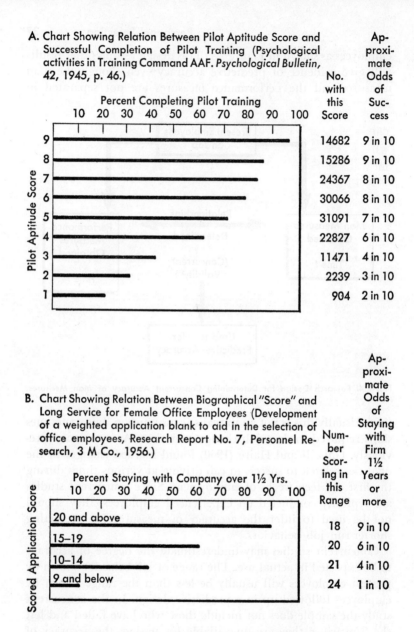

A. Chart Showing Relation Between Pilot Aptitude Score and Successful Completion of Pilot Training (Psychological activities in Training Command AAF. *Psychological Bulletin, 42,* 1945, p. 46.)

Pilot Aptitude Score	Percent Completing Pilot Training	No. with this Score	Approximate Odds of Success
9	(bar to ~95)	14682	9 in 10
8	(bar to ~90)	15286	9 in 10
7	(bar to ~80)	24367	8 in 10
6	(bar to ~78)	30066	8 in 10
5	(bar to ~65)	31091	7 in 10
4	(bar to ~55)	22827	6 in 10
3	(bar to ~40)	11471	4 in 10
2	(bar to ~30)	2239	3 in 10
1	(bar to ~20)	904	2 in 10

B. Chart Showing Relation Between Biographical "Score" and Long Service for Female Office Employees (Development of a weighted application blank to aid in the selection of office employees, Research Report No. 7, Personnel Research, 3 M Co., 1956.)

Scored Application Score	Percent Staying with Company over 1½ Yrs.	Number Scoring in this Range	Approximate Odds of Staying with Firm 1½ Years or more
20 and above	(bar to ~90)	18	9 in 10
15–19	(bar to ~60)	20	6 in 10
10–14	(bar to ~40)	21	4 in 10
9 and below	(bar to ~15)	24	1 in 10

Fig. 2.5. Illustrative Examples of Expectancy Charts Relating Test Scores to Job Behavior.

One further caution: in concurrent studies, we must avoid measures which may *result from* rather than being *predictive of* the job behavior being observed. The danger is greatest with self-description inventories such as interest and personality tests. A highly successful salesman would presumably be more likely to use the adjective successful in describing himself than he would have been when he was first applying for a job fresh out of college. It would obviously be unwise to infer predictive accuracy from such a concurrent finding.

THE STATISTICS OF PREDICTION

Expectancy charts

After we have sized up an applicant through psychological testing and interviewing, how shall we interpret the results? The answer to this question depends upon the inferences we are willing to make about the predictive accuracy of the assessment measures. Ideally, we desire information about the expected job behavior of persons who have obtained certain scores or ratings on each of the selection instruments; in other words, what are the odds of various job outcomes emerging from persons with various different test scores? Such odds are most easily presented in the form of Expectancy Charts; two examples are shown in Figure 2.5.

Chart A summarizes the predictive accuracy for the battery of tests administered to thousands of airmen during World War II. Scores from the tests were combined into a single index (Pilot Aptitude Score) ranging from 1 to 9. It is readily apparent that the large majority (nearly 90%) of airmen with high scores (7, 8, and 9) did successfully complete pilot training. At the other end of the scale, fewer than forty per cent with low scores (3, 2, and 1) completed training successfully. These statistics, gleaned from observing the behavior of airmen with different composite test scores, provided an easily understood and meaningful method for interpreting the scores of future pilot aspirants. Chart A is a rather unusual example, however, because of the very large number of persons involved. We would never encounter such large numbers in a business setting.

Chart B is a more realistic example of the numbers of persons usually available for estimating predictive accuracy of selection devices in business. It shows the results of a systematic study of the biographical histories of female office workers who had proved to be long-term (18 months and longer) or short-term (less than 9 months) employees. The study was undertaken because high turnover is costly; it is obviously inefficient to invest in the hiring of an employee who may stay with the firm only a few months. By comparing the application blanks of short-term girls with those of long-term girls, several factors (e.g., education, birthplace, age, marital status, previous work experience, etc.) were discovered which differentiated between the two groups. Points were assigned to the factors characterizing the long-term girls, and these were summed up to form the distribution of scores depicted in Chart B. It is clear that higher scores are associated with higher odds of staying with the firm 18 months or more.

Cross-validation

At this point you should be wondering about the rather small numbers of persons on which Chart B is based. It is reasonable to suggest that we cannot place much confidence in the odds associated with various scores when they are based on so few people. This is a very wise and legitimate objection, and it points up the necessity of employing an important safeguard called "cross-validation." Cross-validation insures that any special scoring keys (such as those developed on personal history factors or reponses to test items) are stable predictors of differences in job behavior and not just chance differences occurring among the particular people being studied at the time. Cross-validation is the process of seeing how a scoring key works when used with another independently selected group of subjects—not the ones on whom the scoring key was developed.

This technique was applied in the turnover study just described in Chart B. Scoring weights for personal history factors were derived by studying the application blanks of 163 girls hired during 1954. This scoring key was then checked or cross-validated on a different group hired during 1955. The information for the latter group is depicted in Chart B; thus, the effectiveness of the scoring keys for predicting the job stability of future applicants may be viewed with confidence even though based on rather small numbers of employees.

Expectancy charts are perhaps the most straightforward and meaningful method for expressing the predictive accuracy of selection instruments. In practically all situations, however, it is imperative to investigate the stability of selection tests on a group different from the one on which the tests were first identified or developed; certainly the predictive odds associated with different scores should be set on such a cross-validation sample. The only situation in which cross-validation may not be necessary would be in the case of a test or selection technique about which one already knew a great deal. For example, tests of verbal and inductive reasoning abilities have often been shown to be predictive of effective managerial behavior; thus, we would not ordinarily need to cross-validate results of a study showing positive predictive accuracy for such tests on a group of managers, although if the use of a particular cutting score is anticipated for selection, it would be desirable to determine the score on a cross-validation group.

The correlation coefficient

A more general way of expressing the predictive accuracy of a selection technique is by means of the correlation coefficient, r. This is a single index, varying from -1.00 to $+1.00$ which expresses the degree and direction of any covariation between two measures. We have already noted that Sir Francis Galton invented the standard score to express the relative standings of different persons on a single measure. When two measures (e.g., a selection score and a job performance rating) are available on each person, we may express both in the form of standard scores; Galton reasoned that the products of the various pairs of standard scores could be summed and averaged to yield a simple index of covariation, the correlation coefficient.

The formula for r looks like this:

$$r = \frac{\Sigma Z_x Z_y}{N}, \quad \text{where: } Z_x = \text{standard scores on x measure}$$

$Z_y = \text{standard scores on y measure}$
$N = \text{total number of persons for whom measures are available}$

In order to illustrate the values of the correlation coefficient obtained for different degrees of covariation between measures, let us look briefly at the simple examples below (these examples are actually quite unrealistic because they are based on such small numbers of persons, but they do serve to illustrate how r reflects the degree of covariation between two measures):

EXAMPLE A

Person	Test Score	Job Per- formance Score	Z_x	Z_y	$Z_x Z_y$
A	5	5	$\sqrt{2}$	$\sqrt{2}$	+2.0
B	4	4	$1/\sqrt{2}$	$1/\sqrt{2}$	+½
C	3	3	0	0	0
D	2	2	$-1/\sqrt{2}$	$-1/\sqrt{2}$	+½
E	1	1	$-\sqrt{2}$	$-\sqrt{2}$	+2.0
Mean	3.0	3.0		$\Sigma Z_x Z_y = +5.0$	
Standard Deviation	$\sqrt{2}$	$\sqrt{2}$		$r = +1.00$	

EXAMPLE B

Person	Test Score	Job Per- formance Score	Z_x	Z_y	$Z_x Z_y$
A	5	1	$\sqrt{2}$	$-\sqrt{2}$	−2.0
B	4	2	$1/\sqrt{2}$	$-1/\sqrt{2}$	−½
C	3	3	0	0	0
D	2	4	$-1/\sqrt{2}$	$1/\sqrt{2}$	−½
E	1	5	$\sqrt{2}$	$-\sqrt{2}$	−2.0
Mean	3.0	3.0		$\Sigma Z_x Z_y = -5.00$	
Standard Deviation	$\sqrt{2}$	$\sqrt{2}$		$r = -1.00$	

EXAMPLE C

Person	Test Score	Job Per- formance Score	Z_x	Z_y	Z_xZ_y
A	5	3	$\sqrt{2}$	0	0
B	4	5	$1/\sqrt{2}$	$\sqrt{2}$	$+1.0$
C	3	1	0	$-\sqrt{2}$	0
D	2	2	$-1/\sqrt{2}$	$-1/\sqrt{2}$	$+\frac{1}{2}$
E	1	4	$-\sqrt{2}$	$1/\sqrt{2}$	-1.0
Mean	3.0	3.0		$\Sigma Z_xZ_y = +\frac{1}{2}$	
Standard Deviation	$\sqrt{2}$	$\sqrt{2}$		$r = +.10$	

Example A illustrates a perfect positive relationship between two measures (i.e., high scores on x are accompanied by high scores on y) and calculation of r yields a value of $+1.00$. Example B illustrates a perfect negative relationship between two measures (i.e., high scores on x are accompanied by low scores on y) and calculation of r yields a value of -1.00. Example C illustrates no systematic relationship between two measures (i.e., high scores on x are accompanied sometimes by high scores, sometimes by low scores on y) and calculation of r yields a value close to zero ($+.10$). All other values of r between -1.00 and $+1.00$ are possible and indicate different amounts of covariation between two measures. The correlation coefficient between scores on selection techniques and measures of job performance may be used as an index of the predictive accuracy of the selection techniques. Higher values of r (either high positive or high negative) denote high degrees of predictive accuracy.[2]

[2] For large numbers of persons, calculation of standard scores for each person on each measure would be tedious and inefficient. The defining formula for r, given above, through simple algebraic manipulation, yields the following computing formula:

$$r = \frac{N\Sigma XY - (\Sigma X)(\Sigma Y)}{\sqrt{[N\Sigma X^2 - (\Sigma X)^2][N\Sigma Y^2 - \Sigma Y^2)]}},$$

where X and Y are the scores obtained by the persons on measures X and Y, and N is the number of persons.

Unfortunately, the interpretation of the correlation coefficient seems far more simple than it really is. Two problems in particular need to be mentioned. First, r must *not* be interpreted as a proportion. A value of +.50 is not half way between 0 and +1.00 in terms of the accuracy of prediction which may be accomplished. About all we can say is that larger values do yield more accurate predictions than smaller values. Any other interpretation about the relative magnitudes of different r's depends on various assumptions and on the further development of statistical formulas which we do not care to burden you with. Thus, although r does give a single arithmetic index of covariation and of predictive accuracy, we will usually find other statistics more useful for expressing the actual practical importance of the association between selection techniques and performance measures.

A second problem in interpreting r involves the form of the relationship between the two measures. Strictly speaking, the correlation coefficient is applicable only when two measures show a straight line relationship. If you plot the numbers given in Examples A and B on graph paper, you will see that a straight line will connect all the dots; in each case one of the measures is perfectly predicted from the other as is shown by r's of +1.00 and —1.00, respectively. However, example D immediately below also shows an instance in which one measure is perfectly predicted from the other. Yet, if you plot the data, you will see that a straight line does not fit the dots, and the value of the correlation coefficient instead of being +1.00 is only +.87, an underestimate of the true relationship between the two measures. Thus, before using the correlation coefficient as an estimate of predictive accuracy, we should always be assured that a straight line is appropriate for describing the relationship between the measures.

These and other problems make the correlation coefficient undesirable as a practical index of predictive accuracy. True, it yields a convenient summary index of the magnitude of covariation between two measures, and it is widely used and understood (and often misunderstood, as well) by psychologists, but it is *not* easily understood by businessmen and its complex mathematical properties make it inadequate for interpreting the meaning to be attached to different levels of performance on various selection techniques.

EXAMPLE D

Person	Test Score	Job Per- formance Score	Z_x	Z_y	$Z_x Z_y$
A	20	20	+1.33	+1.85	+2.46
B	19	17	+1.17	+1.29	+1.51
C	18	13	+1.00	+0.55	+0.55
D	17	11	+0.83	+0.18	+0.15
E	14	10	+0.33	0.00	0.00
F	10	9	−0.33	−0.18	+0.06
G	7	8	−0.83	−0.37	+0.31
H	6	7	−1.00	−0.55	+0.55
I	5	4	−1.17	−1.11	+1.30
J	4	1	−1.33	−1.67	+1.82
Mean	12.0	10.0		$\Sigma Z_x Z_y = +8.71$	
Standard Deviation	6.0	5.4			

Percentage overlap

As we have already seen expectancy charts are very useful for describing the practical importance of a relationship between measures. A related method, but one which yields a single arithmetic index rather than a picture or chart, is the "percentage overlap, 0." This index gives the percentage of scores from one group which may be matched by scores in another comparison group. For example, if 0 between the scores of two groups is estimated to be 50%, this means that the scores of fifty percent of the persons in either group may be matched with scores from persons in the other group. The measure is of great practical usefulness because it tells us how successfully a selection technique separates different groups showing different levels of performance or different types of job behavior. If the two groups are not separated at all, 0 is 100%; if they are completely separated, 0 is 0%. Percentage overlap between two distributions may be easily estimated by calculating the difference between the means of the two distributions and comparing it with the standard deviations of the distributions. Tilton (1937) has developed a convenient

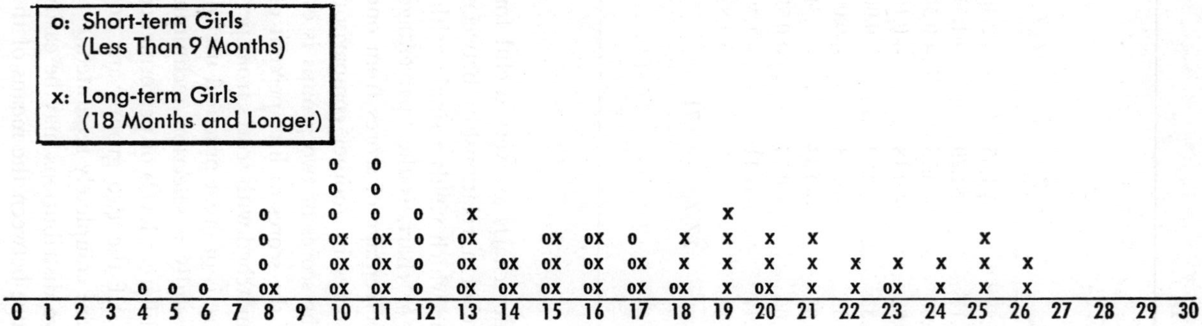

Short-term Girls

Mean = 12.32
Standard Deviation = 3.95

Long-term Girls

Mean = 17.69
Standard Deviation = 4.89

$$\text{Difference} = 17.69 - 12.32 = 5.37$$

$$SD_{av.} = \frac{8.84}{2} = 4.42$$

$$\frac{\text{Difference}}{SD_{av.}} = 1.215$$

From Table 1, $0 = 54\%$

Fig. 2.6. Application Score Distributions for Long-term and Short-term Girls in Cross-validation Sample and Estimation of Percentage Overlap.

table for estimating 0. Table 2.1 presents the relevant parts of Tilton's table. Note that it is only necessary to calculate the means and standard deviations of the two distributions in order to obtain the appropriate estimate of 0 from Table 2.1.[3]

Take a look at Figure 2.6 to see how the overlap statistic looks when applied to actual data. There, we have shown the distributions of application blank scores obtained by the long-term and short-term employees discussed previously. It is apparent both from the actual distributions of scores and from the estimated value for 0 of 54% that the scored application blank succeeded moderately well in separating the two groups of clerical employees. Another method often used for expressing the amount of overlap between two distributions is to count the number of scores in one distribution which either fall below or exceed the middle-most score (median) in the other distribution. In our example only 3 (out of 40) of the short-term girls equal or exceed the median score (18) of the long term group, and only 7 (out of 45) of the long-term girls fall below the median score (12) of the short-term group. However, 0 is the more useful and meaningful measure of overlap because it is a single index and because it also yields estimates of varying degrees of overlap for those cases in which no score in one distribution exceeds the median score in the other distribution.

Since 0 is a percentage and may be directly interpreted as such, it is apparent that it is superior to r as a practical estimate of predictive accuracy. We should remember, however, that 0 is a statistic for comparing just two groups. In many instances only continuous measures of job performance are available. In these the use of 0 requires that we make an arbitrary assignment of persons into two groups based on some cutting score (usually the median) on the continuous measure. This does no great damage to the interpretation of 0, but it does imply that we are willing to

[3] The value of 0 given in Table 2.1 is a theoretical value based on the assumption that the distributions are samples from normally distributed populations with the same standard deviations. This theoretical value is useful because it gives us an estimate of the amount of separation (overlap) which we might expect to encounter in applying the selection technique in future situations to similarly constituted groups.

Diff.* $\overline{\dfrac{}{SD_{av.}}}$	Percentage Overlap, 0	Diff.* $\overline{\dfrac{}{SD_{av.}}}$	Percentage Overlap, 0	Diff.* $\overline{\dfrac{}{SD_{av.}}}$	Percentage Overlap, 0
0.000	100	0.880	66	1.948	33
0.025	99	0.908	65	1.989	32
0.050	98	0.935	64	2.030	31
0.075	97	0.963	63	2.073	30
0.100	96	0.992	62	2.116	29
0.125	95	1.020	61	2.161	28
0.151	94	1.049	60	2.206	27
0.176	93	1.078	59	2.253	26
0.201	92	1.107	58	2.301	25
0.226	91	1.136	57	2.350	24
0.251	90	1.166	56	2.401	23
0.277	89	1.197	55	2.453	22
0.302	88	1.226	54	2.507	21
0.327	87	1.256	53	2.563	20
0.353	86	1.287	52	2.621	19
0.378	85	1.318	51	2.682	18
0.403	84	1.349	50	2.744	17
0.429	83	1.381	49	2.810	16
0.455	82	1.413	48	2.879	15
0.481	81	1.445	47	2.952	14
0.507	80	1.478	46	3.028	13
0.533	79	1.511	45	3.110	12
0.559	78	1.544	44	3.196	11
0.585	77	1.578	43	3.290	10
0.611	76	1.613	42	3.391	9
0.637	75	1.648	41	3.501	8
0.664	74	1.683	40	3.624	7
0.690	73	1.719	39	3.762	6
0.717	72	1.756	38	3.920	5
0.744	71	1.793	37	4.107	4
0.771	70	1.831	36	4.340	3
0.798	69	1.869	35	4.653	2
0.825	68	1.908	34	5.152	1
0.852	67				

* Diff. = Difference between means = $M_2 - M_1$

$SD_{av.}$ = Average of the Standard Deviations = $\dfrac{SD_2 + SD_1}{2}$

SOURCE: Tilton, J. W. The measurement of overlapping. *J. educ. Psychol.,* 1937, **28,** 656-662.

view the persons above and below the cutting score as possessing a common characteristic (e.g., success or failure) rather than showing important differences among themselves which we may desire to predict differentially. Whenever we undertake such a grouping of persons, we should be aware of what we are doing and examine rather carefully whether it is wise or unwise to ignore the various gradations obtained from the continuous measure.

Interpretation of overlap

How low must the value of 0 be to assure the usefulness of a selection technique? The answer to this depends on a number of factors, but two of the most important are the "success rate" and the "selection ratio." Success rate refers to the proportion of employees who perform a job adequately or successfully when no selection test is employed. Selection ratio refers to the proportion of applicants who are actually hired by the firm. If nearly all employees are successful, 0 needs to be very low in order for a selection test to be useful in increasing the success rate among employees hired by the test. For example, suppose that 95% of persons are successful in the job of window washing. We would need an extremely accurate selection test of window washing aptitude before we could hope to increase the relative proportion of successful persons above 95%. It is not likely that any great amount of time and effort devoted to better selection techniques for window washers would be warranted. In contrast, if only 5% of persons usually achieve success in the job of window washing, we could increase the proportion of successful workers on the job even if we used a rather imperfect test yielding a relatively high overlap, 0, between successful and nonsuccessful window washers.

The selection ratio is equally important for interpreting various values of 0. When the supply of applicants is very large, we can afford to be highly selective in staffing the openings in a firm. For example, if we could set a selection ratio of only 1 in 10, we would consider only the applicants scoring among the top 10% on a selection test. Then, the selection test could be rather inaccurate (high 0) and still do an adequate job of increasing the proportion of successful employees on the job. You can see this clearly by referring again to Figure 2.6. A selection ratio of 1 in 10 would result in hiring only those applicants with scores of 23 and above, and nearly all of these (90%) would be long-term employees. In contrast, when applicants are in short supply or when many more new employees are needed by the firm, the recruitment of applicants can be very costly, necessitating a much higher selection ratio, such as, for example 1 in 2. Then we would be compelled to select the best 50% of applicants on the selection test, and it would need to be relatively much more accurate (lower 0) in order to achieve the same degree of selective efficiency. In Figure 2.6, a selection ratio of 1 in 2 would result in hiring all applicants with scores of 15 or above. You can see that the overlap would need to be much less in order to insure the success rate of 90% which we achieved when using a selection ratio of 1 in 10.

In summary then, in order to do an equally effective job of employee selection (i.e., maintain a certain proportion of successful people on the job), we need increasingly accurate selection techniques as the selection ratio and the success rate increase. There is no single answer to the question posed earlier. When selection ratio and success rate are low, we may do well with a selection method yielding a rather high value of 0; when selection ratio and success rate are high, a method yielding a lower value of 0 will be necessary in order to achieve the same level of practical usefulness.

A SELECTION RESEARCH STUDY

Now that we have outlined the basic procedures for conducting selection research, let us look at an actual study carried out by the Employee Relations Department of the Standard Oil Company of New Jersey (Laurent, 1961; Laurent, 1962). Management of Standard Oil undertook support of this research in order to shed light on two questions: (1) how may success in the job of managing be measured, and (2) how may employees who possess the potential to be successful in management be identified early in their employment careers? In our terminology the problems bear directly on questions of performance measurement, man measurement, and the relationship between the two. This is exactly what we have been discussing; thus, the study is a good one for illustrating and summarizing the points we have made.

A total of 443 managers working for Standard Oil Company (N.J.) and five of its affiliate companies comprised the persons studied. Because a major purpose of the study was to investigate the broad core of what constitutes managerial success and potential, the sample included managers in many different functions ranging across marketing, research, production, accounting, and various staff specialties such as medicine and law. Since all these functions were represented in the sample, it was decided not to consider separately the job responsibilities and job behaviors in each of the functional groupings, and it was necessary to be satisfied with a rather general measure of managerial success. As we have seen, such a global approach to performance measurement is usually not advisable; the failure to do a careful analysis of the actual behaviors leading to job success or failure can seriously confound the estimates or measures of success finally obtained. In this case, however, careful study of managerial behavior in the diverse functions represented was not feasible and a global composite estimate of job success was necessarily adopted. Even so, the factors finally decided upon as measures of overall success are appealing and reasonable criteria of management success. They are:

Position.   This was the relative level in the organizational hierarchy to which a manager had advanced.

Salary History.   Each manager's salary history during his entire career was studied. Various adjustments for the effects of inflation, age, and rate of salary progress were made so that the final index could be regarded as a reflection of actual differences in the worth of various managers to the organization.

Effectiveness Ranking.   Managers at similar levels in the organizational hierarchy were grouped together and ranked on the basis of overall managerial effectiveness by company officials who were at higher levels in the organization and who had observed the job behavior of the managers being ranked.

These measures were combined to form an Overall Success Index, and precautions were taken to assure its independence from both age and length of experience in the firm. This point is important because the use of any success measure highly correlated with age or experience would suggest that success was simply a matter of staying in the firm a sufficiently long time, thereby subverting one primary aim of the study—the *early* identification of management potential. Therefore, even though the study utilized a concurrent validation design, precautions were taken to increase the likelihood that the results would also be useful in prediction situations.

Each of the managers took a lengthy battery of tests and completed a background survey covering home and family background, education, vocational planning, finances, hobbies and leisure time activities, health history, and social relations. The tests included measures of verbal ability, inductive reasoning, management judgment (the ability to size up and choose an effective action in different human relations situations), an inventory of managerial attitudes, and personality measures similar to those described in our discussion of personality tests. The scores on the tests were correlated with the standings of the managers on the Overall Success Index. In addition, each of the items in the background survey was examined to discover the elements of biographical information related to the success measure. Since many items and even more responses were examined, it was imperative that the stability of relationships be checked by cross-validation. In this study, a technique called "Double Cross-Validation" was used. The total of 443 managers was divided randomly into two subsamples of 222 and 221. Then, only those responses showing the same relationship with the Overall Success Index in *both* subsamples were retained and scored in the background survey. The importance of this step cannot be overemphasized. Cross-validation is absolutely necessary in order to give an empirical check on the stability of the relationships between predictors and performance measures in any selection study—particularly when many items are correlated against the success measure as was done in this study. One further precaution was taken to assure independence between predictors and age and experience: no item from the background survey was scored if it showed a significant relationship with either age or experience.

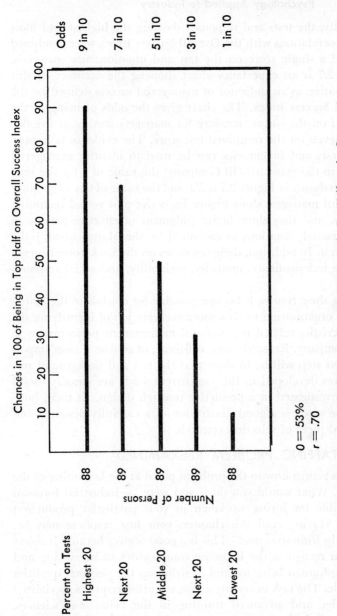

Fig. 2.7. Expectancy Chart Showing Chances of Being in the Top Half on the Overall Success Index for Standard Oil Managers with Different Composite Test Scores.

$O = 53\%$
$r = .70$

Chances in 100 of Being in Top Half on Overall Success Index

Percent on Tests	Number of Persons	Odds
Highest 20	88	9 in 10
Next 20	89	7 in 10
Middle 20	89	5 in 10
Next 20	89	3 in 10
Lowest 20	88	1 in 10

Finally, the tests and responses showing the highest and most stable correlations with the Overall Success Index were combined to yield a single score on the test and questionnaire materials. Figure 2.7 is an expectancy chart showing the accuracy of this combination as an indicator of managerial success defined by the Overall Success Index. The chart gives the odds of being in the top half on the success measure for managers scoring at five different levels on the combined test score. The evidence is impressive. Tests and inventories can be used to identify managerial success in the Standard Oil Company; the value of r for the relationship shown in Figure 2.7 is .70, and the value of 0 is 53%. More successful managers show higher inductive and verbal reasoning abilities, and they show better judgment of effective actions in interpersonal situations as measured by the Management Judgment Test. In addition, their responses on the background survey indicate independence, maturity, sociability, and social responsibility.

Using these results, it became possible for officials of the Standard Oil organization to do a more accurate job of identifying the characteristics related to successful management performance in their company. Research must continue, of course; a most important next step will be to show that the test and background survey scores developed in this concurrent study are equally useful when investigated in a predictive research design. In total, however, the study is a good illustration of a carefully designed and executed piece of selection research.

THE STAFFING PROBLEM REEXAMINED

Let us return now to the problem posed at the beginning of the chapter. What would you do if you were an industrial foreman responsible for hiring workmen in your particular production setting? Having read this chapter, your first response may be, "Get help from someone!" This is a good answer because it shows that you recognize the immense complexities of measuring and assessing human behavior and of sizing up the personal qualities of people. The task of staffing an organization requires specialized knowledge and advanced training in the behavioral sciences. Fortunately in recent years, more and more firms have begun to recognize this, and they have established departments manned by experts with special training and experience in the functions we have discussed. But even if, as a foreman, you do get help from such experts, the final decision about accepting or rejecting an applicant must still be yours. It is you and you alone who must live and work with the people who become a part of your organization. Since the ultimate responsibility for selection is yours, you need to evaluate the procedures used by the persons in your employment or staffing department. We hope this brief chapter on staffing problems and methods will help you evaluate not only their procedures but also your own. With what we hope is now an increased awareness of the importance of careful procedures of job, performance, and man measurement, you should ask the following questions: Has careful thought been given to analyzing the jobs in your unit? Are the measures of job performance carefully designed and comprehensive? Most important, what kind of validity information is there on the selection techniques (tests, interview, application blanks, etc.) being used, and how accurate are the hiring recommendations based on them? By now you also should have gained a feeling for using systematic rather than haphazard procedures to determine how well you are doing in making selection decisions. By demanding always to see the evidence of the relative accuracy of staffing decisions, you will create a strong pressure on yourself and on the employment experts in your firm to plan and to maintain a continuing program of personnel selection research. This, in turn, should assure constant improvement in selection methods and an increasing level of accuracy in making staffing decisions. The net outcome will be to move a step closer to the major objective of industrial psychology—the maximum utilization of human resources in industry.

Suggested Additional Reading

Albright, L. E., Glennon, J. R., and Smith, W. J. *The use of psychological tests in industry.* Cleveland: Howard Allen, Inc., 1963.

Cureton, E. E. Validity, reliability, and baloney. *Educ. Psychol. Measmt.,* 1950, **10,** 94-96.

Dunnette, M. D. A modified model for test validation and selection research. *J. appl. Psychol.,* 1963, **47,** 317-323.

Dunnette, M. D. A note on *the* criterion. *J. appl. Psychol.*, 1963, 47, 251-254.

Dunnette, M. D., and Kirchner, W. K. Validities, vectors, and verities. *J. appl. Psychol.*, 1964, 46, 296-299.

Gellerman, S. W. Personnel testing: what the critics overlook. *Personnel*, 1963, 40, 18-26.

Ghiselli, E. E. Dimensional problems of criteria. *J. appl. Psychol.*, 1956, 40, 1-4.

Krug, R. E. Personnel selection. In Gilmer, B. von H., *Industrial psychology*. New York: McGraw-Hill, 1961. Ch. 6.

Nagel, B. F. Criterion development. *Personnel Psychol.*, 1953, 6, 271-289.

Stone, C. H., and Kendall, W. E. *Effective personnel selection procedures.* Englewood Cliffs, N.J.: Prentice-Hall, 1956.

Thorndike, R. L. *Personnel selection: test and measurement techniques.* New York: Wiley, 1949.

Wilson, J. W. Toward better use of psychological testing, *Personnel*, 1962, 39, 55-62.

3

PERSONNEL TRAINING AND DEVELOPMENT

TRAINING AND EDUCATION

An institution created to produce goods and services does so through the efforts of its employees who have job responsibilities defined by the goals and subgoals of their institution. *Personnel training* is the process by which individuals learn the skills, knowledges, attitudes, and behaviors necessary for carrying out the job responsibilities assigned to them. This definition implies that training in industry consists of formal learning programs designed and carried out to serve the particular needs and objectives of the organization. In contrast, *education* is designed to fit persons to take part in the many institutions of society rather than only a specific one. Thus, industrial training has specific purposes whereas the goals of education are multifaceted and not always specifically defined.

TRAINING IN INDUSTRY TODAY

In the first chapter we said that training is inextricably intertwined with personnel selection. It would be inefficient to attempt to staff an organization with persons already possessing *all* the knowledges, skills, and attitudes required by the jobs in a firm. Instead, we try to employ persons who will profit from the training they will receive. Thus, training programs must be designed to take account of the aptitudes and learning capabilities of the persons available for training, and selection programs should be designed, in part, to provide candidates who are optimally suited for the training they will receive. Today, it is rare in industry to find selection and training programs tailor-made to fit one another in this idealized fashion. The result is that the effectiveness of both are much less than they might be. The quality of selection and of training varies greatly from firm to firm. Even the best conceived training program is severely weakened if a poor selection system brings poorly qualified trainees into the firm. Similarly, the selection of highly qualified people may be for naught unless they are helped to realize their high potential through good training. Of the two, training has the greater potential for assuring the effective utilization of human resources, for it is through training that human skills and knowledges are developed and behavior is changed. In its most extreme form, selection simply takes the individual as given and declares him either suitable or unsuitable insofar as his qualities either do or do not match the requirements of the job in question. Training implies a less rigid stance and holds greater hope for upgrading and changing human qualities to fit the changing requirements of industry.

The stake of industry in effective training has always been great, but the impact of automation has made it even greater. McGehee and Thayer (1961) suggest three of automation's effects which have direct implications for industrial training. First, some jobs will be enlarged thereby requiring additional skills and knowledges. Others will change in the direction of requiring a narrower range of skills. Finally, many jobs will disappear entirely and other new jobs emerge. Many employees will need to learn new skills to meet the requirements of the changing and emerging jobs of the future. Perhaps the most significant aspect of automation is the tremendous rapidity of change accompanying it. Only through effective programs of industrial training supplemented with carefully coordinated programs of personnel selection can sufficient flexibility be maintained to assure wise and efficient utilization of our human resources in the firms of the future.

THE DESIGN OF TRAINING

Designing effective industrial training programs is no easy task, and the problems involved in doing it are far from solved. The typical pattern in most firms consists of on-the-job training; new employees are put into jobs and given sporadic explanations and instructions with no systematic management of the learning process. Even when formal programs have been developed, their design has rarely been based on a thoughtful and thorough analysis of training goals, techniques, and results. The careful design of a good training program demands answers to the journalist's questions: *what, who, how, where, when* and *why*. In the language of the training manager:

• What skills, knowledges and attitudes should be trained?
• Who should be trained?
• How should training be carried out?
• Where and when should training be done?
• Why should training be carried out? What evidence is available showing the efficacy of a particular training program?

The remainder of this chapter is devoted to an effort to answer these questions.

DETERMINING TRAINING REQUIREMENTS

Specifying the content of training requires an analysis of the operations necessary for satisfying the goals of the organization. These goals may be learned by interviewing key people and by direct observation of the flow of work and sequence of operations. The focus of the entire study is to be able to spell out desired employee behaviors in operational terms; the specification of behaviors must include the specific actions and duties to be performed, and these behavioral specifications constitute the terminal behaviors to be developed through training. The importance of this step cannot be overemphasized; specification of organizational goals and the correlated task requirements is absolutely crucial to the determination of the content of training. This is no easy task; in fact, it is a grubby, sweaty job which demands great precision and a limitless attention to detail. The final specifications must include not only the terminal behaviors desired but also detailed descriptions of the allowable range over which each desired job behavior may be asserted, the conditions surrounding the tasks being performed, and the functional relations between humans, materials, and machines and their relevance for training. Our discussion in the last chapter on methods of job measurement and performance measurement are relevant here also—with the further stipulation, however, that the measures be directed not only toward identifying patterns of successful job behavior but also toward analyzing and specifying the sequence of behaviors leading to the acquisition of successful task performance.

Classifying task performance

Unfortunately, psychology has not yet developed a uniform taxonomy for classifying task performances. However, Miller (1962) has suggested a useful scheme, including the following task functions:

Nomenclature and Locations of Work Objects and Symbols. Ability to recognize work objects by appearance, name, and function is crucial to learning about them and their relationships to the tasks to be performed.

Scanning and Detection of Relevant Cues. Every task involves some type of inspection for information required for taking action whether it be actual manipulation of equipment or decision making.

Identification of Cue Patterns. Proper identification of relevant information depends on scanning and detection but includes, in addition, the withholding of judgment until sufficient information has accumulated to direct the appropriate action (e.g., the identification of machine malfunction).

Short-Term Recall. Any one of a series of task behaviors may require the kind of short-term retention of information such as that required of the typist who perceives a series of words and then types them as a group.

Long-Term Recall of Procedures. This refers to the memory of relationships and procedures applicable to any occasion on which the task is performed.

Decision Making. Decision-making behaviors are usually defined by the processes involved; thus, training specifications will strive for learning by concepts or through generalized procedures from which deductions for specific task conditions may be made.

Motor Response. Motor responses demand appropriate differentiation and coordination of body members and muscle groups, factors which need to be specified for training.

The first step in determining training requirements is to analyze all the tasks in the organization according to a classification scheme such as the one outlined above. From this may be derived statements of training objectives. It is not enough to state that training should produce successful salesmen, good supervisors, or accurate keypunch operators. The behaviors making up these definitions must be spelled out in detail. Unfortunately, it is rare that behaviors can be quantified with complete precision, but this does not negate the desirability of trying. For example, accuracy in keypunching (e.g., number of errors per 100 cards) may seem to be an objectively specified behavior, but it does not provide clues for training designed specifically to increase accuracy. Further study enables us to classify the kinds of errors commonly committed by a keypunch operator into *motor response* errors (e.g., hitting a different key from the one intended), *scanning* errors (e.g., misreading the copy—punching P instead of R), and *mediational* (or short-term recall) errors (e.g., reversing a pair of numbers—punching 52 instead of 25). As specifics are increased performance standards are easier to establish, and the necessary content of training may be more clearly inferred.

In many jobs (managing, conducting research, teaching, selling, etc.) performance includes behaviors which seem incapable of being reduced to objective behavioral formulae; cooperation, decisiveness, improvisation, enthusiasm, and invention are examples. It is possible that such performances might be stated as specific behavior sequences or incidents, but the task of translating these into training content is extremely difficult. Miller (1962) calls these kinds of performances "heuristic variables." It may sometimes be desirable, because of their importance, to include heuristic variables in the specification of task and training requirements. This should be done with great caution, however, for as Miller states ". . . they confess an inadequacy of description by the analyst which is likely to be compounded by an equivalent inadequacy in training technique" (1962, p. 50). Where possible, instances and illustrations of the required behaviors should be spelled out in detail.

WHO SHOULD BE TRAINED

Assigning training priorities

The total analysis of organizational goals, operations, and task requirements will yield instruments (checklists, questionnaires, performance rating measures, etc.) to be used in determining areas of training need. Ideally, the job behavior of employees can be compared with these performance specifications and discrepancies and their consequences noted. Decisions may then be made about the relative seriousness and the relative costs of discrepancies between performance specifications and employee behavior; improving performance by other means (e.g., through improved selection) may prove less costly or be more certain than by developing and conducting a training program, or, with the less important jobs, cost comparisons may dictate against the feasibility of trying to improve performance at all. Ideally, the organizational analysis will yield a listing of training need priorities based on cost and feasibility factors which will be the basis for developing actual training programs for different task requirements in the firm. In addition to pinpointing specific job functions for which training programs should be developed, the priorities checklist will help to identify employees who may profit from training. The mere fact that an employee may not be satisfying all the performance requirements of his job is no assurance that training is the only answer. Some employees will profit from and change their job behavior through training; others will not. Decisions about who is to be trained requires research evidence relating different human qualities to different training outcomes. Typical of studies showing relationships between aptitude variables and achievement in training is the one by Cook (1947) in which girls with high finger dexterity gained proficiency as spoolers much more rapidly than girls with low finger dexterity. Cook estimated that the additional cost of training the low aptitude girls was $10,000. Thus, it is well, before undertaking training, to determine rather carefully the aptitude requirements for profiting from the training program and to take account of this in choosing trainees to enter the program.

But what of the employees for whom a specific training program appears *not* to be economically feasible? It is likely that they could profit from a different training approach designed to fit their aptitude patterns. What is needed is knowledge about the interaction between different aptitude patterns and different types of training approaches. No single training program would usually be sufficient to assure the prescribed terminal behaviors for all trainees. Instead, trainees should be divided into relatively homogeneous aptitude groups, and training programs individualized to fit their different aptitude requirements. Admittedly, this is an idealized state of affairs—particularly since so little research has been done on the relative appropriateness of various methods of training for different aptitude patterns and levels. A few studies point the way for further research. Allison (1960) discovered significant relations between learning behaviors and different levels of ability factors and Edgerton (1956, 1958) showed that the accuracy of tests for predicting success in learning aircraft nomenclature differed according to the particular training method used. Thus, deciding *who* should be trained is not just a simple matter of exposing everyone to training who seems to need it. Cost factors are important, and it will usually be desirable for the training manager to develop knowledge about who may profit most from training and under what conditions.

METHODS OF TRAINING

The design and conduct of training must, therefore, be intimately intertwined with research. This is apparent from our foregoing discussion of whom to train, and it becomes even more apparent as we consider *how* training should be done. Learning a new skill, knowledge, or behavior demands an increasing precision and organization of responses. The major question for the training manager is how to *sequence* the training steps so as to develop the desired terminal responses in the most efficient way for each learner. In developing a training program he must answer a number of additional practical questions bearing on the relative difficulty of topics, the optimum order of the subject matter, the time required for various topics, how to allocate time for practice, review, and testing, and how to take into account individual differences among the learners (Covner, 1946). These questions are difficult and their answers depend largely upon the specific conditions and research information garnered from each particular training project. However, learning theory and previous training research do provide a number of principles which are helpful during the design of training. They constitute broad guidelines for the programming of training even though they may not all apply to each and every training problem.

Principles of learning

First of all, programming and sequencing of training must be introduced into the learner's motivational system. Psychologists agree that no change in performance due to training will occur if the responses making up the performance are not tied directly to the desires or wants of the learner. However, psychologists do not agree on the exact nature of the desires or motives important in human learning. Some seem willing to assume that the same basic motives act for all persons; others adopt the more complex (and probably more realistic) view that persons differ in the things they desire and in the intensity of effort they will expend in order to gain them. We shall choose a course midway between these two views by suggesting that people in industry are motivated by certain common desires but that they differ from one another in the relative importance they attach to them at any given time. Some of the possible desires which motivate industrial employees are:

• Desire for security of employment and pay
• Desire for safe and pleasant working conditions and surroundings
• Desire for friendly relationships with other persons
• Desire for recognition as an important or worthwhile person
• Desire for interesting work
• Desire for a sense of worthwhile accomplishment
• Desire for independence (i.e., the freedom to plan one's own activities)

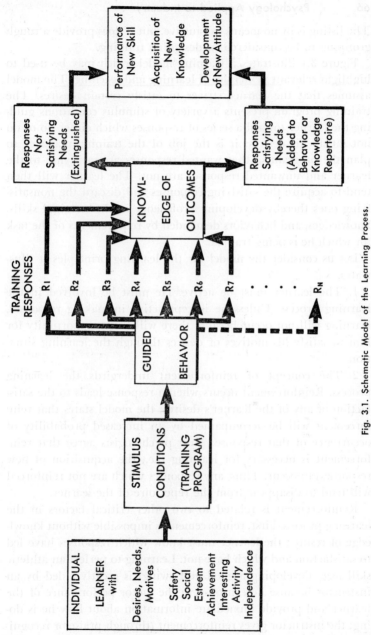

Fig. 3.1. Schematic Model of the Learning Process.

The listing is by no means exhaustive, but it does provide a rough grouping to be considered in designing training.

Figure 3.1 illustrates a learning model which may be used to highlight relevant principles of learning and teaching. The model assumes that the learner strives to satisfy certain desires. The training program presents a variety of stimulus conditions guiding the learner toward a series of responses which either do or do not satisfy his desires; it is the job of the training manager to plan the program so that wanted responses are satisfying to the learner and unwanted responses are not. The learner will then tend to acquire the satisfying responses and discard the nonsatisfying ones thereby developing proficiency in the terminal skills, knowledges, and behaviors demanded by requirements of the task for which he is being trained.

Let us consider the model for the learning principles it illustrates.

1. The learner must be active. He must be involved in the learning process. Unless he is kept active in making responses, learning will not occur because there will be no opportunity for him to satisfy his motives or desires through the learning situation.

2. The concept of reinforcement undergirds the learning process. Reinforcement occurs when a response leads to the satisfaction of any of the learner's desires; the model states that reinforcement will be accompanied by an increased probability of occurrence of that response. Most psychologists agree that reinforcement is necessary for learning (i.e., the acquisition of new responses) to occur. Thus, any responses which are not reinforced will tend to disappear from the repertoire of the learner.

Reinforcement is related to two other critical factors in the learning process. First, reinforcement is impossible without knowledge of results; the learner must know which responses have led to satisfaction and which have not. Learning to perfect an athletic skill (e.g., developing a good golf swing) is greatly aided by an instructor because he can observe the motor performance of the learner and provide immediate information about how he is doing; the instructor gives reinforcement (through praise or recognition) for responses leading to the perfection of the skill and he withholds reinforcement for inappropriate responses.

Secondly, the material presented in the training program should be meaningful to the learner; otherwise, he will not know how his responses are related to the stimulus conditions of the training program. Not all psychologists agree that the learner must necessarily understand the sequence of stimulus response relationships in order to learn them, but they do agree that such understanding probably does increase interest in the learning task and that it does, therefore, take on motivating properties. Most studies of human learning show that meaningfulness of material greatly increases the efficiency of learning.

Planning appropriate reinforcement schedules is a difficult part of designing industrial training programs. The training manager must discover the desires or motives of his learners, and he can only do this by inferring them from their behavior during training. At the very least he will try to present a program with intrinsic interest, but he also must plan reinforcement for the "right" responses by appealing to human desires and motives (e.g., achievement or esteem). Thus, some form of recognition or praise usually works well as a reinforcer; or, very often, simply telling the learner that he has responded correctly is sufficiently rewarding to increase the probability of the response recurring. In many industrial situations man's need for physical safety may be utilized effectively in training. When a job is surrounded by hazards, such as high voltage equipment, vats of molten metal, or perilous heights, training must be designed to show vividly the link between safe actions and the maintenance of physical safety.

It is not usually desirable to use punishing circumstances in an effort to facilitate learning. Studies have shown that a wrong or unwanted response is more effectively extinguished simply by the absence of reinforcers than by presenting adverse or punishing consequences. Thus, a training manager can expect to control learning more effectively through stressing satisfying consequences for correct performance than through developing penalties for incorrect performance. The greatest danger in using punishment is that emotional reactions may be elicited in the learner and negative associations developed against the job, the training situation, and the trainer.

3. Practice and repetition is also implied by our learning model. Active responding by the learner must continue until appropriate responses have been learned and inappropriate responses have disappeared. Not all learners will need the same amount of practice; therefore, the training program should provide for constant testing and evaluation to determine, at each stage of training, how well the learners are doing and how much more practice may be necessary.

4. Finally, the learning model points up the critical importance of constant guidance and management of learning by the trainer. He must guide the active responding of the learners, reinforce appropriate responses, administer evaluation measures and, in general, be "on top of" the learning process at all times while the learners are gaining the skills, knowledges, and behaviors defined by the task requirements.

The foregoing principles provide the broad framework for answering the *how* question. Ideally, our design of a training program will capitalize on the learner's desires, use meaningful material, provide immediate knowledge of results to reinforce the learner's active responding, and give sufficient practice and guidance to shape the learner's acquisition of new knowledges and skills.

Some actual training methods

This leads us to another aspect of the *how* question. How well do existing training procedures incorporate the above principles into the training program?

The traditional training method, still by far the most widely used in learning situations, is the lecture. Considered in the context of our learning principles, the lecture appears poor. There is no provision for the active responding of the learners; no practice is possible; feedback of results and reinforcement occurs only after lengthy intervals in the form of examinations which, more often than not, are not based on a careful formulation of course objectives. Still, a skillful lecturer who has planned his course objectives, can often capture at least a sizeable segment of his audience and assure their active listening. Through careful sequencing of his material, he may stimulate curiosity and create a strong desire to learn. He may even employ methods calling for periodic audience response so that he may use feedback and reinforcement procedures. However, most persons lack the ability to overcome the inherent weaknesses of the lecture method. The usual classroom lecture merely exposes learners to subject matter with no assurance at all that any actual acquisition of knowledge will occur.

Several training methods designed to assure more learner participation have been devised. Among these are group discussion, case study, and role-playing techniques. The group discussion or conference method, as the name implies, simply involves an active group discussion of the principles to be learned. The training manager or leader of such a discussion obviously plays a critical role. He must have the course objectives well in mind and be able to direct the discussion toward responses related to the objectives. This is an unusually difficult job because of the difficulty of controlling reinforcement in a group situation. The trainer who simply reinforces participation will have trouble with some of the vocal but perhaps less effective participants. On the other hand, the trainer who tries to reinforce only useful or correct responses runs the risk of engendering the antagonism of the less effective participants, and they may fall into a passive, morose, and unmotivated mood with obviously deleterious effects on their learning of the subject matter. It is not surprising that Planty, McCord, and Efferson (1948) have described the conference as a conversational boatride on uncharted seas to an unknown port. More often than not, this is the direction that a group discussion takes.

The case study method utilizes a case or problem which the trainees discuss in an effort to discover the underlying principles involved in its solution. Role playing involves a simulated situation in which participants play the parts of specific persons involved in the situation. Both methods possess the advantages of high intrinsic interest, active learner participation, and heightened meaningfulness of the instructional materials. But again reinforcement is extremely difficult to control, not only for the reasons mentioned in discussing conference methods but also because feedback or knowledge of results is often ambiguous and hard to handle. McGehee and Thayer (1961) illustrate this difficulty with a role-playing example drawn from a sales training program. In this training a film was used showing a prospect with various arguments designed to resist the arguments of the sales trainee. The filmed prospect would talk to the trainee to try to get rid of him; then the trainee was given time to respond during which he tried to overcome the objections of the prospect. His time was measured by a white time bar at the bottom of the screen which became shorter as time ran out. Altogether, the trainee had five or six chances to talk to the prospect, and the prospect would stall in various ways between every time bar. The intent was that the trainer would offer feedback bearing on the effectiveness of the trainee's responses thereby developing patterns of concise, forceful, and winning sales arguments. It soon became clear, however, that the time bar was by far the most compelling stimulus in the training situation. Although many trainees learned to time their responses with great precision, they failed to develop good arguments. What they learned was not what the trainer wanted them to learn; the training situation suffered because trainees received feedback about responses irrelevant to the purpose of the training. This often occurs in role playing through uncontrolled feedback and differing patterns of reinforcement due to different types of audience reaction.

The effort to incorporate all the learning principles implied by our learning model (Figure 3.1) into training has resulted in a new method called "Programmed Instruction." Programmed Instruction formalizes the guidance, feedback, and reinforcement features of learning; training content is organized into logical steps which demand active responding from the learner for which he receives immediate knowledge of results and reinforcement. The careful sequencing of the material is called *programming* and the various steps comprising the program are called *frames*. It is assumed that a form of reinforcement occurs simply from making the right response—giving the right answer undoubtedly is satisfying to desires for achievement, esteem, and learning (i.e., curiosity drive) and acts, therefore, to increase intrinsic interest in the learning task. Thus, it is important that the learner nearly always obtain the right answer. This is achieved by giving him the knowledge necessary to respond correctly or by providing cues or prompts. Typically, the learner may write his answer in a blank whereupon he is provided the correct answer which, in a good program, will nearly always (say, for example, 90% of the time) agree with his own; this knowledge is reinforcing and he proceeds, at his own pace, through the series of frames increasing in complexity until he has mastered the subject matter of the training program. What we have just described is the "linear" type of program developed by Skinner (1954; 1958). He likens the method to that of a private tutor. As with a tutor, there is constant interchange between the program and the learner. The program insists on a given point to be learned, presents just the material for which the learner is ready, helps him respond with the right answer, and reinforces him immediately for the correct answer. An example of the Skinner linear type program taken from a program in high school physics is shown below (Skinner, 1958, p. 973):

Sentence to be Completed	*Word to be Supplied*
1. The important parts of a flashlight are the battery and the bulb. When we "turn on" a flashlight, we close a switch which connects the battery with a _____.	bulb
2. When we turn on a flashlight, an electric current flows through the fine wire in the _____ and causes it to grow hot.	bulb
3. When the hot wire glows brightly, we say that it gives off or sends out heat and _____.	light
4. The fine wire in the bulb is called a filament. The bulb "lights up" when the filament is heated by the passage of a(n) _____ current.	electric
5. When a weak battery produces little current, the fine wire, or _____, does not get very hot.	filament
6. A filament which is *less* hot sends out or gives off _____ light.	less
7. "Emit" means "send out." The amount of light sent out, or "emitted," by a filament depends on how _____ the filament is.	hot

8. The higher the temperature of the filament the   brighter,
   _____ the light emitted by it.   stronger
9. If a flashlight battery is weak, the _____ in the bulb   filament
   may still glow but with only a dull red color.
10. The light from a very hot filament is colored yellow or
    white. The light from a filament which is not very hot
    is colored _____.   red

A second type of program used in programmed instruction is Crowder's "multiple choice branching method" (Crowder, 1960). The system provides frames in which a paragraph or whole pages may be presented. The learner responds to a multiple-choice question at the end of each frame; if he answers correctly, he proceeds to new material in the program. But, if he answers incorrectly, he is directed to a frame explaining why he was wrong; often he will be led through a short remedial *branch* of the program giving him the knowledge which his incorrect answer showed he lacked. Shortly, he will be referred back to the original question, answer it correctly, and proceed to the remainder of the program. It is apparent that reinforcement is less direct in the branching method than in the linear method. Crowder believes that learning occurs during the reading phase and responses are used simply to establish the fact that learning has occurred. Skinner believes that response and reinforcement are crucial to learning and responses are employed to get learning to occur. It is obvious that branching programs depend more heavily on intrinsic task interest as a motivating factor in learning and that actual reinforcement is more definitely present in the linear programs. The differences between these two major methods of programmed instruction are minor, however, when viewed against the similarities. Both require active responding; both are self-sufficient and are designed to develop mastery of the subject matter; both are based on careful sequencing of material and provide automatic guidance of the learner's responses; both allow the learner to proceed at his own rate—a form of individualized instruction; both use immediate feedback or knowledge of results.

Industry's interest in programmed instruction is recent, dating directly from Skinner's 1958 article in *Science,* but already it has been used in varying degrees by an impressively large number of firms (e.g., American Telephone & Telegraph, DuPont, IBM, Raytheon, Sperry Rand, Monsanto, Dow Chemical, Union Carbide, Standard Oil Co. (N.J.), Proctor and Gamble, and Pfizer Laboratories, to name but a few). So far it has been employed almost exclusively for teaching relatively short and specialized courses such as Basic Russian, Fundamentals of Electricity, products knowledge courses (for salesmen), and machine and equipment nomenclature (e.g., IBM familiarization courses on the SAGE and 7070 computers). To date, industrial experience with programmed instruction suggests that it is an extremely efficient means of training employees. When evaluated, it has yielded higher levels of knowledge of the course content in shorter time periods than more conventional methods of instruction (such as the lecture). Murphy and Goldberg (1964) give some illustrative examples of the increased efficiency often realized from using programmed instruction. Their data are shown in Table 3.1. This record of results is impressive, but so far there seem to be many subjects or areas of knowledge that have not proved to be amenable to the technique. These include the attitudinal and heuristic factors discussed previously. At the level of managerial jobs, for example, no programmed courses have been written to teach managers how to inspire their subordinates or how to bring imagination or ingenuity to bear in sizing up a tough problem. Since the method is, however, still in its infancy, it is not unlikely that such programs may be developed and utilized successfully in the future. Certainly, the method appears to be the most suitable one for the learning principles outlined previously, and the years ahead should witness many innovations in the method and evaluative studies to define more thoroughly its appropriate role in industrial training.

Summary of methods

Table 3.2 summarizes our discussion of various training methods. The chart illustrates an important rule in training—that is, that different methods are useful for different purposes. The programming of course materials for any given training task will, therefore, usually employ many different methods carefully designed and sequenced according to the learning model shown in Figure 3.1. In this way, the total training package will take account of results of training research and will be built around blocks of instructional materials utilizing methods shown to be optimal for each particular purpose. The total sequence hopefully will be independent of instructor skill, will allow for individual learner differences where necessary and will include a number

TABLE 3.1. SOME ILLUSTRATIVE EXAMPLES OF
IMPROVED PERFORMANCE AND SAVINGS IN TRAINING TIME
ASSOCIATED WITH THE USE OF PROGRAMMED INSTRUCTION

Course	Average Performance Score		Average Length of Time (hours)	
	Conventional Instruction	Programmed Instruction	Conventional Instruction	Programmed Instruction
7070 Computer Nomenclature	86.2	95.1	15	11.0
Reading Engineering Drawings	81.2	91.2	17	12.8
Dermatology & Mycology	60.1	91.9	Information not available	
Basic Electricity Facts:	64.9	76.8	Information not available	
Concepts:	47.5			
Analog Computation	Information not available		40	11.0
Package Billing	Information not available		40	26.0

* SOURCE: Murphy, J. R. and Goldberg, I. A. Strategies for using Programmed Instruction. *Harvard Business Review*, 1964, 42, 115-132.

of evaluation check points to assure the efficient acquisition of the knowledges, skills, or attitudes desired in the terminal response repertoire of the trainee.

TABLE 3.2. SUMMARY CHART SHOWING DIFFERENT TRAINING METHODS CONTENT APPLICABLE TO THEM AND WHETHER THEY DO OR DO NOT INCLUDE VARIOUS LEARNING PRINCIPLES

	Active Participation of Learners	Knowledge of Results	Meaningful Material	Reinforcement	Practice and Repetition	Instructor Guidance	Motor Skills	Cognitive Knowledges	Development and Change of Attitudes
Lecture	No	Only Periodically	Yes for Some; No for Others	Possibly through Intrinsic Interest	No	Yes, but Poorly	No	Yes	Rarely
Group Discussion or Conference	Yes	Difficult to Apply	Yes	Difficult to Apply	No	Yes, but Poorly	No	Difficult	Yes
Case Study	Yes	Difficult to Apply	Yes	Ambiguous and Difficult	No	Yes	No	Difficult	Yes
Role playing	Yes	Yes	Yes	Ambiguous and Difficult	No	Yes	Yes	Difficult	Yes
Linear Program	Yes	Yes	Yes	Yes	Not Needed	Yes	No	Yes	Not at Present
Branching Program	Yes	Yes	Yes	Indirect (Intrinsic Interest)	Yes	Yes	No	Yes	Not at Present

TRANSFER OF TRAINING

Design decisions about the training package must consider *where* and *when* the training will be done. Essentially these questions depend on the degree of transfer to the actual job situation of the skills, knowledges, and attitudes acquired during training. Complete transfer would be most readily assured if all training were done on the job; the apprentice system used in the skilled trades and the interneship and residency requirements in medical training are examples of such on-the-job training. However, one of the common difficulties with on-the-job training is that little systematic attention is paid to it and new employees may receive only sporadic explanations and instructions rather than the careful guidance necessary to efficient learning. Furthermore, it may be impossible, in a real job situation, to compress examples of all the required job behaviors into a relatively short period of training time. Thus, the actual site of training often is away from the job, occurring in a school or job-simulated setting. It is important, of course, always to remember that the purpose of training is to develop certain behaviors on-the-job; thus the design of training procedures must encompass a measure of how effectively the desired behaviors actually do transfer to the job. This, in turn can probably be most definitely assured by designing training to include a judicious combination of school and on-the-job training. Systematic coverage of skill, knowledge, and attitude requirements through a series of carefully developed school or job-simulated situations can be tied into an on-the-job "tryout" as the final step in the training program.

Training by simulation

Unfortunately, industry has often supported expensive training procedures without always demanding a demonstration of the transfer of classroom behavior to the actual job setting. This has been nowhere more evident than in managerial development programs—ranging from "human relations training" to "sensitivity training" and "business games." Most such programs are essentially simulation exercises; sensitivity training simulates the interpersonal or human relations aspects of executive performance. Business games, often programmed on electronic computers, deal with the quantitative aspects of managerial performance such as pricing, investment, production scheduling, and marketing. The heart of sensitivity training is a small group of about 15-20 persons. Most groups begin with an embarrassing silence until one of the participants expresses himself even if it is only to state his name and the company he works for. A rambling conversation begins during which feelings are vented and reactions of the members to the other participants aired; the trainer's role is one of aiding the participants in achieving a free and open expression of feelings, anxieties, tensions, and frustrations. In theory, the participants come to see themselves in a new light; they begin to be aware of their impact on other persons, and they develop a greater openness and flexibility of social action patterns based on a more accurate knowledge of the dynamics of interpersonal behavior. Continued use of the method for managerial training demands an answer to the question of how well the behavior developed in the simulated social situation of sensitivity training transfers to the business setting.

Business gaming is another widely used simulation technique designed primarily to compress a great deal of managerial experience into a relatively brief period of time. The business game has been characterized by Campbell and Wernimont (1962) as follows:

> A certain portion of the real world, whether it be a firm, industry, or labor-management bargaining group, is abstracted and represented by a set of mathematical, theoretical, or rational relationships. These relationships dictate the interaction of a certain set of variables (e.g., amounts spent for sales promotion, research and development, etc.) which are manipulated by the players with a set of resultant variables (e.g., unit costs, amount sold, net worth, inventory level, profits, etc.). The players' manipulation of these variables is governed by a set of rules, and their success in "playing the game" is determined by how well the changes in resultant variables reflect the goals set forth by the rules of the game. The interrelationships among the variables, or the "model," are typically derived from general business and economic theory.

It is clear that business gaming is designed to teach participants many of the fundamental principles of operating a business. Once again, however, the crucial question revolves around the degree of transfer between the behavior acquired during the simulation exercise and the desired behavior in the actual business setting.

EVALUATION OF TRAINING

In answering the question, "Why should a training program be conducted?" the major concern is with evaluating the behavioral outcomes of the training. Obviously, this cannot be an after-the-fact enterprise; evaluation procedures must be planned at each stage during the research and development leading to the design of the training package. It is necessary to develop a number of behavioral measurements for estimating progress during the course of training and for pinpointing possible inadequacies in the training program. These measures may be of many types ranging from written examinations to attitude scales or, most important, direct observations of the trainee's actual ability to do the job. The tests must, of course, reflect the objectives of the training program; as in developing measures of job success (discussed in Chapter 2), the design of training proficiency tests depends on essentially qualitative comparisons between desired task behaviors and the behavior elicited by the tests. As Glaser (1962) points out, the essential question is, "To what extent does this test require performance by the trainee of the behaviors which constitute the objectives of the training program?"

Such behavior measures are used, then, to estimate the organizational gains resulting from the training procedures—increased employee proficiency, decreased costs, shortened training time, or the realization of other organizational goals, which may provide the training program with its *raison d'etre*.

Much has been written about the evaluation of training programs (for example, MacKinney, 1957; Kirkpatrick, 1959; 1960). Everyone agrees that evaluation of training should take the form of an experiment, utilizing "before" and "after" proficiency measures on control (untrained) and experimental (trained) groups. Presumably, if training has had the desired effect, persons in the experimental group should show much greater changes in the direction of acquiring the desired terminal behaviors than persons in the control group. If no change occurs in *either* group, one may well question the efficacy of the training package. Or, if equal changes occur in *both* groups, one may certainly conclude that the training program is not the primary or even necessary causative agent in changing behavior. Obviously, anyone asking the *why* question would be somewhat disenchanted with either of these outcomes. Perhaps this is one reason why training directors in industry have so infrequently carried out experimental evaluations of their programs; they have been uneasy and fearful of the possibility of obtaining negative results.

Experimental evaluation of training—answering the *why* question—is essential; we cannot emphasize this too strongly. However, it should also be clear that any training director who has designed his program in the systematic way we have described and who has been constantly concerned with defining and measuring training outcomes will have automatically included evaluation procedures as an integral part of his training package. For him, the *why* question constitutes no threat, for the question will have been central to the entire process of designing and implementing his training procedures.

A TRAINING RESEARCH STUDY

An excellent illustration of the total sequence of activities involved in developing a training program is the account given by Crawford (1962) of the military training project known as task SHOCKACTION undertaken to devise revised procedures for training tank crewmen. In 1954 an army survey of armor officers showed widespread opinion that the training of tank crewmen was not achieving the level of crew proficiency desired, and psychologists of the army's Human Resources Research Office (HumRRO) were asked to study the problem with the objective of developing a program to train enlisted men for handling all of the three task assignments (i.e., driver, gunner, and loader) necessary for operating a tank in combat.

The project began with the review of current training procedures and training manuals and detailed interviews with armor officers about the responsibilities and knowledges required of tank crewmen. Preliminary forms of interview schedules, activities checklists, observation checklists, and proficiency measures were developed, pretested on 200 members of an armored cavalry regiment, and revised. During the fall of 1955, the revised instruments were used to gather information from 256 highly experienced tank crewmen in Europe. The Activities Interview Form was used as a guide for asking questions about various tasks, their frequency of performance, and the degree of difficulty involved; from this, elements of job duties were identified and the proficiency with which crew members performed them was measured by actual performance checks. Finally, the various crewmen kept a daily Activities Log for a period of one week. From these rather exhaustive job analyses a final listing of job duties for each position was derived; under each duty was given the related operations, responsibilities, and knowledges necessary for its proper performance.

At this stage a preliminary training research project was conducted to determine the effect of instructional time and repetition on the degree of knowledge gained by trainees. The lesson content was kept constant, but instruction and practice time was varied from as little as four hours to as long as sixteen hours for each of eighteen subject areas. After training, achievement tests were given to 2500 armor trainees. The results showed little increase in proficiency even with very large increases in instruction time and gave important information about the optimum time to be spent on various subjects and the areas in which training time might be conserved for use with new kinds of training on the more difficult subjects or remedial instruction for the slower, lower aptitude learners. The importance of conducting a preliminary investigation of this kind deserves special emphasis. Decisions about the final design and conduct of almost any training program can be greatly improved by conducting preliminary research of this sort during the design stage of training.

A new course was then developed on the basis of all the accumulated research evidence and with careful attention to the major principles of learning outlined previously. Conditions of positive motivation to learn about armor were assured by means of films and demonstrations, orientation sessions, compulsory make-up periods for trainees with deficiencies, and by providing plenty of time for organized athletics and recreation. The actual training was as realistic as possible; situations were specially designed to simulate combat conditions closely. Knowledge of results was maximized by incorporating performance tests into the program after each stage of instruction; trainees in small groups learned by active responding under the close guidance of instructors and assistant instructors; thorough understanding was aided by using empirically developed picture guide books showing the job procedures for each of the three crew positions. The total training effort was rigidly sequenced with carefully programmed periods of instruction, performance testing, remedial instruction, and strict adherence to the course objectives of developing tank crewmen qualified to perform the jobs of gunner, driver, and loader.

During the planning, the Armor Mastery Performance Test was built, consisting of 21 subtests designed to ascertain whether each trainee had developed the essential skills for satisfactory performance; 9 subtests were devoted to gunnery, 6 to driving, 4 to loading, and 2 to special weapons used by all crewmen.

In order to evaluate the new program, two equivalent companies of 160 trainees each were trained, one with the new procedures requiring only six weeks and the other with the conventional program requiring eight weeks. At the completion of training, both companies were tested, under simulated combat conditions on a new driving course, with the Armor Mastery Performance Test. The company taking the new six-week course was superior to the other company on the 11 subtests measuring the more complex skills involved in gunnery, driving, and communication; the two companies did not differ on 7 tests; and the company taking the old eight-week course was superior on only 3. Thus the overall proficiency of the graduates from the new course was greater than that of graduates from the old course, and this gain occurred in conjunction with a saving of 25 percent in the amount of time necessary for training. The new program was, therefore, instituted by the Army and is now utilized for the training of all tank crewmen.

CONCLUSION

The foregoing description of task SHOCKACTION illustrates the ideal pattern to be followed in developing every training program. The HumRRO task force diagnosed training needs, conducted exhaustive job analyses, designed training procedures based on learning principles and on empirical research, and conducted a rigorous evaluation of the degree of transfer between the training situation and actual performance of the newly acquired skills in the real job setting. This training research program is, therefore, an excellent example of a training effort devoted toward one primary purpose—that of assuring the acquisition and maintenance of desired behaviors by the learners. Too often, industrial training just simply happens; training design is based on fads, fashions, and haphazard notions of what should be taught rather than on knowledge of the learning process or on fundamental research bearing on the behaviors to be learned.

Effective training in firms should be flexible; the major concern must be with bringing *individuals* up to the desired standards of job performance. Ideally, the training package will include no single training method or technique, but many—carefully pre-tested, programmed, and sequenced to instill desired job skills, knowledges, and attitudes in the repertoire of *all* trainees. This demands a subtle change of emphasis from the prevalent view of training in industry today. Employees in firms of the future will not just be exposed to learning opportunities during which their individual motives and capacities result in wide differences in the acquisition of training content; instead, they will be guided under individually tailored programs to a uniform level of acquisition. To the extent that this idealized outcome can be realized, we may look to the area of personnel training for vastly improved utilization of human resources in the firms of the future.

Suggested Additional Reading

Deterline, W. A. *An introduction to programed instruction.* Englewood Cliffs, N.J.: Prentice-Hall, 1962.

Gagne, R. M. (Ed.) *Psychological principles in system development.* New York: Holt, Rinehart and Winston, 1962. See especially: Chapter

6, Task description and analysis; Chapter 9, Concepts of training; Chapter 10, Training programs and devices; Chapter 11, Team functions and training; Chapter 12, Proficiency measuresment: assessing human performance.

Glaser, R. (Ed.) *Training research and education*. Pittsburgh: The University of Pittsburgh Press, 1962.

Hughes, J. L. *Programed instruction for school and industry*. Chicago: Science Research Associates, 1962.

Kirkpatrick, D. L. Techniques for evaluating training programs: Part 1, Reaction; Part 2, Learning. *J. Am. soc. Training Directors*, 1959, **13**.

Kirkpatrick, D. L. Techniques for evaluating training programs: Part 3, Behavior; Part 4, Results. *J. Am. soc. Training Directors*, 1960, **14**.

Lumsdaine, A. A., and Glaser, R. (Eds.) *Teaching machines and programed learning: a source book*. Washington, D.C.: National Education Association, 1960.

MacKinney, A. C. Progressive levels in the evaluation of training programs. *Personnel*, 1957, **34**, 72-77.

McGehee, W., and Thayer, P. W. *Training in business and industry*. New York: Wiley, 1961.

Murphy, J. R., and Goldberg, I. A. Strategies for using programed instruction. *Harvard Business Review*, 1964, **42**, 115-132.

Skinner, B. F. The science of learning and the art of teaching. *Harvard Educational Review*, 1954, **24**, 86-97.

Skinner, B. F. Teaching machines. *Science*, 1958, **128**, No. 3330, 969-977.

4

COUNSELING IN INDUSTRY

INTRODUCTION

It is difficult to say exactly how many psychologists are engaged as counselors in or for industry. Brayfield (1961), in a survey of overlapping membership of psychologists in Divisions 14 (Industrial) and 17 (Counseling) of the American Psychological Association, found that only 7% of psychologists (N = 68) who were in the Counseling Division held joint membership in the Industrial Division. Brayfield further indicated that of these, he could identify only 10 members of Division 17 who actually were involved to any great extent in vocational counseling. He suggested that these data show something of an indifference to industrial psychology on the part of counseling psychologists. Putting it another way, it would appear that there are not a great number of psychologists whose primary interest is counseling in industry. This further suggests that much of the counseling being done in industry is being done by industrial and clinical psychologists or by non-psychologists, none of whom hold membership in the counseling psychologist group.

It is also difficult to find much research in the psychological literature related to industrial counseling. There are many journals of counseling, but nearly every article or research study is a report of activities being carried out in nonindustrial settings.

Our overview of counseling in industry begins, then, with the fact that there are very few trained counseling psychologists in business and industry today and that of those psychologists or nonpsychologists, who are doing industrial counseling, few are engaged in research of any kind.

That there is a need for counseling, of course, is only too evident. Fraser (1947) has reported a revealing study of the incidence of neurosis among factory workers. He drew a sample from nearly 3,000 male and female factory employees and gave them various psychological tests; they were also interviewed by social workers, and had a complete medical and psychiatric examination. From the analyses of these data, 10% of the male and female employees were judged to be severely neurotic and 20% as having minor neuroses. It was also estimated that neurotic and emotionally based illnesses caused between one-quarter and one-third of all absences from work due to illness. It is rather obvious that there are many people working in industry today who have emotional problems, and it is probable that these emotional problems affect the job performance of these employees.

It has been estimated also that industry loses about $500,000,-000 a year because of employee alcoholism, another example of employee maladjustment. As we shall see later in the chapter, maladjustment on the part of employees can lead to such things as increases in absenteeism, number of grievances, number of accidents, and many other types of undesirable job behaviors.

Other statistics could be cited, but in general, the point is clear. Many people have many problems that affect performance on the job. Whether industry approaches counseling from an humanitarian point of view or from an economic point of view really doesn't matter. The need to help these people in order to increase job performance is evident.

Brayfield has suggested, however, that business firms are not ideally suited to helping individuals who have personal problems. His contention follows Argyris' theme (1960) which is outlined further in Chapter 7 on Organizational Psychology. He argues that the needs of the employee are basically in conflict with the needs of the organization and that this conflict is a major reason for the widespread problems of mental health in industry.

HISTORY OF INDUSTRIAL COUNSELING

In order to set the scene for discussing some of the methods used by industrial conselors, it is well to review briefly some of the history of counseling in industry. According to Bellows (1961), the first counseling program in industry was introduced in January 1914, by Henry Ford at the Ford Motor Company. At that time, a so-called educational department, which later became the Department of Sociology was set up to advise workers on such things as legal and family matters and on personal affairs. The department also had the additional duty of discovering whether or not employees were "living right" according to rules that Henry Ford had set down. Not too surprisingly this was not a popular program and the employees did not like it. Probably they did not appreciate being told how to live during their leisure hours. Ford, too, at that time, did not believe in what might be labeled a human relations approach.

Another company that was a pioneer in counseling for mental health was R. H. Macy & Company, the New York department store. Using psychologists, social workers, and other professional people, they tried to provide some aid and assistance to employees with various problems.

The employee counseling program conceded to be the best known and perhaps the best run in the late 1920's and early 1930's was that of the Western Electric Company. Over nearly a decade about 20,000 interviews were conducted with employees in an effort to learn what they were thinking, how they felt about their work, and the like. The interviewing program, under the direction of social scientists from Harvard University, began with formal, systematized, and highly structured interviews. These proved unsuccessful because employees apparently did not feel at ease to answer such direct questions. As a result, the interviewers turned to an informal approach and urged the workers to discuss anything that came to mind. They hoped, of course, that the typical worker would bring up the things that bothered him the most.

Because the intent of the interview was to get at problems of morale and because of possible dissatisfaction, these early interviews too, proved rather discouraging. What appeared to be happening was that people were getting things "off their chests." This idea, however, turned out to be a good one, for the employees responded with eagerness and enthusiasm. As a result the program became one of employee adjustment counseling, beginning formally in 1936 and supplanting the original interviewing program. It is of some interest to note that over the years Western Electric employed over 50 full time counselors in this program. Each department had a counselor assigned to it, and the counseling was done on company time and on company premises.

The attitudes and methods employed by the Western Electric counselors have been described as follows by Dickson (1936):

1. Interviewer's Attitude
   a. One of interest and sympathetic curiosity.
   b. Quite as much interested in interviewing satisfied employees as those who are dissatisfied.
   c. An employee's interpretation of his own personal situation can be changed only by an internal or psychological change within the employee.
   d. An employee will take the necessary steps to correct a situation when he has clarified his thinking by talking over his problem in detail with the interviewer. This employee will initiate his own action and assume the responsibility for his acts.
   e. Any action initiated by the employee will tend to relate him to other people in the situation in question.
   f. The supervisor's relationship with his employees will be strengthened rather than weakened by the interviewing process.
2. Methods Used
   a. The employee is put at ease by the general surroundings and attitude of the interviewer.
   b. Strict confidence is guaranteed the employee in reference to anything he may say.
   c. The employee is encouraged to talk freely and to continue to talk until he is talked out.
   d. The employee is never interrupted while he is talking.
   e. The interviewer never argues with the employee or gives him advice.
   f. The interviewer strives to discover how the employee thinks and feels, and why.

The Western Electric program was unusual because of its size and the intensity of effort expended by management to "hear out" all employees with problems. After a number of years, the program suffered from economy drives and other internal company problems, and, finally, it was dispensed with entirely. Large-scale programs are not the rule in industry today. Instead, most companies simply support a relatively small counseling department within their Personnel division. For example, Minnesota Mining and Manufacturing Company maintains a Personnel Services Department. It is the function of this department to help employees with financial, military, and emotional problems; the members of the department act as counselors in referring employees to community agencies of one kind or another or to private consultants such as psychiatrists and psychologists where professional help may be obtained. None of the persons in this department has the job title of counselor, however, and this follows general industry practice today.

As can be seen from this sketchy historical resume, counseling in industry is relatively new and relatively limited. It will take some time before the proper role of counseling within industry can be established and this will occur only if research is done to evaluate the results and establish the appropriate goals of counseling programs in industry.

DIRECTIVE VERSUS NONDIRECTIVE COUNSELING

Two major techniques of counseling have been called "Directive" and "Nondirective." While they do represent two different approaches to counseling, they are not as clearly distinct from one another as many writers indicate. Actually, they represent two ends of a continuum of counseling techniques with most actual counseling probably falling somewhere in between these two extremes.

For definitional purposes, however, directive counseling is counseling that has been described as counselor-centered, somewhat authoritatian in approach and highly specific in nature. Here the counselor gives direct advice to the counselee.

In contrast, the nondirective approach does not feature advice from the counselor. This kind of counseling has been called counselee-centered and generally involves letting the individual attempt to gain insight into his own problems by talking them out to the counselor.

Both types of counseling, however, are quite clear in emphasizing that the individual himself, in the long run, has to solve his own problems. Both techniques, too, stress the advantages of letting the counselee talk. It is mainly in the use of advice or guidance that the two techniques differ.

Which is better for industrial purposes? It is likely that a more nondirective approach is more useful. This would follow the approach used at Western Electric, where employees were allowed to talk about any problems that they might have or anything that came to mind with their counselors. It is likely that employees and companies, too, would be more happy about nondirective counseling techniques rather than having the counselor and the company in the role of telling the employee what to do, off the job, as well as on. It is also likely that in the majority of counseling cases in industry where the problem is not one of extreme maladjustment, there is not much need for actual direct advice.

Thorne (1948) has given a rule of thumb concerning the use of directive and nondirective counseling by stressing quite strongly that the healthier the personality, the less the need for direction. In other words, the more normal an individual is, the less he needs direct advice on how to solve his problems. He may need information and he may need counseling in the sense of being able to sit down and talk about his problems, but he will not always profit from direct advice. Yet, in such areas of counseling as retirement counseling, the counselor acts to give direct advice on such matters as Social Security benefits. Nondirective counseling in this situation would be almost impossible.

The industrial counselor then probably leans toward the nondirective approach which most clearly puts the burden of problem-solution on the employee himself. However, he cannot and should not avoid the giving of direct advice and information where it is needed. Both directive and nondirective approaches have their place in industrial counseling.

TYPES OF COUNSELING PROGRAMS

There are many ways of categorizing the kinds of counseling that are done or can be done in industry. Bellows (1961), for example, has listed five different kinds of programs as follows:

1. Provide information to employees, to supervision, and to top-management.
2. Give assistance to foremen in handling the special problems of women workers.
3. Coordinate personnel policies in production departments and, by interview indoctrinating and training, improve workers' understanding of management objectives and personnel policies.
4. Provide employee adjustment counseling.
5. Provide help in job improvement.

As Bellows indicates, the first three of these five are not particularly important and have been done on a more or less informal basis. For our purposes, a more useful categorization of types of counseling should include the following four areas:

1. *Adjustment counseling.* This involves helping the employee to achieve better mental health. It implies the solution of emotionally based problems such as neurotic behavior.
2. *Executive counseling.* This is the counseling of a specific high-level group of individuals who are presumed to be under greater stress and strain than others in an organization.
3. *Guidance counseling.* This also could be called vocational counseling. It generally implies helping an individual to find the right job within the company. It is closely related to the placement function.
4. *Retirement counseling.* Clients for retirement counseling are those individuals, usually 60 years of age or older, who are approaching retirement age. It involves preparing people for the changeover from work to leisure, helping persons financially, and giving information on benefits available.

Each of these counseling areas is considered further in the following sections.

Adjustment counseling

This particular kind of counseling definitely requires a trained psychologist because it involves the counseling of persons with emotional difficulties. The aim of this kind of counseling is to improve employee mental health. Without question, this is probably the major area of counseling in industry today and it is the area that requires the greatest amount of professional trained help.

It cannot be questioned either that emotional maladjustment of employees is a major problem of American industry. Definite relationships have been established between such things as absenteeism and personality characteristics of employees. For example, Newton (1950), in a study of absenteeism, compared machine shop employees who tended to have more absenteeism over a two-year period with those who tended to be relatively absence-free. The two groups were matched as far as possible on age, length of service, and other variables. He found that the high-absence employees were less emotionally stable than the ones with low-absence rates.

Another study of absenteeism among female employees in a telephone company was conducted by Plummer and Hinkle (1952). They compared 20-year service employees who had the highest absence records with 20-year service employees who had the lowest absence records in terms of medical case histories. It was found very definitely that the high-absence group had a much greater number of emotional disorders and other kinds of disorders which had an underlying emotional basis.

In addition, many studies have been conducted of so-called accident-prone individuals. These are individuals who tend to have a higher rate of accidents than other employees. It has been found by Shannon and Burgett (1960) that male employees who tended to have more than their share of plant accidents, also tended to be persons who received more garnishments, took more leaves of absence, received more reprimands, and tended to visit the plant hospital more frequently. The same type of pattern was found by the same two investigators (1959) among females who tended to file more insurance claims than others. This particular group also tended to have more accidents, had more grievances, and had a significantly different history of mental illness than the so-called nonproblem employees. All of these data and other studies substantiate the point as well as suggest quite strongly that many employees are emotionally maladjusted and that this very definitely affects their performance on the job.

Fortunately, however, it has been shown also that employee maladjustment quite often is only a temporary phenomenon. Schulzinger (1956), who gathered accident statistics and data in his medical practice for a number of years, states that there are persons who tend to have more accidents, but that this group is a continually changing one. He feels, therefore, that maladjustment is relatively temporary in terms of its effects on employee job behavior.

Because of this, it would seem that counseling could be quite beneficial in a majority of such cases. Many employees do have problems of an emotional nature but with some help it is likely they could overcome and solve these problems. It is here that adjustment counseling should play its greatest role. It is not likely that adjustment counseling would help much with persons who are psychotic or severely disturbed mentally, but in these cases the function of the counselor would be to refer these individuals for psychiatric help or to refer them for possible institutionalization.

The approach in adjustment counseling is best described as nondirective and therapeutic in nature. It is important in these cases for the counselor to attempt to get the individual to recognize the underlying causes of his particular problems and to bring up possible solutions by himself. A problem does arise, however, because it is very likely that the more maladjusted an individual is, the less likely he is to solve his own problems. The counselor walks something of a tightrope between having to be somewhat directive in terms of his approach yet being as nondirective as possible.

In any case, it is becoming quite clear that individuals who in the past would be considered troublemakers on the job because they have more grievances, are away from work more often, and the like, are actually people who need help and support from their company and can usually benefit from such help.

Executive counseling

Executive counseling is concerned with the counseling of persons close to the top of the management ladder, and it has come into prominence only within the last decade. Generally speaking, the one basic premise for this kind of counseling is that the man at the top is singularly alone. His problems, whatever they may be, are problems which he finds difficult to share with other persons in the organization. Many writers say these top executives literally have no one with whom to talk. Certainly, it is clear that the executive is somewhat isolated from the day-to-day activities of a company or organization, particularly in a large one. In a sense, the information that does get through to the top executive is probably filtered through a great number of screens, including his secretary and his subordinate executives and so on down the line. It is likely, in fact, that this filtering removes much unpleasant information. Some writers have suggested that executives live in something of a dream world, both in terms of their economic knowledge and their knowledge of their own company, for they do not get all necessary information nor do they associate with people who are likely to offer conflicting views.

Many psychological consulting firms specialize in executive counseling. Counseling of this type has been referred to facetiously as executive hand-holding. The primary function of the psychologist or the consultant is to act as a good listener. The executive in turn gets things "off his chest" and talks about problems he would not ordinary reveal to other people in the company. A good illustration of this would be the case of a vice-president who sees himself competing strongly with another vice-president or several vice-presidents for the top job in a company. He, obviously, cannot go to the other vice-presidents and talk about the problems of competition, the stress that arises from this, and the unpleasantness that might arise from tactics some of his competitors might be using. Neither can he go to the president of the company and talk about it because he might be considered a poor sport, bad loser, or one not stable enough to take over the top job. In this case, it would seem that a psychological consultant might be of great help. Probably the major counseling technique that would be used in these situations would be the nondirective approach, where little attempt is made by the psychologist or counselor to give advice but a strong effort is made to act as a sounding board so that the executive himself can see his problem and his possible course of action more clearly.

It should not be assumed, however, that all such executive counseling is nondirective. In some companies psychologists and psychiatrists, too, have been making decisions about such things as budgets, which are generally thought of as functions belonging to other professions. In these cases, it is obvious that the counselor gives direct advice to the executive.

Another function that has been reported in this counseling area is where the psychologist has carried out the unpleasant assignment of actually firing people from the company. It is assumed that he would be more diplomatic, more able to explain reasons more clearly, and would also remove this unpleasant task from the shoulders of persons in the firm. As is apparent, interesting ethical problems can arise when a consulting psychologist is asked to do this; it is difficult to say exactly what his response should be.

In terms of benefits to be derived from executive counseling, we know of no evaluative studies that have been conducted. For one thing, the number of executives being counseled in any one company is rather small, making any kind of evaluative study quite subjective. Secondly, the counselor-counselee relationships in these situations bring up many problems and much information that most companies would not like to see made public. Executive counseling, then, because of the people involved, tends to be a research-free area. Any conclusion about its relative merits can only be based on speculation.

It is likely that executive counseling sessions can be beneficial primarily because of their therapeutic effects upon executives. Many of these counseling sessions become extremely cathartic for the executive and he probably is able to relieve tension, stress, and anxiety through the counselor who, as indicated above, tends to act usually in a highly nondirective fashion in this counseling.

Guidance counseling

The aim of guidance counseling is to help people make better vocational decisions. Generally speaking, this kind of counseling is associated with schools, colleges, and rehabilitation agencies. However, there is a great emphasis today in industry upon helping individuals who feel they are in the wrong jobs to be placed on jobs that they would both enjoy more and do better. This is the function of guidance counseling in industry. Quite often it is done by personnel staff members who also have the responsibility for selection.

The need, of course, for such counseling in industry is obvious. Barry and Wolfe (1962) have stated that there is no such thing as a single, early, wise, intellectual vocational decision and that as a person matures, develops, and broadens his experiences his interests change and his earlier vocational decisions falter. Because this is undoubtedly true for many persons, it is common in industry to find people who perhaps have started out in a field such as engineering, obtained a job in this field, and discovered after some time on the job that they really don't like being engineers. In guidance counseling the psychologist determines an individual's vocational interests and his major aptitudes and skills through techniques of man-measurement discussed in Chapter 2.

Because vocational decision making is such a crucial aspect of an individual's life, it is very unlikely that any industrial counselor would favor strongly directive counseling where the counselor indicates to the individual what vocational choice he ought to make. Rightly or wrongly, an individual must make his own occupational choice. The function of a counselor is to provide and secure information for the individual to help him make a better choice.

As far as we know, no company today has a career guidance department. However, great stress is being placed by industry on management development, and this suggests that guidance is taking on added importance. While most vocational guidance and job transfers in industry today are being arranged by persons who have little training in psychology or counseling, this is an area in which a greater need and demand for such trained psychologists will be occurring in the future.

Retirement counseling

There is one main reason for retirement counseling—preparing an older employee for retirement. Because of the increase in longevity of U.S. citizens due to such things as better medical techniques and better living conditions, there has been a rapid increase in the percentage of persons attaining the normal retirement age of 65. Because of this, it is likely that retirement counseling is going to become more and more important in the industrial scene as time goes on.

What is involved in retirement counseling? For the most part, this type of counseling features a directive approach and the giving of information to employees. Companies vary in their general approach to this problem of retirement, but one company's procedure is fairly typical of that followed by many others: An initial interview with employees is set up about five years ahead of their scheduled retirement dates. At that time emphasis is given to the general question of retirement benefits that the individual will be entitled to, and his general reactions and thoughts about forthcoming retirement are solicited. During the five-year period between the initiation of this program and the actual retirement date, more sessions are held, and the employee is helped by the counselor to wind up his work affairs and to prepare for leisure.

It is obvious, of course, that this particular counseling can involve severe problems of emotional readjustment. It is a common reaction for people to fear retirement. Nobody likes to be put "on the shelf." Research studies, however, suggest that most people adjust rather favorably to retirement, particularly those who have made advance preparations. It is clear, therefore, that retirement counseling can be greatly beneficial in helping employees to adjust to the sudden cessation of work which they may have been doing for 40 years or more.

Few retirement counselors are psychologists or trained counselors. It should be noted, however, that this kind of counseling is also on the increase and presumably will attract more highly trained individuals in the years ahead.

Limitations of counseling

As can be seen from the foregoing discussion, there are problems and limitations concerning industrial counseling. First, and perhaps the most important is the general question of whether or not it is actually a company's duty to provide counseling services to employees. Certainly, the primary aim of a company is to produce goods and services at a profit so that the business or industry can remain in business. There is no question that a counseling program of one kind or another is going to cost money and whether or not this outlay of money actually results in better performance or better value to the company is a question that is hard to answer. There are many persons in industry today who would argue that the problems an employee has outside of work ought to be his own and not those of his company.

Secondly, counseling programs have been criticized as too paternalistic. The first counseling program, in fact, at Ford Motor Company in the early 1900's was highly paternalistic in nature and failed, in part, because of this. It is obvious that employee dissatisfaction can occur if employees feel that the company is looking over their shoulders, outside of work as well as at work. Company suggestions to employees indicating that they ought to see a psychiatrist probably are not going to be overly popular. As a result then, counseling programs may be regarded as overly paternalistic by employees.

Thirdly, a major limitation of counseling in industry today is the fact that little or no evaluation whatsoever is being made of the effectiveness of such counseling. Figures are cited, for example, to indicate that alcoholism costs industry a great deal of money every year. It is suggested that a dried-out alcoholic thereby saves the company money. A hardheaded cost accountant might well scoff at this and suggest that a simpler way to save money in the situation is merely to get rid of the alcoholic completely rather than to spend money on his rehabilitation, and to hire someone to replace him who does not have this problem. In terms of cold cost figures, it may be difficult to argue with such an opinion. It is difficult also to prove that counseling programs are highly effective, and, unfortunately, there seems to be little interest on the part of most counselors in industry to make the effort to do so. Psychologists in industry should undertake the difficult task of actually evaluating the counseling that is being conducted by both themselves and other less well-trained persons.

A final major problem or limitation of counseling is that counseling is being done all too often by untrained, psychologically naïve persons. It is *not* true that anyone can be an effective counselor. It would be much better if companies who engage in these activities were to hire persons who were actually trained in the counseling field, who are familiar with the tools and techniques of counseling, and who have some idea of the limitations of counseling. More problems probably arise because of what might be called amateur counseling than because of a lack of counseling in industry.

FINAL STATEMENT

Regardless of limitations, however, counseling in industry is here to stay and will increase in the future. The fact alone that executive counseling is becoming so widespread suggests that counseling will probably filter down from executives who perceive it as beneficial to other employees in the organization. It is unlikely that counseling will disappear from the industrial scene.

With this in mind, a final statement should be made about counseling in industry. It seems to us that the one purpose of industrial counseling is to help the employee do a better job. If problems outside of work are causing detrimental work performance, then counseling may help him solve the problem and help him adjust better at work. Certainly there are humanitarian motives for carrying out industrial counseling programs, and we heartily endorse these. However, if it can be shown that counseling actually does help employees to become better and more effective workmen, it will not be necessary to argue for the utility of counseling programs solely on humanitarian grounds.

Suggested Additional Reading

Birren, J. E., Butler, R. N., Greenhouse, S. W., Sokoloff, L., and Yarrow, Marian R. (Eds.) *Human Aging.* Bethesda, Md.: U.S. National Institute of Mental Health, 1963.

Black, J. D. *Some principles and techniques of employee counseling.* Stanford: Stanford, 1955.

Blum, M. L., and Balinsky, B. *Counseling and psychology.* Englewood Cliffs, N.J.: Prentice-Hall, 1951.

Borow, H. (Ed.) *Man in a world at work.* Boston: Houghton Mifflin, 1964.

Crook, G. H., and Heintein, M. *The older worker in industry.* Berkeley, Calif.: Univ. of Calif. Institute of Industrial Relations, 1958.

Freeman, G. L. A high-level interest values preference test for counseling pre-retirants. *J. Psychol.*, 1958, **46**, 121-139.

Hahn, M. E., and MacLean, M. S. *Counseling psychology* (2nd ed.). New York: McGraw-Hill, 1955.

Hoslett, S. D. Listening to the troubled or dissatisfied employee. *Personnel*, 1945, **22**, 52-57.

McKinney, F. *Psychology of personal adjustment.* New York: Wiley, 1960.

McLean, A. A., and Taylor, G. C. *Mental health in industry.* New York: McGraw-Hill, 1958.

McMurray, R. N. Mental illness in industry. *Harv. Bus. Rev.*, 1959, **37**, 79-86.

Ohmann, O. A. Executive appraisal and counseling. *Michigan Bus. Rev.*, 1957, **9**, 18-25.

Sadler, L. E. The counseling psychologist in business and industry. *Voc. Guid. Quart.*, 1960, **8**, 123-125.

Stryker, P. How to retire executives. *Fortune*, 1952, **45**, 110 ff.

5

ENGINEERING PSYCHOLOGY

MAN-MACHINE SYSTEMS IN INDUSTRY

Elements of production systems

Industry as a producer of goods and services may be viewed as consisting of an array of production systems differing widely in levels of complexity and in the breadth of operations they are designed to perform. Regardless of its level of complexity, however, any system devoted to the production of goods and services includes three essential elements: a mechanical or machinery subsystem, a power source, and a control element. With the exception of the most simple systems (e.g., a bicycle-man system), human beings function at the control point of the production system. Thus, the role of a human operator is one of maintaining surveillance over the system to assure the specified outcome of the production process. A human operator, functioning as the control element of a system, must keep a running account of the operation of the system, and he must utilize this information to make whatever adjustments are necessary for continued satisfactory operation. In this way, men and machines become intimately intertwined in the processes of industrial production. It is the essential job of the engineering psychologist to see to it that the systems of industrial production are optimally designed to allow their human operators to run them with minimum error and maximum efficiency.

Are humans necessary?

It is relevant to ask how important human operators will be in the industrial world of the future. Since electronic computers are playing increasingly important roles as control devices, it might be argued that humans will one day be entirely supplanted as the primary control elements of industrial production. Such an occurrence is extremely unlikely. No computer yet devised operates without human surveillance; although some very complicated industrial processes have been automated, the ultimate overseer of such processes is and always will be a human operator. The nature of control decisions made by humans is changing rapidly, but this is not the same as saying that humans are, in any sense, disappearing from the scene as the control masters of industrial production. In regard to man's capability as a control mechanism, it has been said: "Nowhere else can one obtain a self-maintaining computer with built-in judgment, which can be mass produced inexpensively by unskilled laborers who like their work so much." This remark should not be viewed as entirely facetious for it does sum up rather nicely some of the special advantages for the continuing use of humans as the ultimate elements of control in our industrial production systems.

What do humans bring to the system?

Granted that humans will always be necessary, what important strengths and limitations are brought to the system by the human operators. Sinaiko and Buckley (1961) have summarized these factors, along with a discussion of the design implications for each:

1. *Physical Dimensions.* The capability of the human operator obviously is limited somewhat by his own physical dimensions such as height, weight, arm length, sitting height, strength, and ability to resist tensile forces. Human dimensions must be considered at each stage of the design process in order to be certain that the operating requirements of the machinery are compatible with the operator's physical makeup.

2. *Capability for Data Sensing.* The human being is a remarkably sensitive detecting organism. Through his senses an operator detects information about the operation of the production system. He sees, smells, hears, tastes, and feels. Human factors engineers (or engineering psychologists) study human sensory capabilities in order to display information patterns which are optimal for detection by the operator. The absolute sensitivities of human senses, their relative efficiencies, their

load capacities, and their capacities for discriminating among various stimulus configurations are all crucial for deriving design specifications. In detection, humans greatly excel computers in their abilities to perceive the environment selectively—to attend to the relevant and to filter out the irrelevant; this is an important asset to be taken advantage of in equipment design.

3. *Capability for Data Processing.* The most unique, but unfortunately also the least understood, feature of man is the richness and variety of his ability to process information. As Sinaiko and Buckley point out, man's thinking includes arithmetic calculations, quantitative and qualitative estimations, comparative judgments, translation, coding, inductive and deductive reasoning, abstraction and concept formation, memorization and recall, prediction, and decision making. Computers falter and fall by the wayside when confronted with information processing problems such as these. The thinking flexibility of humans is, however, also accompanied by a greater potentiality for variability and error. Thus, the systems designer seeks to learn what the sources of error in a system may be so that his design will wed machinery and men to assure that each compensates for the other's shortcomings. In this way, the machines will "play into" man's overriding strengths of planning, supervision, flexible processing of information, and creative thought, and they may also be used to provide high-speed checks on the effectiveness and accuracy of the decisions and judgments made by man.

4. *Capability for Motor Activity.* Humans obviously possess the abilities to respond to their environment in the form of muscular actions. Through motor actions an operator manipulates devices to assure proper operation of the system. To a rather large degree automation is enabling man to restrict his motor activities to push button control, but until automation is much more complete than it now is, engineering psychologists will seek to influence the design of machines so that the speed, accuracy, strength, and load limitations of operators' motor abilities will not be exceeded.

5. *Capability for Learning.* As pointed out in Chapter 3, humans, through training, can modify their abilities. Thus, it is obvious that the design of any production system may capitalize on the potential modifiability of the human operators. It is imperative, of course, that training and design specifications be worked out simultaneously rather than making the unrealistic after-the-fact assumption that training will be able to achieve whatever is demanded for effective operation of the equipment.

6. *Physical and Psychological Needs.* The production process must be designed to allow operators to replenish their physical systems when

necessary. In addition to the obvious physical needs for food, water, and sleep, operators must be guarded from the debilitating effects of fatigue and boredom. Man's psychological needs are less clearcut, but they include such factors as social, esteem, and status needs; these also must be taken into account by human factors engineers and systems designers.

7. *Sensitivity to the Physical Environment.* The environment within which an operator functions may affect his performance for good or ill. Engineering psychologists attempt to discover and map the allowable range of environmental variation in such factors as temperature, humidity, noise, acceleration, radiation, vibration, etc.

8. *Human Versatility.* The operator is seldom used as an element in only one production system. Instead, he may be required to function in many systems simultaneously or intermittently, and he may be required to do many things at once. He behaves as a coordinated unit—detecting information, processing it, responding, and modifying his behavior as the occasion demands. Systems design may capitalize on this human quality of versatility, but it should also be careful not to overload the operator. Research should determine the production conditions which can be efficiently coordinated by a single operator and the conditions under which backstop controls or additional operators may be necessary.

9. *Human Differences.* Human variation is so great it must be given prime attention during the design stage of every production system. Frequent interchange of operators is the rule, and systems must be designed to allow such interchange without disrupting the production process. One way of coping with individual differences is to design the system with the average operator in mind and to develop a "wide-band" design—that is, design a system which will tolerate a rather broad band or range of differences in operators. Naturally, such a design is often impossible; thus, the engineering psychologist must specify the operator characteristics necessary for efficiently maintaining the system, and these specifications may then be incorporated into the company's programs of selection and training.

The job functions of the engineering psychologist

The above special functions and qualities brought to a system by its human operator help to define the job activities of the engineering psychologist. First, through *systems analysis,* he seeks to identify and measure each of the sources of variability in the system. Secondly, after establishing the nature and locus of system variability, he seeks to reduce it by appropriate systems design modifications. In so doing he will examine at least three broad areas, including *input factors, output factors,* and *operator variables.* Input factors refer to all the elements of equipment having anything to do with providing information (input) to the operator. In many cases, the engineering psychologist will carry out experiments to be certain that existing or anticipated display components are designed and arranged so that the operator may use them with minimum error. Output factors refer to all the elements of equipment having anything to do with necessary responses (output) made by the operator to maintain or to change the functioning of the system. In considering output factors, the engineering psychologist will often conduct experiments to be certain that existing or anticipated control components (levers, wheels, switches, etc.) are designed and arranged to be compatible with operators' motor capabilities. Finally, operator variables refer to the differences among humans. Here the engineering psychologist must learn how much system variability may be due to the interchangeability of operators, and he either redesigns equipment or standardizes the operators (through selection, training, or both) to assure a reduction of error due to operator variation.

Having discussed very generally the major activities of engineering psychologists, let us now consider the specific methods employed and some examples of research done in each of the areas mentioned above.

SYSTEMS ANALYSIS, THE STUDY OF ERROR

Quality control

It is important in any industrial process to maintain the quality of the final product. Quality is a loosely defined attribute referring to the sum of all characteristics which make a product desirable and useful to consumers. These characteristics include a wide range of possibilities. For example, quality in the production and operation of a radar scope is measured ultimately by the accuracy with which highly skilled operators are able to detect targets and to estimate their nature, bearing, and range. In contrast, in a study of the production of women's nylon hose, Coakley (1947) measured quality by determining the weight of nylon yarn in stockings of different machine-determined sizes. He found that stockings purportedly of the same size differed widely in the amount of yarn they contained, thereby demonstrating faulty quality control in the production process. Thus, when the product or the product's use shows deviation from a desired standard, excessive error is present in the system; the engineering psychologist sets out, through an analysis of the total system, to identify and remove its cause.

Constant error

Errors are of two general types, constant and variable. Constant errors are illustrated by rifle shots which all penetrate the same hole in the target but with a constant deviation from the bull's-eye. Constant errors are not serious because they may nearly always be easily corrected. A simple adjustment in the sighting mechanism of the rifle would bring all the shots directly into the bull's-eye. If Coakley had found that all stockings, sized 9, uniformly contained the amount of yarn necessary for size 10 stockings, it would have been an easy matter to reset the machinery or even easier to simply resize the stockings. However, Coakley found vaiable error to be present in the nylon products, and this is much more serious and difficult to cope with.

Variable error

Variable error is illustrated by rifle shots which scatter all over the face of the target. Variable error in a production system is serious because the final product is not uniform; therefore, no simple readjustment or resetting will standardize the product. When this happens, the engineering psychologist is faced with a detective job of finding the source or sources of variable error. How does he go about this? In order to answer this, we must first discuss how variable error is measured.

There are many possibilities (such as the *range* of the values or their *average deviation* from the mean) for measuring variable error, but the most usual one is the *variance:*

$$S^2 = \frac{\Sigma[X_i - M]^2}{N} ,$$

where: S^2 is the variance of the measures,
X_i is the magnitude of any given measure,
M is the Mean of all measures; and,
N is the number of measures.

It is apparent that the variance is the average of the squared deviations of the measures about their mean value. A distribution of values clustering closely about their mean would illustrate a small amount of variable error, and their variance would be small. In contrast, a distribution of values scattering widely about their mean would illustrate a large amount of variable error, and their variance would be large. Thus, the variance has a good deal of merit simply as a description of the amount of variable error. In addition, however, the variance is particularly useful because the total variance of a system is a simple algebraic summation [1] of variances due to all sources of error in the system. Thus,

$$S^2_{total} = S^2_{operator} + S^2_{machine} + S^2_{other sources}.$$

This property of variances enables the engineering psychologist to "partial out" the total error of a system among the various contributing components and to identify the relative importance of each.

For example, let us see how we might set up an experiment to examine the relative error contributed by operators and machines in a production system. Coakley faced such a problem in his effort to reduce error in the production of nylon stockings. An efficient way of approaching this problem would be to ask different operators to produce a batch of stockings on each of several different machines. The variance (error) due to operator variation and due to machine variation could then be measured and compared with the total variance to show the relative contribution of each.

[1] The accumulating of errors in a system is more complicated when errors due to different components are correlated with one another. For our purposes we will assume that errors from various sources are uncorrelated (independent) with each other; this is usually a fairly realistic assumption.

An example of variance analysis

Table 4.1 is a hypothetical set of production figures for four operators who produced four items each on four different machines. We may use these numbers to illustrate how Coakley might have proceeded in solving his problem.[2]

First, the total variance of the system may be computed[3] from the total set of 64 units produced by the operators. This value is equal to 3.103.

Next, we calculate the variance due to machines. This is done simply by calculating the variance of the means for each of the machines. The variance of these values (4.938, 5.500, 4.750, 5.125) is 0.077 which is only a very small fraction (slightly over 2%) of the total variance. Since the variance between machines is small, we can conclude that machines are not contributing much error to the system, and we turn our attention to the possibility of operator variation.

The variance between operators is given by calculating the variance of their mean values (3.625, 5.379, 4.938, 6.375); it turns out to be 0.975, which is 31% of the total variance. Since this is a rather substantial portion of the total variance, we conclude that operator error is contributing a large amount to product variability. For example, the products produced by operator D have a relatively large mean, and those produced by Operator A a relatively small one.

Now that we have identified variance due to machines and operators, we may examine *interaction variance*. Interaction variance refers to the possibility of error resulting from the interaction of men with machines (i.e., variability resulting from the differential behavior of operators on different machines). The

[2] For a similar illustration drawn from industrial data, the interested reader may want to refer to Chapanis, A., Garner, W. R., and Morgan, C. T. *Applied Experimental Psychology, Human Factors in Engineering Design.* New York: John Wiley & Sons, Inc., 1949.

[3] For the purpose of computation, it can be shown that

$$S^2 = \frac{\Sigma(X_i - M)^2}{N} = \frac{\Sigma X_i{}^2 - \dfrac{(\Sigma X_i)^2}{N}}{N}.$$

This identity has been used in computations presented in this section.

TABLE 4.1. HYPOTHETICAL DATA SHOWING PRODUCTION FIGURES FOR
FOUR OPERATORS ON EACH OF FOUR MACHINES

	Machine I	Machine II	Machine III	Machine IV	Means for Operators
Operator A	3 1 3 4 $M_c = 4.343$ $M = 2.750$	3 2 4 3 $M_c = 4.031$ $M = 3.000$	3 3 4 2 $M_c = 4.781$ $M = 3.000$	5 6 7 5 $M_c = 7.156$ $M = 5.750$	3.625
Operator B	5 6 6 7 $M_c = 5.844$ $M = 6.000$	5 7 7 7 $M_c = 5.781$ $M = 6.500$	6 5 8 7 $M_c = 6.531$ $M = 6.500$	4 2 3 1 $M_c = 2.156$ $M = 2.500$	5.375
Operator C	5 5 4 5 $M_c = 5.031$ $M = 4.750$	5 5 5 5 $M_c = 4.719$ $M = 5.000$	5 4 5 6 $M_c = 5.469$ $M = 5.000$	5 6 5 4 $M_c = 5.094$ $M = 5.000$	4.938
Operator D	6 7 7 5 $M_c = 5.094$ $M = 6.250$	6 8 8 8 $M_c = 5.781$ $M = 7.500$	5 5 4 4 $M_c = 3.531$ $M = 4.500$	5 8 8 8 $M_c = 5.906$ $M = 7.250$	6.375
Means for Machines	4.938	5.500	4.750	5.125	Total Mean 5.078

production results of Operators A and B illustrate this kind of effect. Note that Operator A, with a low average production on machines I, II, and III, showed a rather high mean production on machine IV. Operator B, on the other hand, with high average production on machines I, II, and III, suddenly showed a very low mean production on machine IV. Thus, the operator performance differs depending upon the machine being used; this kind of variability is indicated by interaction variance. We may calculate it by first correcting each mean for the effects due to operators and machines. Operator A, for example, shows a deviation from the total mean of 1.453 (5.078 — 3.625). We may correct the mean in the upper left hand cell of the table for this operator effect by adding 1.453 to it. In the same way, the correction for the effect due to machine I would be 0.140 (5.078 — 4.938). Thus, the corrected mean is 4.343 (2.750 + 1.453 + 0.140). In the same way, the means in the other cells of the table have been corrected for operator and machine effects and they are shown in the table as the M_c values. If there were no variability due to interaction, these values would all be the same. Interaction variance may be calculated, therefore, by computing the variance of these corrected means. It amounts to 1.352 which is nearly 44% of the total variance and constitutes a very substantial portion of the error in the system.

Finally, the last source of error is given by the variance of the four units produced by each man on each machine. This is called *within cells variance* and is calculated by computing the average of the sixteen cell variances, which is 0.699 or about 23% of the total variance. This may be viewed (in this experiment) as an indication of the degree of intraoperator variability (i.e., the amount of variability in the products produced by any given operator on a single machine).

Let us summarize the sources and magnitudes of variance which have been identified:

Between Machines	0.077
Between Operators	0.975
Interaction	1.352
Within Cells (average)	0.699
Total Variance	3.103

Removing sources of variability

The engineering psychologist, faced with the above results, would proceed to examine the production process in detail in an effort to discover the reasons for the errors being contributed by the operators to the system. His first step might be an examination of the apparent lack of uniformity in the interaction between different operators and different machines. It is likely that he would soon discover an optimum placement of men on certain machines so as to reduce the interaction variance which was discovered. He would then turn his attention to the possible differences between operators leading to the high interoperator variance, and finally he would turn to the question of intraoperator uniformity. Throughout, the investigator would be trying to learn how he might change the machine design or set each machine to overcome the various sources of operator variability. He would also, of course, be alert to possibilities for training the operators to work toward greater uniformity of production. It is apparent that this systems analysis of error is only a starting point. The engineering psychologist must still learn the *why* of each of the sources of error he has discovered. However, he has at least pinpointed the sources and their relative magnitudes, and this shows the direction and presumably makes more efficient his continuing investigations.

We have used the above hypothetical example simply to illustrate how the total variance (error) in a system may be partialed out among its various sources. However, the reader must be cautioned that the example is oversimplified in that it does not indicate the tests of statistical significance which would ordinarily be employed in such an analysis of variance. The interested reader is urged to consult any of several widely used statistics texts for a more complete treatment of the procedures involved in the analysis of variance.

Discovering errors through critical incidents

In addition to examining systems errors through the analysis of variance procedures, the critical incident technique (see Chapter

2) is often used. In applying this method the engineering psychologist simply asks operators to tell him about so-called critical incidents involving errors or mistakes which might have led to a malfunctioning of the system. A content analysis of such incidents leads to the discovery of error sources which presumably might be rectified through improved equipment design or through better selection and training of operators. Fitts and Jones (1947) used the technique to investigate incidents of accidents or near-accidents reported by U.S. Air Force pilots. A total of 270 incidents was reported ranging from errors involving human illusions to the misreading of aircraft instruments. The results pinpointed the *kinds* of errors made and yielded recommendations for equipment design modifications. Thus, the critical incident method, though imprecise for measuring the magnitude or relative importance of errors, does give a qualitative flavor to the error analysis and comes closer to answering the *why* question of system variability.

THE STUDY OF INPUT FACTORS

After completing his systems analysis, the engineering psychologist knows something of the magnitude and nature of variable errors affecting the production process. Next, he reanalyzes the operator's task with special emphasis on input and output factors and operator variables.

In looking at the input area, he is concerned with man's sensory apparatus; he wants to learn whether or not the system is adequately designed for conveying information to the operator via his sensory receptors. In the study by Fitts and Jones (1947) mentioned previously, one of the most frequent kinds of error involved misreading the altimeter by 1000 feet or more, an error which was often accompanied by disastrous results. The altimeter in use at the time (and still used in many aircraft today) demanded that the pilot read and interpret three pointers (10,000's, 1000's, and 100's of feet) on the face of a single dial. It is little wonder that this complex task often resulted in a faulty input of information to the pilot, particularly under conditions of stress when he had to be concerned with many competing stimuli. As a result, Grether

(1948) studied the relative accuracy of other altimeter designs and showed that a dial with an open window to indicate thousands of feet and a single pointer to show the hundreds was highly superior to the standard altimeter in the accuracy and speed with which it could be read.

An example of input research

Let us take a better look at Grether's study, for it illustrates the strategy and methods of the engineering psychologist in working with an input problem. In order to study alternative altimeter designs, Grether prepared a number of booklets, one each for nine different dial designs. Each booklet, after giving directions on how to read the particular dial, reproduced that dial design with twelve different settings, and a space was provided for writing in the reading. The booklets were then presented, in carefully counterbalanced order (in order to equate possible learning or fatigue effects), to 97 experienced Air Force pilots and to 79 college men, none of whom had flying experience. The accuracy of their readings and the time required for each were recorded. The results confirmed the difficulty of reading the three pointer altimeter; both pilots and students required nearly 10 seconds for each reading and over 15% of *both groups'* readings were in error, 12% by 1000 feet or more. These poor performances are particularly noteworthy because they occurred in the relatively relaxed atmosphere of a classroom experimental setting rather than under the potentially stressful and certainly more complicated environment of an aircraft in flight. In contrast to the standard altimeter design, the dial with the open window and single pointer was read very accurately and very quickly; an average of only 3 seconds per reading was required and fewer than 5% of the readings were in error, fewer than 1% by 1000 feet or more. Based on these results, Grether recommended that the new dial design be adopted as standard equipment in aircraft, and this has been done in many of the aircraft now being built.

The experiment by Grether illustrates a number of important points about engineering psychology. First, it demonstrates the engineering psychologist's bias for basing design recommendations on empirical evidence gained from experimental manipulations rather than on arguments, so-called expert judgments, or simply on the way things have been done in the past. Secondly, the Grether experiment shows the relative ease with which good information about equipment design may be obtained. In this case, a paper-and-pencil experiment was adequate; in fact, it was the preferred approach because it made possible rather careful experimental controls (e.g., the counterbalanced order of presenting the different dial designs) and saved large amounts of time and money by avoiding the necessity of actually designing and building each of the altimeters to be tried out. Naturally, however, the final test of the experimental recommendations will always be the actual trial of the new design in a real-life, operational setting. Finally, the experiment illustrates how action may be taken to solve an immediate applied problem rather than necessarily being directed toward the discovery of basic knowledge about human response characteristics.

Fundamental research in engineering psychology

This last point may seem to imply that no lasting knowledge is being contributed by human factors research. Even though such a charge may, to a limited degree, be true, the large number of instances of improved machine design stemming from such direct applied research are sufficient testimony to the importance of continuing the emphasis on such activities in the future. However, human factors studies do also develop and expand basic knowledge. In the input area, for example, psychophysical methods [4] have been widely utilized to define the basic sensory capacities of human beings. Thus, the absolute magnitudes of physical stimuli (sound, light, etc.) necessary to assure detection by human operators have been mapped. More important, psychophysical methods have aided in the analysis of complex sensory tasks demanding far more than simple threshold determinations. For example, a series of classic studies by Baker and Grether (1954)

[4] A detailed discussion of the psychophysical methods is beyond the scope of this book. The interested reader will find an excellent presentation of these methods in Chapanis (1959).

related the probability of target detection on a radar scope to such factors as the size of the target blip and the amount of brightness contrast necessary between the blip and the background brightness of the scope as a function of the background brightness and of the level of dark adaptation of the eyes of the operator. The interested reader will find that Wulfeck and Zeitlin (1962) [5] have done an excellent job of presenting the results of basic sensory experiments and summarizing their implications for equipment design considerations.

THE STUDY OF OUTPUT FACTORS

Output factors constitute a second important potential source of operator error; the production process and the equipment design may often need to be modified so that the operator can more efficiently and more accurately do the things to the system which are required for proper control. For example, Coakley discovered nearly 20 ways—such factors as the order and manner in which the machine controls were set and the techniques used in inspecting and stretching the hose during knitting—in which the weaving machine operators were influencing the weights of stockings produced. In this instance, the solution to the problem involved training the operators to standardize their output behavior. However, in many if not most instances, the solution would involve recommendations for equipment redesign.

A classification of output errors in operating aircraft

Recommendations for equipment redesign were the primary outcome of the classification by Fitts and Jones (1961) of 460 critical incidents involving pilot output errors in operating aircraft controls. They classified the errors according to the following six categories:

1. *Substitution errors:* confusing one control for another, or failing to identify a control when it was needed; for example, mistaking a wing flap control for the landing gear control or vice versa

[5] Wulfeck, J. W. and Zeitlin, L. R. Human Capabilities and Limitations. In Gagne, R. M., *Psychological Principles in System Development.* New York: Holt, Rinehart and Winston, 1962.

2. *Adjustment errors:* operating a control too slowly or too rapidly, moving a switch to a wrong position, or following the wrong sequence in operating several controls; for example, turning the fuel selector to the wrong gasoline tank

3. *Forgetting errors:* failing to check, unlock, or use a control at the proper time; for example, forgetting to lower the landing gear upon landing

4. *Reversal errors:* moving a control in a direction opposite to that necessary to produce a desired result; for example, activating the wing flap control in the wrong direction

5. *Unintentional activation:* inadvertently operating a control without being aware of it

6. *Unable to reach a control:* errors caused by placement of controls too far away to be reached easily by the pilot

Equipment design principles

The above classification of output errors leads readily to a number of practical principles to be followed in the design of equipment. First, it should be obvious that controls should be positioned for easy accessibility by the operator; he should be able to reach them and operate them without assuming uncomfortable or awkward positions. Second, controls should be readily and accurately identifiable. Color and shape coding should be used wherever possible, and ingenuity should be employed to relate the coding scheme to the use of the control; for example, the landing gear control for an aircraft might have a knob in the shape of a pair of wheels. Third, safety mechanisms should be employed to insure against unintentional activation of control devices. The safety lock on a rifle is an example of this. Fourth, the arrangement of controls should be carefully planned. Unusually important and frequently used controls should receive priority placement. Controls which "go together" functionally should be grouped together and controls related in some way to an input display should be located near that display. For example, it makes sense to locate the ignition switch of an automobile near the gas gauge. The arrangement of controls should also be uniform. Fitts and Jones found that one major reason for substitution errors was the lack of uniformity of control placement in different aircraft. Although in the same general location, the throttle and propeller controls were exactly reversed (in a left-right sequence) in the B-25 and C-47. Such lack of uniformity renders interchangeability of operators inefficient if not downright dangerous. Finally, controls should be designed so that their positions or settings are clearly apparent; thus, on-off positions should be shown on switches and the effect of an indicated direction of movement should be displayed on all knobs, levers, or continuous tracking controls. Consider, for example, how much easier it would be to change an automobile tire if auto manufacturers would simply indicate on the wheel rim the direction the wheel nut should be turned for loosening it.

These practical principles of control design seem to be based on little more than common sense reasoning. However, since they are derived from the study of critical incidents involving actual human output errors (often leading to accidents and near accidents) it is painfully apparent, unfortunately, that these common sense principles have all too rarely been employed in the initial design of systems control devices. By whatever label we choose, therefore—common sense or informed judgment—it is clear that the engineering psychologist is in a central position to foster an improvement in the design of such systems control components.

Fundamental research on psychomotor abilities

On the other hand, these practical, common sense principles contribute little to a fundamental understanding of human response characteristics. As mentioned in Chapter 3, we still do not possess an adequate task taxonomy for classifying activities according to human motor modalities. Fleishman has contributed most to our knowledge here (Fleishman, 1962), but a great deal of fundamental research relating Fleishman's findings to the requirements of industrial systems still needs to be accomplished. After performing scores of factor analytic investigations extending over nearly a decade, Fleishman has identified eleven psychomotor abilities which appear to cut across muscle groupings and which strongly refute earlier notions about the possible existence of such things as general physical proficiency or general manual dexterity. The eleven abilities identified by Fleishman are:

1. *Control Precision:* common to tasks requiring finely controlled muscular adjustments involving large muscle groupings
2. *Multilimb Coordination:* ability to coordinate the movement of a number of limbs simultaneously
3. *Response Orientation:* involving the ability to make the correct movement in relation to a stimulus under highly speeded conditions
4. *Reaction Time:* representing simply the speed with which an individual is able to respond to a stimulus when it appears
5. *Speed of Arm Movement:* representing the speed with which an individual can make a gross arm movement where accuracy is not required
6. *Rate Control:* involving the ability to make continuous motor adjustments relative to a moving target changing in speed and direction
7. *Manual Dexterity:* ability to make skillful arm and hand movements in handling rather large objects (such as blocks) under speeded conditions
8. *Finger Dexterity:* involving skillful manipulations of small objects (such as nuts and bolts) with the fingers
9. *Arm-Hand Steadiness:* involving the ability to make precise arm-hand positioning movements which minimize strength and speed (such as threading a needle)
10. *Wrist-Finger Speed:* rapid tapping movements with the wrist and finger
11. *Aiming:* a highly restricted ability involving the placing of dots in circles

What is now needed is further industrial research designed to define the output requirements of production systems in terms of these eleven psychomotor groupings. With such information, the engineering psychologist, in making equipment design recommendations, will be capable of a much greater generalizability than is now possible with the important but rather narrowly restricted common sense principles outlined previously.

OPERATOR VARIABLES

We have already noted that the use of human operators in production systems is greatly complicated by the fact of individual differences. Since people differ widely from one another, they are far from perfectly interchangeable as systems components. The engineering psychologist is painfully aware of differences in the sensory and motor capabilities of people and also of broader differences in aptitude, personality, motivation, and morale, etc.— the many dimensions of difference are too numerous to list. Because of these many differences, the engineering psychologist must wear a variety of different hats. As the occasion demands, he becomes a selection expert or a training specialist or he may even find himself giving attention to the question of how different operators may best be motivated to do a good job. Because other chapters are devoted to each of these areas, we shall not discuss them separately here; instead we shall simply comment briefly on one rather interesting operator variable which we hope will serve to give the flavor of research on operator variation.

A research study on alertness as an operator variable

During World War II, the question of operator alertness received a good deal of attention. A war machine or a defense establishment does not stop to rest at night; constant operator surveillance is necessary. Yet alertness fluctuates greatly over time; any student who has struggled to stay awake during a boring lecture is well aware of these changes, but most people may not know that the alertness cycles differ rather markedly for different persons. Some are at their peak of alertness early in the morning; others don't "get going" until nearly midmorning, but they may sustain a high level of efficiency and alertness far into the night. The curve of alertness for any given person typically follows a 24-hour cycle which is associated with a corresponding daily fluctuation in body temperature (ranging over 1° F). It is obvious, therefore, that when operators are assigned to night work or to early morning watches, many may be at a low point of alertness and efficiency. Concerned with this problem, Kleitman (1949) studied the patterns of sleep-wakefulness and alertness among the 74 crew members of the submarine, U.S.S. *Dogfish* for a period of two weeks. He kept careful records of the amount of time each man spent in sleeping, working, eating, and recreation, and he obtained ratings from the men of their overall feelings of alertness during various waking periods. He also obtained body temperature readings every four hours from a small subgroup of crew members. The watches aboard the craft followed the traditional "4 on 8 off" routine, and the watch remained fixed for the entire duration of the cruise. Kleitman found, as he had expected, that crew members failed to adjust their individual alertness cycles to the patterns dictated by their work assignments. In other words, most men standing watch during late night and early morning hours were sleepy and unalert. According to Kleitman, the men failed to shift their individual cycles primarily because a shore-type schedule of meals was retained. On the basis of his observations, therefore, Kleitman suggested a number of changes in meal and watch schedules to take better account of operator differences in alertness cycles. This research and many of his recommendations are now proving particularly useful in formulating schedules for present-day crews of nuclear submarines and in planning the schedules to be followed by future operators of interplanetary space craft.

A HUMAN FACTORS ANALYSIS LEADING TO EQUIPMENT REDESIGN

Shackel (1962) provides a good example of a human factors analysis directed toward redesigning the console of the EMIDEC 2400 computing system. The operator's task, in running a computer, is to oversee the entire operation. Shackel describes the operator's job as being "analogous to that of a nursemaid; he has to see that the machine is fed correctly with all the required data at the right times, to watch over the life of the machine at work, to prevent it hurting itself or its data if something goes wrong, and to cure minor ills and call in the specialist to deal with major ones" (page 229). Thus, the operator is himself the ultimate controller of the computing system, and the design of the console or control board of the computer is a critically important part of assuring complete accuracy of operation. A brief listing of the problems considered by Shackel and the way he solved them should give the reader a good view of what an engineering psychologist does. The actions taken by Shackel are summarized below under the categories of *input factors, output factors,* and *operator variables:*

INPUT FACTORS

1. *Displays.*   The console included over 150 lights to indicate to the operator the operational mode of each one of 25 magnetic tape units, the availability of the units for further storage, and the operating characteristics of data input and output machines. Shackel divided the three types of indicators (i.e., operational mode of tape units, their availability, and input and output machinery) into separate banks of lights and developed an overall color code for the lettering beside the indicators.

2. *Warning Systems.*   Originally, the console had no integrated warning system but merely a number of red lights located at various points, some of which indicated the need for attention to a minor problem, others showing the need for immediate attention to correct a dangerous fault in the computer operation. Shackel integrated all the warning lights into a single display panel and provided for a two-level warning system combining simultaneous visual and auditory signals. Thus, the lights for the more important components glowed green for satisfactory and red accompanied by an alarm bell for a state requiring immediate action. Lights for the components requiring less immediate action were normally off but changed to amber accompanied by a pleasant ding-dong chime (sounded at 30 sec. intervals) for conditions requiring action within the next 5-10 minutes.

OUTPUT FACTORS

1. *Push Buttons.*   One panel on the console had three rows of push buttons with which the operator manually operated various components of the computer. The layout was confusing, however, and was improved by regrouping the buttons and by using the same color code as for the display units discussed previously.

2. *Selector Switches.*   Another manual action panel used symmetrically shaped knobs for five selector switches with only a thin white line on each to show the direction the knob was pointing. Furthermore, the knobs were located in a confusing way (three above and two below) so that the sequence of their numerical settings was not immediately clear. In fact, the engineer who had designed the panel made an error when asked to set a five-digit number with the knobs. He, as would most operators, simply set the first three digits with the upper knobs and the last two digits with the lower knobs.

The correct sequence followed an alternating pattern between upper and lower knobs, but few operators would be aware of the proper sequence, and it was not shown in any clear way on the panel. Shackel's redesign of the panel made use of arrow-shaped knobs (to show more clearly the direction they pointed) sufficiently small to be lined up in a single horizontal row. In addition, the numbers were placed in a standard clock-face arrangement about each dial, thereby taking advantage of the operators' obvious familiarity with clocks to aid them in making accurate numerical settings with the switches.

3. *General Layout of Workspace.* Bodily measurements were then used to help plan the spatial arrangements of the various panels. A rather simple analysis using a drawing board and anthropometric data was sufficient to plan the panel placement so that 95% of all operators would be able to view all portions clearly and reach the control buttons and switches without bending, stretching, standing, stooping, or in any other way contorting themselves.

OPERATOR VARIABLES

Operator variables were not dealt with to any degree in this specialized project. This is probably because the typical operator of a computer is a highly trained and skilled technician who is selected for the job only after careful screening and a sizeable amount of experience. Thus, any operator differences apt to affect the accuracy of the operation are, in effect, not allowed to enter the system. Certain environmental factors were, however, dealt with. Lighting was carefully designed to afford adequate illumination without introducing glare, and noise was reduced by using sound-absorbing surfaces whenever possible. In addition, the human operators profited from the computer's own requirements for an air-conditioned, temperature-controlled, and dust-free environment. Thus, the major considerations given to operator variables occurred in the form of simply making the environment a pleasant place in which to work, thereby contributing possibly to a general feeling of well-being and favorable morale for any operator assigned to the position.

A FINAL WORD ABOUT RESEARCH IN ENGINEERING PSYCHOLOGY

In the above illustration, it is clear that no actual research was performed. However, the focus of the analysis and many of the recommendations were obviously based heavily on Shackel's own experience as an engineering psychologist, including his ability to draw on the accumulated body of human factors research results bearing on design problems similar to this one. Shackel's work represents, therefore, nearly the full range of human factors considerations including the analysis of anticipated systems errors, display problems, the design of controls, anthropometric measurements, and environmental considerations. But it does not, unfortunately, represent a careful validation of the procedures recommended. To do this would have required a carefully designed experiment with appropriate scientific controls assigned to the many potential variables which might have affected the operation of the computer. In many instances the time pressures of practical design work preclude carrying out a well-designed scientific investigation, in which case the engineering psychologist must be content to base his recommendations (as Shackel did) on his own experience and knowledge of the field. However, he must not be content to do this for all his design problems; the better engineering psychologists will press always for research and for carefully designed studies to add to the total fund of knowledge concerning man-machine systems and their interactions. Only in this way will the field of engineering psychology continue to be able to support its claim of offering scientifically-established principles to take the place of guesses, opinions, hunches, and intuitions.

Suggested Additional Reading

Bennett, E. Degan, J., and Spiegel, J. (Eds.) *Human factors in technology.* New York: McGraw-Hill, 1963.

Chapanis, A. *Research techniques in human engineering.* Baltimore: Johns Hopkins, 1959.

Chapanis, A., Garner, W. R., and Morgan, C. T. *Applied experimental psychology, human factors in engineering design.* New York: Wiley, 1949.

Committee on Undersea Warfare. *A survey report of human factors in underseas warfare.* Washington, D.C.: National Research Council, 1949.

Gagne, R. M. (Ed.) *Psychological principles in system development.* New York: Holt, Rinehart and Winston, 1962.

McCormick, E. J. *Human engineering* (2nd ed.). New York: McGraw-Hill, 1964.

McFarland, R. A. *Human factors in air transportation.* New York: McGraw-Hill, 1953.

Morgan, C. T., Cook, J. S. III, Chapanis, A., and Lund, M. W. (Eds.) *Human engineering guide to equipment design.* New York: McGraw-Hill, 1963.

Sells, S. B., and Berry, C. A. (Eds.) *Human factors in jet and space travel: a medical-psychological analysis.* New York: Ronald, 1961.

Sinaiko, H. W. (Ed.) *Selected papers on human factors in the design and use of control systems.* New York: Dover, 1961.

Woodson, W. E. *Human engineering guide for equipment designers.* Berkeley: University of California Press, 1954.

6

HUMAN MOTIVATION
IN INDUSTRY

MOTIVATION: AN IMPORTANT
BUT DIFFICULT CONCEPT

In previous chapters, we have referred occasionally to human motivation, as, for example, when we said (in Chapter 3) that learning could only occur when the learner was motivated. So far, however, we have handled motivation in a rather cavalier way—as if a simple listing of human wants and desires might be sufficient for completely understanding human motivational processes. Unfortunately, understanding motivation is not nearly so easy. The motivation of employees in industry is one of the most important but one of the least understood areas of industrial psychology today.

Motivation is important to industry because it involves the *action* phase of behavior. An old saying states that you can lead a horse to water, but you can't make him drink. Like the horse, an industrial employee may be liberally endowed with all the physical equipment, abilities, and machinery necessary to perform a task, but this does not guarantee that he will indeed perform that task. The mysterious quality impelling him to undertake action to actually get the task done is what we are studying when we direct our attention to problems of human motivation in industry.

A motivation model

Motivation is poorly understood because it is an extremely complex and subtle phenomenon. Some of its complexities may be more readily outlined by referring to the motivation model shown below:

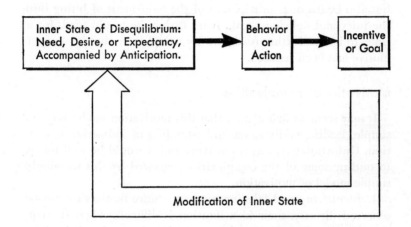

In this model, it is assumed that a person behaves in response to stimuli associated with a hypothesized internal state of disequilibrium. The behavior is directed at attaining an incentive or goal which the individual anticipates will be satisfying in the sense of restoring equilibrium. The state of disequilibrium may stem from deprivation or pain (e.g., going without food or water for a time) or simply from anticipating a sense of enjoyment if the incentive is attained (e.g., a preference or appetite for different kinds of foods or liking to engage in certain activities). The attainment of the goal, as shown by the model, leads to a change in the degree of disequilibrium and an accompanying change in the level of the force impelling the individual toward action. It is clear that these inner states of disequilibrium or motives cannot be observed and measured directly; instead their presence and their nature must be inferred from observing the kinds of behavior occurring in relation to different kinds of incentives and antecedent circumstances. For example, if we were to withhold all food from a person for two days and then present him with a huge T-bone steak, his behavior (voracious eating) would lead us to infer that he was impelled by an inner motive (state of disequilibrium) which common usage has labeled hunger. Presumably, our subject's eating behavior would be directed not only toward satisfying his body's physiological need for nourishment but also by his own anticipation of the enjoyment of biting into the juicy and delicious steak. After eating, he would tend, for a time, to ignore further food, and we would infer that his hunger motive had been reduced.

Motivational complexities

It may seem, at first glance, that this motivation model is quite simple, leading easily to an understanding of industrial motivation. Unfortunately, this is not true, and it would be well for us to outline some of the complexities suggested by this seemingly simple model of motivation.

1. *Identifying and labeling motives.* Since motives cannot be observed directly, their identification is difficult. Their description must be derived from inferences based on other behaviors, and these inferences are rarely as easily or as well-specified as those related to the so-called hunger motive discussed above. We know, for example, that people may work hard to earn more money. But what underlying motive does this reflect? Money may be an incentive for some because it helps to satisfy their desires for status; for others, because it gives them a greater sense of security (saving for a rainy day); and, for still others, because it can become a symbol of their power over other people. Thus, the necessity to infer motives from behavior greatly complicates our understanding of human motivation; similar behaviors may stem from quite different underlying motives, and different behaviors may often result from the same underlying motive.

2. *Mapping the configuration of motives.* A motive rarely exists alone or in isolation. Any individual may experience a wide range of inner desires or anticipations. They may presumably

exist at differing levels of strength, waxing and waning as they are differentially satisfied or frustrated. Further, some may be in conflict with others; that is, striving to satisfy one motive may be done only at the expense of not satisfying another. In industry, accepting a promotion may help to satisfy needs for status or for power while at the same time frustrating social needs for acceptance by members of one's immediate peer group. The changing relative importance of various motives is illustrated by the amorous young man who may wine and dine the object of his affections in the hope that satisfaction of certain of her physiological motives (i.e., hunger and physical comfort) may be accompanied by a relative strengthening of other motives (e.g., affiliation or sex). Thus, the patterning and configuration of motives within any person is undoubtedly in a constant state of change. Human motivation can only be completely understood by adopting a dynamic rather than a static point of view, and this obviously further complicates the observation and measurement of human motives.

3. *Differences among individuals.* Undoubtedly, people differ in the nature of motives impelling them to action. Because of this, the same incentives are responded to differently by different persons. Not only do they differ in *what* they seek in their jobs, but people also differ in the ease with which their motives may be satisfied. One man, motivated to achieve status, may appear rather easily satisfied and rest on his laurels after a single promotion. Another, also motivated by status needs, may show an apparently insatiable striving to advance in the business hierarchy either because he derives enjoyment from the act of striving for advancement or perhaps as a means of gaining increased socioeconomic advantages. Certainly, individual differences such as these must be considered in our effort to understand human motivation.

4. *Nature of changes in motives after goal attainment.* Still another complication arises from the way in which motives are changed after incentives have been reached. Some motives such as hunger, thirst, sex, and sleeplessness are temporarily diminished after being gratified. In fact, as long as they are satisfied,

such motives remain insignificant as activators of behavior. However, those motives which have their basis in the anticipation of
enjoyment are often actually strengthened by goal attainment.
Such motives may not be susceptible to being appeased, and they
may take on motivating properties of their own. For example,
the need to achieve something of consequence or the related
need for a sense of personal esteem are not usually diminished
for long by being satisfied. In fact, their attainment is often accompanied by a heightened sense of anticipation and a setting of
new and higher goals of achievement whose attainment may involve greater heights of exhilaration and ever increasing feelings
of personal esteem. Thus, for many motives, the attainment of
the goal serves simply to whet the appetite for still more of the
same. Beyond the purely physiological motives, it is difficult to
determine whether a given motive should be classified as a *satisfier*
(that is, one which is appeased by being satisfied) or a *motivator*
(that is, one which is not appeased by being satisfied and which
takes on increased motivating properties through the very process
of striving to achieve the goal). The accuracy of such a classification is obviously important if we are to make recommendations
about the industrial environment most likely to elicit and maintain certain desired employee behaviors. Here too, we must expect that persons may differ in the way their motives change or
are modified after goal attainment, and it becomes extremely
difficult, therefore, to predict the behavioral consequences that a
given set of incentives may have for any given individual.

It should now be clear why psychologists and other behavioral
scientists have had trouble understanding the motivation of employees in industry. Why does one employee work eagerly, maxi-
mally utilizing his abilities while another employee, equally
endowed, lets his abilities fall into disuse in favor of adopting an
apathetic or even hostile behavior in the work setting? Obviously,
the question is not answerable in the abstract; in fact, the complexities of human motivation have made it difficult even to do
well-designed research studies on the matter. Consequently, many
early investigators adopted the easy alternative of making unrealistic and oversimplified assumptions about the nature of man and
his participation in industry. Even so, the early research stimu-

lated thinking on these complex problems and, more recently, numerous studies, characterized by ingenious and sophisticated research designs, have been and are being conducted. The result is a rapidly accumulating body of knowledge and a number of new insights concerning industrial motivation. We want to review these studies in some detail. First, however, it is well to gain perspective on the present by briefly reviewing the history of thinking and research concerning human motivation in industry.

BRIEF HISTORY OF MOTIVATION IN INDUSTRY

Preindustrial revolution

Before the industrial revolution in the mid 1800's, no one gave much systematic thought to questions of employee motivation. The units of production were small and production techniques were simple. By and large, employees owned their own tools and capital investment by employers was relatively small. Since capital resources had not yet been introduced on any broad scale into the production framework, no strong pressure was created for high quantity production. The marketing process was not sufficiently advanced nor efficient to be able to handle high output. The workday was long, to be sure, but the tempo was relaxed and easy, and questions about the utilization of human efforts or the motivation to work were not particularly important or significant.

Scientific management

All this changed under the impact of the industrial revolution. Capital investment in land, factories, and machinery spiraled upward; innovations in the marketing process not only met but began to create widespread consumer demand. Under the threat of keen competition, in order to protect their capital investments, and trying to meet burgeoning consumer demands, owners pressed harder and harder for increased productivity. Suddenly, almost overnight, attention was directed at the individual employee and questions concerning his efficiency and motivation became very important. At the time, the easiest view of the worker was as just another element of the production process. It seemed that his efficiency might most easily be increased by giving him a single best method for doing his job and that his strongest efforts could be elicited by the simple expedient of using money as an incentive. The major proponent of these ideas was Frederick Taylor, the Father of Scientific Management. Taylor developed systems of time and methods analysis whereby each employee was, in effect, "standardized." Along with the standardization, he introduced wage incentive schemes so that workers could receive increased wages in return for increased production. He argued that scientific management would increase satisfaction to the worker *and* reduce unit costs of production. Note, however, that a major premise of scientific management was that employees were all essentially identical elements in the production process, to be studied and manipulated as any other cog in the machinery of production. Moreover, in spite of early warnings by some of the so-called efficiency experts, it was assumed that employees were uniformly motivated by a desire for money and that other motives were either nonexistent or of little consequence. Certainly, these simplified assumptions and early methods of scientific management were sharply at odds with what we have already said about the complexities of human motivation.

Negative reactions

In spite of these simplified and erroneous concepts, most workers seemed, for a time, to "buy" the incentive schemes that were set up. Large production increases were recorded, and scientific management came to be regarded by some as an industrial panacea. Unfortunately, however, most owners had their own assumptions about the ultimate worth of workers, and they resisted the idea of paying them *too much*. They were willing to pay for increased production only up to a certain point, and, if the point was exceeded, it was often the signal for a restudy of the production standards and the setting of new, more conservative incentive payments. Workers soon learned that it was unsafe to produce over a given level and negative pressures leading to the restriction of output became common. Employees also came to learn that "runaway" production might exceed market demands and lead to the necessity for temporary layoffs; thus, the need for security and steady earnings came to be expressed in the form of a slowing down or restriction of output. In other words, the fallacies inherent in the early assumptions of scientific management began to be all too apparent; the true complexities of human motivation began to show up, and scientific management came to encounter an increasing number of failures.

The human relations movement

One such failure occurred in a Philadelphia textile mill in the early 1920's. Hounded by employee antagonism and excessive labor turnover, the management of the firm hired efficiency experts to study the jobs and to institute methods of incentive payment. However, the effort to implement the recommendations of this scientific management study was accompanied by increased turnover and a heightened incidence of griping and grievances by the workers. At this point, a Harvard sociologist, Elton Mayo, was called in to see if he could stem the tide of labor discontent. His solution was startlingly simple. He reasoned that the difficulties arose out of the monotony of the work, and he suggested that the workers be allowed to take rest periods according to their own agreed-upon schedule. Utilizing Mayo's suggestion, management was pleased to note a sharp decrease in turnover, accompanied by rapidly increasing productivity. It is clear, of course, that Mayo solved this problem successfully because he stood ready to discard mechanistic notions of man's nature in favor of more humanistic assumptions. He recognized that employees sought more than money from their jobs—that money probably could only be effective as an incentive if it were used in conjunction with rather than in opposition to man's other needs. Stimulated by this early success, Mayo set out to discover what these other needs might be. Conveniently, at about this time, he was asked to study employee productivity at the Hawthorne works of the Western Electric Company; thus, he undertook the series of studies which are regarded by some as classics in the study of employees' motivation.

In order to gain greater experimental control over the work setting, a group of six female employees was asked to work in an experimental production room where production could be observed and measured and which also allowed for the ready manipulation (with the assent of the workers) of working conditions, such as rest periods, the length of the work day, etc. It soon became apparent that the productivity of the experimental work team shot upward quite without regard to the experimental variables being manipulated. In the words of Gellerman (1963), "The research team realized that in trying to maintain the scientific purity of the experiment, they had inadvertently ignited a powerful, dormant motivator." Gellerman (1963, pp. 21-22) goes on to describe the results as follows:

By singling a few workers out from many to participate in an experiment, the Mayo group had given them a sort of "elite" feeling among themselves; when this was compounded by giving them control (through assent) of their own workday, morale soared and production with it. The experimental group was operating under motivational conditions that were vastly different from those in the rest of the plant—these workers were treated as if they were important and unique. They had a major voice in deciding on the management of their own time, and they were insulated (by the researchers) from the routine demands and restrictions of management. The evidence was beginning to mount, in other words, that in "treating workers like human beings," allowing them to coalesce into natural groups and relieving these groups of impersonal controls, motives were being harnessed which could improve production dramatically.

Thus, the human relations movement in industry was set off. Mayo interpreted the Western Electric results in terms of man's peculiarly human need to belong to and to be regarded as a significant member of a group. In so doing, he was able to explain both the enhancement of productivity when the group's goals and pressures were congruent with the desires of management *and* restriction of productivity when the group's goals and pressures were in opposition to the desires of management. Mayo's explanation cast our understanding of human motivation along a new dimension, but it too was a greatly oversimplified one.

Where scientific management had been content to assume that man's most basic motives were economic, Mayo and his "Human Relations School" made the equally oversimplified assumption that group membership and affiliation were the most fundamental and essentially the only human needs of any consequence.

Nonetheless, Mayo's research stands today as a landmark in our efforts to understand human motivation in industry. It made evident to all observers the unique characteristics of the human being in industry and made obvious the necessity and desirability of studying the complexities of human motivation rather than merely relying upon easy assumptions about the nature of man. The impact of Mayo's research was heightened by the zealous manner in which he publicized it. His strong opinions about man's so-called fundamental desire to affiliate in groups caused others to question and to reinterpret his findings and to undertake widespread research studies of their own.

A reanalysis of Mayo's findings

A second look at Gellerman's description of the Western Electric experiments will show that much more was occurring in the experimental production room than could be subsumed under Mayo's own interpretation of his results. For example, the workers gained an increased sense of personal worth; they participated in decisions affecting their work, and they came to like the actual duties of their jobs because the jobs had been broadened to include participating in an important scientific experiment. They were able, thereby, to gain an increased sense of accomplishment; they probably felt more secure in their jobs because of the permissive and friendly manner of the experimenter; on top of all this, they had the opportunity to earn more money because a group incentive pay scheme had been introduced at the very beginning of the experiment. Thus, on the basis of the many different types of incentives present in the Western Electric experiments, we could infer that many different motives might be acting, including, for example, security, affiliation, esteem, intrinsic job interest, and achievement. It is clear, then, that Mayo's research was much less precise for specifying a single human motive than he believed it was. Subsequent research has dealt more systematically with each of the motives mentioned above. We will summarize some of the more important of these investigations in order to lay the groundwork for our later discussion of the measurement of human motivation.

FOUR HUMAN MOTIVES

Security

When faced with a threat to their well-being, most people do whatever is necessary to avoid injury. The threat may arise not only from such obvious factors as hazardous working conditions threatening to one's physical welfare, but also from more subtle factors such as a threatened loss of employment or the loss of a settled and familiar working environment. Thus, to varying degrees, people behave in order to preserve their security. The relative importance of security obviously differs from time to time. During the Great Depression set off by the stock market crash of 1929, economic conditions made it impossible for most employers to assure their workers of the continued security of steady employment. For a time, security became perhaps the most important element in industrial motivation. In contrast, the industrial scene of today is strongly characterized by plans designed to insure the security of employees—pensions, hospitalization and insurance provisions, and company policies protecting employees against arbitrary discharges and job changes. However, even though such plans are widespread, they are far from universal; for this reason, it is possible to observe quite marked differences in employee behavior which presumably arise partly from their differing needs for security. For example, many persons move into jobs which seem to offer little in the way of security. Anyone who enters life insurance selling has obviously made a decision, either consciously or unconsciously, that other incentives are more important than the immediate security of an assured future and a defined environment within which to work. Other persons seem to be extremely security-minded. Such people behave as if they had vague and ill-defined misgivings about life, and they try to allay these uneasy feelings by seeking a protecting job environment—one which defines very precisely what will be demanded from them and offers a sort of paternalistic protection to them in return for their efforts. Obviously, such persons will not usually show any eagerness to strive for goals which may require giving up the security of the known for the insecurity of the unknown. It would seem, therefore, that such an employee would not be easily motivated by opportunities to advance or to gain increased success in the firm.

We should remember, however, that human motives may be dynamic and changing rather than fixed. It is possible, for example, that a so-called security-minded person could be enticed into utilizing other (probably dormant) motives or taught to anticipate satisfaction from behaviors seemingly antagonistic to his security motive. This is what most probably occurred during the Western Electric experiments, and we shall want to discuss the possibility further after first mentioning some of the other human motives.

Affiliation

The desire of people to establish and maintain interpersonal contacts is a strong urge which nearly everyone shows at one time or another. As we have seen, Mayo made this the central theme in his effort to understand industrial motivation. Recently, other investigators, notably Schachter (1959), Shipley and Veroff (1952), and Herzberg, Mausner, and Snyderman (1959) have thrown new light on the "affiliation motive." Schachter's research suggests that one major reason that people come together is to share their opinions with like-minded individuals. In a sense, groups often form, then, in order for individuals to gain the security of hearing their beliefs confirmed by other people. Schachter has also shown that *anxiety* may be an important determiner of affiliative tendencies. In a series of experiments with college coeds, he demonstrated that subjects who were threatened with the possibility of a physically painful experiment (electric shock) chose more often to get together in groups than girls who were not so threatened. He concluded that affiliative tendencies stem, in part, from a strong desire to allay anxiety by talking things over or otherwise sharing one's worries or beliefs with other people.

Shipley and Veroff, working with subjects belonging to a college fraternity, asked each man, in turn, to stand up while his fraternity brothers rated him on a number of adjectives such as aggressive, friendly, conceited, intolerant, modest, and sympathetic. This was followed by having each member write down the names of the three brothers whom he would most prefer as his closest personal friends. Later, when the members of the fraternity were asked to make up stories about a number of rather ambiguous pictures, similar to those in the Thematic Apperception Test (TAT), they tended more often to choose themes involving affiliative tendencies than did the members of a second fraternity who had merely been asked to check a list of food preferences prior to their writing the TAT stories. Apparently the stimulus of being rated by one's peers was sufficient to arouse the affiliation motive among members of the first fraternity. In another study, Shipley and Veroff showed that freshmen who were rejected by fraternities they had wished to join showed higher affiliative needs (in TAT stories completed a month after the rushing season) than freshmen who had been accepted by the fraternities of their choice. Both these studies are consistent with Schachter's results in that they suggest that the affiliation motive is often aroused by conditions involving some degree of anxiety—based either on the threat of physical harm (as in Schachter's experiments) or on the possibility of interpersonal rejection (as in the Shipley and Veroff experiments).

It seems, therefore, that the affiliation motive may arise out of circumstances rather similar to those involving a need for security. In industry, the difference is that security needs usually involve the physical or material circumstances of one's work environment whereas affiliation motives involve the social and interpersonal environment. Herzberg, et al. (1959) learned more about this social side of work when they interviewed 200 engineers and accountants about unusually satisfying and unusually dissatisfying job occurrences. Somewhat surprisingly, they found that relationships with co-workers were mentioned only rarely as being important elements in these critical job incidents. In fact, only 3% of the unusually satisfying situations were based on affiliative relationships; about 8% of the unusually dissatisfying situations involved such relationships.

Thus, the results obtained by Schachter, Shipley and Veroff, and Herzberg, et al. lead to a number of generalizations about the affiliation motive. First, it is probably far less important, in and of itself, as a factor in industrial motivation than Mayo concluded it to be. Secondly, affiliation, defined as the anticipation of warm and friendly relationships with other persons, seems in part to be a response to anxiety instead of a positive striving for enjoyment. Referring again to the motivation model outlined previously, it appears that affiliation might best be classified as a *satisfier* because affiliative needs probably are appeased and diminished by goal attainment rather than being increased or strengthened. It should, of course, be equally apparent that persons differ widely in the degree to which they seek affiliative associations and the extent to which their anticipations can be satisfied. In the industrial setting, then, the affiliation motive probably is most powerful in affecting behavior when circumstances are such as to frustrate the normal affiliative needs of employees, thereby resulting in anxiety and a strong tendency to seek group succor. This fact, in turn, helps us understand how the group may exert a strong influence on an individual worker; he fears the anxiety of losing the emotional support of his peers, and he looks to the group as a source of psychological or "social" security. Thus, a group motivated (probably by other more important needs) toward production (as in the Western Electric studies) may well bring subtle pressures, in the form of threats of anxiety inducing loss of acceptance, to bear on each of the group members. The same sort of pressure may be brought to bear toward the restriction of production. A third generalization concerning affiliation is that, as with other motives, people differ a great deal from one another in the degree to which they may seek the emotional security of affiliation with others. Schachter showed this to be true, and he was even able to relate such differences to various biographical variables such as the birth order of a person among her siblings. As with security, we may note that different jobs or job settings may differ in providing circumstances satisfying to persons with highly affiliative needs; thus, persons may move differentially into job situations on the basis of these *emotional* security needs as well as on the basis of *material* security needs. Finally, then, we are able to cast Mayo's findings in their proper perspective. Affiliation and the desire for group belonging is one important factor in understanding industrial motivation, but probably much less important than Mayo believed it to be.

Competence and esteem

A great deal of what we do as adults involves patterns of behavior learned as children. In particular, we spend much of our childhood learning to cope with the people and objects making up our environment. Even young infants seem to show a strong sense of curiosity as indicated by their continual investigation of their ever-expanding worlds.

In fact, laboratory studies have shown that animals, too, appear to possess strong curiosity or exploratory drives. Glanzer (1958) has summarized a number of such experiments, and it is clear that animals tend to seek out and to explore new or novel situations in preference to situations in which the stimuli are less complex or familiar. Thus, it is probable that opportunities to investigate complex situations or to explore novel stimuli serve as strong incentives to both animal and human learning.

White (1959) believes this demonstrates and is the basis for a fundamental human motive toward mastery of the environment which he calls the "competence motive." White does an excellent job of tracing the development of the competence motive through the successes and failures of childhood and adolescence to the behavior patterns shown by adults. We need not speculate with White about the onset of this motive; for our purposes, it is sufficient to state that many adults do behave *as if* they seek to confirm their own feelings of competence. Those who have successfully overcome many obstacles in the past strive mightily to confirm this history of competence by continuing to seek and to overcome obstacles in the present and future. People who have not encountered much success in the past may be less ready in the present to try difficult jobs because they fear just another failure, and they seek to avoid the pain of confirming once again their own relatively low estimate of themselves. It should be apparent that the idea of a competence motive may help to explain some important aspects of industrial behavior. First, it is clear that a high sense of personal worth and competence will not often be served adequately by jobs demanding little in the way of skill and knowledge from the individual employee. Thus, if an employee *is* motivated by a desire to demonstrate his overall competence and his job does not allow him to do so, his response to the job may well become one of apathy, and he will instead seek to show his competence in other areas, for example, by pouring himself into hobbies and other avocational pursuits. Secondly, a sense of competence or personal worth is not measurable in any absolute sense. Instead it depends to a large degree on feedback from the people and objects in the environment. A star quarterback who completes a 30 yard pass for a touchdown is granted immediate feedback both in the objective form of seeing the ball caught by his teammate for the touchdown and in the more subjective form of the confirming roar of approval from his team's supporters in the stands. Can you imagine how he might feel if his spectacular performance were greeted by stony silence from the stands? Certainly, he would wonder what had gone wrong. He might even question momentarily whether or not he actually had scored a bona fide touchdown. In essence, his own feelings of personal worth, competence, esteem, and success would be influenced strongly by the behavior of other people toward him. Thus, it is also in the industrial setting. Employees experience esteem only through feedback from the work environment. To be sure, part of the feedback may be based on fairly objective evidence of success (such as the football landing perfectly in the outstretched arms of the receiver). More important by far, however, is feedback in the form of recognition or praise received from other persons in the work environment. It is easier now to understand one of the factors which probably was operating in Mayo's Western Electric experiments. What had been a routine and perhaps rather onerous job contributing little to a feeling of competence became, in the experimental setting, a task which was valued in the eyes of the experimenters; hence, the work situation was changed overnight into one capable of providing the employees with feelings of competence, personal worth, and esteem.

We may summarize what we have said about the competence motive as follows: People behave as if they seek to confirm their feelings about their own personal worth and competence. It is likely that many industrial jobs provide little opportunity for employees to gain a sense of competence. Instead, they either stifle the competence motive or merely confirm a lack of competence for those who have not formed strong competence needs. However, it is possible that ingenuity may show how jobs and job situations may be restructured to give greater opportunities for gaining feelings of personal worth and even, perhaps, to educate or show employees how to respond constructively to incentive situations designed to elicit the competence motive.

Achievement

Highly related to the desires for esteem or competence is the more general desire to achieve something of consequence. Many of the important goals of our industrial society fall under the general label, *achievement*. As we look about us, it is apparent that people differ greatly in the degree of satisfaction they derive from accomplishment. Some seem to strive strongly to gain a sense of having achieved a difficult goal; others, apparently less intent on achievement simply for achievement's sake, seem to need constant prodding in the form of more tangible rewards. It may be, therefore, that achievement, per se, can be viewed as a fundamental human motive. Certainly, this is the view held by McClelland (1961) and his colleagues (McClelland, Atkinson, Clark, and Lowell, 1953; Atkinson, 1958), and they have devoted over a decade to the study of what they term the "achievement motive." Their early experiments were designed to elicit the achievement motive and to develop a way of measuring it. To do this, they asked groups of college students to take a number of short tests under several different conditions. Although several conditions were employed, a description of two of them should be sufficient to convey the major elements of the experiment. One condition, the relaxed condition, used directions designed to convince the students that the tests, and not the students, were being tested; presumably the achievement motive would not be heightened by such directions. Another group was told that the tests were important measures of general intelligence, that they were strongly indicative of leadership ability and that they had been used to select people for high administrative posts in government and business; presumably these directions would heighten the achievement motive. After the tests had been taken, the subjects were asked to make up stories about what they saw in the rather ambiguous pictures of the Thematic Apperception Test (TAT). As expected, they differed substantially in the degree of striving or achieving attributed to the central characters of the stories. Groups in which the achievement motive had been experimentally induced wrote stories with more achievement content than the relaxed group, and it was possible, by comparing responses made by the two groups, to develop a scoring system to account for the achievement motivation reflected in the TAT stories.

Subsequent research has shown that high concern with achieving in the TAT stories is accompanied by strong desires for accomplishment in a person's day-to-day pursuits. For example, persons with high TAT achievement scores tend to be more ready to stick with an achievement-related task, whereas persons scoring lower on the TAT test are more ready to quit a project if they don't receive other rewards (such as money) for continuing. In other words, for persons high on the achievement motive, the accomplishment resulting from the process of striving or seeking to achieve is reward enough, in and of itself, making the whole effort meaningful and worthwhile. It should be obvious, of course, that something which constitutes achievement for one person may be entirely meaningless to another. The choice of what may seem to constitute achievement for any given individual depends, in part at least, on the probability of being able to accomplish a desired task. A person with high achievement needs will usually strive harder for things that seem important and also reasonably capable of attainment. He will tend to ignore the easy goals because their attainment would give no real sense of accomplishment, and he will also tend to put aside the extremely difficult goals because the possibility of their attainment may seem so remote that the probability of gaining a sense of accomplishment is just too low. The major problems, then, in relating these findings to industrial motivation become first one of learning just how important achievement may be for any given employee and, second, one of determining the *kinds* of goals that for him seem to be worthy of his efforts and yet reasonably attainable. Although these problems may seem, at first, to be immense, we should remember once again that human motivation has many dynamic properties. In particular, it is likely that the industrial setting can be structured so as to appeal to employees' achievement motives. For example, jobs can be designed to be more difficult—that is, many of the unusually simple, easy, and routine jobs, beneath the "dignity" of the achievement motivated employee, can be eliminated. In similar fashion, it may be possible to convince some employees that jobs which they originally thought were out of their reach may really not be, and that the probability of their accomplishing them successfully may be higher than they suppose. Thus, the achievement motive, like the desire for competence or esteem, seems capable of manipulation. It may be possible to structure jobs so as to give achievement motivated employees greater opportunities for self-expression; even more important, it may be possible to develop the motive to achieve among employees who are not otherwise so disposed.

Names of motives are summary devices

By now, it should be abundantly clear that human motivation is many faceted. We have chosen to discuss briefly the four motives of *security, affiliation, competence,* and *achievement* simply because they have received a good deal of attention and because they seem among the most useful for helping us understand human behavior as it has been observed in industry. The reader should be cautioned that these four are merely illustrative of any number of others—power, autonomy, social service, etc.—that might have been chosen. In fact, the labeling and listing of so-called human motives is potentially an endless chore because such labels can only be inferred from observed behavior; thus, the listing could presumably be as long as the number of inferences made by different observers. The four we have discussed do, however, sum up many of the inferences that have been made about the motivated behavior of industrial employees. In particular, these four motives provide a good shorthand for classifying and discussing the kinds of goals or incentive situations which may be important in the industrial setting. At the same time, the reader should be cautioned against reifying these behavioral abstractions. The names—security, affiliation, competence, and achievement—are helpful for summarizing certain incentive conditions and behaviors, but they are *nothing more* than just summary devices, and they are treated as such in our subsequent discussion. With this in mind, let us turn to a consideration of how we might measure motivation and relate it to behavior in industrial settings.

THE MEASUREMENT OF HUMAN MOTIVATION

Some false starts

The measurement of human motivation in industry has proceeded slowly and with great difficulty. Until quite recently, most psychologists tended to skirt the issue by utilizing rather crude measures of so-called *job satisfaction*. Job satisfaction was defined simply as the verbal expression of the feelings held by employees about different aspects of their jobs. In essence, then, the usual measures or *employee attitude scales* (as they came to be called) were nothing more than checklists of job conditions about which an employee was asked to express feelings of satisfaction or dissatisfaction relative to his particular job situation. In view of our discussion up to this point, it should be clear that such measures were and are entirely inadequate for providing information about the motivated behavior of employees. The major difficulty is that different employees might obtain the same score on such checklists for quite different reasons. For example, employee A, with strong needs for a sense of personal esteem, might express high satisfaction with his job if his supervisor and co-workers do give him the recognition he seeks. On the other hand, a second employee, with lesser needs for esteem, might express equally high satisfaction with a job in which he is accorded little recognition—

a job, incidentally, which undoubtedly would prove unusually dissatisfying to Employee A. Thus, these early crude measures of job satisfaction seriously confounded the measurement of employee motivation with efforts to estimate the objective realities of the employees' job environments. It is little wonder that over the years scores of studies designed to demonstrate relationships between employee performance (such as productivity) and job satisfaction have failed to do so (Brayfield and Crockett, 1955).

More recently, some investigators (Rosen and Rosen, 1955; Glennon, Owens, Smith, and Albright, 1960; and Weiss, Dawis, England, and Lofquist, 1964) have modified job satisfaction measures by asking employees to indicate the relative importance to them of various job circumstances. For example, an employee might be asked to respond *Very Important, Important,* or *Not Important At All* to the statement: "To have my supervisor give me a pat on the back for doing a good job." Conceptually, this modification seems closer to what we are really after. It is designed to obtain employees' own estimates of the job factors they regard as most important; thus, the results could form the basis for classifying the needs and expectancies workers have about their job environments. However, in asking such direct questions of employees, it is assumed that they can detach themselves sufficiently from their present job situations to give accurate self-appraisals of their own motives. This is probably an unrealistic assumption. For example, if an employee's present job is providing him with plenty of recognition, recognition may seem, temporarily, to be much less important to him than if he were on a job providing him very little recognition. (Food seems somewhat less important immediately after eating than when one is very hungry.) Therefore, although importance ratings are obviously better than straight job satisfaction measures (particularly if they can be obtained from the same persons repeatedly over a period of many years), it is doubtful that they yield entirely accurate estimates of employees' needs and expectancies concerning their jobs. Recognizing this difficulty, other investigators (Porter, 1961; Carlson, Lawrie, Rosensteel, and Crissey, 1963) have asked employees to make *two* responses to each item of a job situation checklist. An example of this response format is shown below:

1. My supervisor provides recognition for a job well done.

a. To what extent
does this *now* oc-   Not at   Very   Almost
cur on your job?   all   Occasionally   Usually   often   always

b. To what extent
should this oc-   Not at   Very   Almost
cur on your job?   all   Occasionally   Usually   often   always

Advocates of this procedure claim that the two responses allow separate estimation of an employee's needs (part b.) *and* description of the job situation in which he is working (part a.), and that the differences between the two responses gives a useful index of the degree to which the job is fulfilling the employee's needs and expectations. Although this is an appealing argument, it suffers from the same potential inaccuracies as the importance format, and it is also quite likely that the employee's own present feeling of job satisfaction will seriously distort his perceptions of the realities of his job situation; thus, it is probable that nothing more than a simple measure of job satisfaction is really obtained from this more elaborate procedure.

The ultimate aim of motivation measures

As we have seen, McClelland and his associates have used fantasy (stories elicited by TAT pictures) to measure various human motives. Their method, disguised as it is, probably overcomes the errors of self-description arising from the imperfect perceptions most persons have of their own underlying needs and motives. Thus, their methods should be useful for measuring human motivation in industry. Unfortunately, they have been applied only rarely in industrial settings. Moreover, the stability of the fantasy measures over time and in different situations has not been studied adequately. For example, we have little or no evidence of how the TAT measures may relate to on-the-job behavior or how they, in turn, may be affected by different job situations and differing degrees of opportunity for obtaining motivational satisfactions. Although the methods developed by McClelland do point the way, they have not, therefore, been sufficiently exploited or tested in industry.

Requirements of an adequate measure
of job motivation

What is needed is a series of measurements accurately getting at the job-related needs, desires, and aspirations of people. Ultimately, we want to be able to describe the kinds of job environments—activities, types of people, modes of behaving on the job, etc.—which an individual approaches, or wants more of, and the kinds of job environments which he seeks to avoid or wants less of. To be useful, however, measurements yielding such descriptions will need to possess certain properties. First, they must be as exhaustive as possible of the domain of possible variations in job environments. In addition to measurements involving job opportunities for satisfying security, affiliation, competence, and achievement needs, many others will be necessary. These, in turn, must be determined by a more thorough study of the range of possible variations in job environments than has yet been accomplished. Herzberg and his colleagues (1959) have made a good start in this direction; their research is discussed in more detail in a following section. Second, the measurements must be studied in a developmental context. The preferences of persons for different kinds of job environments must be investigated during the period over which such preferences are developed. Thus, it will be necessary to learn about their time of onset, and, more importantly, about the intensity and relative stability of such preferences as a person encounters various vocational experiences throughout his work career. In a sense, the studies which have asked workers to gauge the relative importance of different aspects of their job environments are a first step, but, as we have seen, they have not yet been used to study environmental preferences developmentally, and they have suffered from a failure to tap the enduring or stable qualities of individual preferences for different types of job environments. Third, it will be necessary to study how amenable these preferences may be to change. Do such preferences become set and unchanging at a certain age or may they be developed even rather late in one's work career? We have already suggested that job situations might be designed to teach employees to value new goals; in particular, it seems that competence and achievement motives may be developed or at least allowed to emerge by an appropriate structuring of jobs. However, at present, these inferences are essentially untested assumptions which must be submitted to research as we proceed toward developing the measurements we have been discussing. Finally, it will be necessary to relate employees' preferences for different job environments to other personal and biographical characteristics. Only then will we know the kinds of things that different types of people (e.g., men vs. women, old vs. young, PhD's vs. high school graduates, etc.) seek in their jobs and be able to design their job environments accordingly.

In summary, then, any measure of the motivational or preferential properties of different job environments must provide a broad sampling of the job environment domain and we must have information about the developmental trends, relative stability, and educability of these preferences; finally, we must seek out the important personal and biographical correlates of different types of preference.

Relationship of motivation measurement to vocational interest measurement

In Chapter 2, the *Strong Vocational Interest Blank* (SVIB) was said to measure the motivation of persons to enter and to persist in different occupations. Now, in the context of the above outline of the requirements for adequately measuring and understanding human motivation, the SVIB looks particularly good, for Dr. Strong, in his lifetime of research, did demonstrate that vocational interests are highly stable and that they do an excellent job of predicting vocational persistence and, to a lesser degree, vocational satisfaction (Strong, 1955). On the average, male college students scoring high on a specific occupational scale (e.g., lawyer, engineer, psychologist, physician, etc.) are about four times as likely to be in that occupation nearly twenty years later as college men scoring low on the same scale. Moreover, Strong showed that the men who were most satisfied with their chosen occupations were those whose measured interests in college were most compatible with their actual career choices. The item content of the SVIB includes a broad sampling of school subjects, hobbies, pastimes, and occupations, but it does *not* include different aspects of the employee's immediate job environment such as differing opportunities for finding affiliation, achievement, autonomy, and the like. The result is that the SVIB is probably measuring those stable human likes and dislikes which are related to differences in the actual activities intrinsic to various occupations, rather than the stable preferences of people for different types of motivating circumstances from job to job *within* any given occupation or line of work. In a very important way, then, the results obtained with the SVIB are "straws in the wind" for directing future research in the measurement of human motivation; both Strong and McClelland have provided promising leads which need to be broadened to include more specific elements of the job environments of people.

A STUDY OF THE MOTIVATION TO WORK

By interviewing employees (engineers and accountants), Herzberg, Mausner, and Snyderman (1959) learned a good deal about the aspects of job environments which are differentially satisfying and dissatisfying. As we have said, this is an important step toward developing an adequate measure of work motivation; thus, Herzberg's research is an important step forward in our efforts to understand human motivation in industry.

Herzberg and his colleagues used the Critical Incident Method to collect stories from employees about job situations which had been either unusually satisfying or dissatisfying. Their directions to respondents were as follows:

Think of a time in the past when you felt especially good or bad about your job. It may have been this job or any other. Can you think of such a high or low point in your feelings about your job? Please tell me about it.

It is clear that employees were being asked to describe job occurrences or situations which had made an important difference in their feelings toward their jobs. It is likely, therefore, that the employees' responses constituted a rich source of information about the motivating qualities of different job environments.

The "flavor" of the information obtained is shown by three of the respondents' stories which are summarized below:

An accounting supervisor felt wonderful as a result of being assigned the special job of supervising the installation of new IBM equipment. He took pride in seeing the equipment in good working order and was gratified by knowing that the installation made a big difference in the overall functioning of his department.

As his first job out of school, an engineer was hired as an assistant to a contractor. His job involved keeping tabulation sheets and managing the office when the boss was gone. The boss was too busy to train him and was annoyed whenever the young engineer asked questions. The engineer reported feeling frustrated because he was just a "flunky" and he felt that he was in a dead end job.

An industrial sales engineer enjoyed visiting the construction site of a building for which he had developed many of the specifications for materials to be used in the construction. He felt that he had done a good job and that his role had been important to the success of the venture.

Stories such as these, obtained from 200 employed engineers and accountants, were classified according to the job factors reflected in them. Brief definitions of the job factors and the results of the classification are shown in Table 6.1.

TABLE 6.1. PERCENTAGES* OF STORIES OF SATISFYING AND DISSATISFYING JOB SITUATIONS IN WHICH VARIOUS JOB FACTORS WERE MENTIONED

	Satisfying or "Good" Situations	Dissatisfying or "Bad" Situations
1. Achievement To complete a job successfully or to fail to do a job adequately	41	7
2. Recognition To be singled out for praise or for criticism and blame	33	18

* Percentages add to more than 100% because many situations involved more than one factor.

TABLE 6.1 (*Continued*)

	Satisfying or "Good" Situations	Dissatisfying or "Bad" Situations
3. Work Itself To like or to dislike the actual tasks involved in getting the job done	26	14
4. Responsibility To gain responsibility for own or others' work or to lack responsibility in a job	23	6
5. Advancement To change status through promotion or demotion or to miss an expected promotion	20	11
6. Salary To obtain a salary increase or to lose out on an expected one	15	17
7. Possibility of Growth Changes in a job which could lead to further growth or which could be stultifying	6	8
8. Interpersonal Relations with Subordinates To experience either satisfying or dissatisfying social interactions with one's subordinates	6	3
9. Status To obtain some actual sign or appurtenance of status or to lose it	4	4
10. Interpersonal Relations with Superiors To experience either satisfying or dissatisfying social interactions with one's boss	4	15
11. Interpersonal Relations with Co-workers	3	8

TABLE 6.1 (*Continued*)

	Satisfying or "Good" Situations	Dissatisfying or "Bad" Situations
To experience either satisfying or dissatisfying social interactions with one's co-workers		
12. Technical Aspects of Supervision To have a competent supervisor or to have an incompetent one	3	20
13. Company Policy and Administration To be in a company with good policies and administrative procedures or to be in one with poor ones	3	31
14. Working Conditions To have good physical surroundings on the job or to have poor ones	1	11
15. Personal Life To have one's personal life affected for good or ill by occurrences on the job	1	6
16. Job Security Objective indications of security such as job tenure and company stability	1	1

Satisfiers and motivators

These results are important for a number of reasons. First, they suggest rather clearly that especially satisfying and, therefore, potentially motivating job situations differ *in kind* from especially dissatisfying job situations. Satisfying situations are characterized by opportunities to experience achievement, recognition, a sense of responsibility, and advancement in jobs which are themselves intrinsically interesting to the respondents. In contrast, dissatisfying situations most often involve incompetent or "cold" supervision, poor company policies and administration, criticism or blame (negative recognition), and poor working conditions. It is noteworthy that unusually good supervision or good company policies are only rarely mentioned in describing the especially satisfying situations. Thus, Herzberg, et al., concluded that certain job factors (notably supervision, company policies, and working conditions) cannot be utilized to motivate employees; they can only be expected, at best, to prevent negative feelings and dissatisfaction. The findings are remindful of the distinction made earlier in this chapter between *satisfiers* (desires which are, for a time, appeased after being satisfied) and *motivators* (desires which may take on increased motivating properties through the actual process of being satisfied). Apparently, job circumstances must include opportunities for achieving and for gaining recognition and increased responsibility if they are to constitute a motivating state of affairs. If valid, Herzberg's findings carry strong implications for the industrial psychologist, not only for selecting employees who evidence various motivational preferences but also for the structuring of jobs and job environments to provide greater motivational stimulation in the industrial setting.

A taxonomy of job situations

Although these conclusions are important, a more fundamental contribution of the study is that the job factors so identified were allowed to emerge from descriptions of actual job situations rather than being based exclusively on responses to checklists or sets of statements developed ahead of time by the investigator. The job factors derived by Herzberg's classification are more likely, therefore, to reflect things in the job environment leading to employees' approach and avoidance behaviors. As such, the factors seem to be a logical starting point for developing the measures of job motivation we discussed in the previous section.

Weaknesses in the Herzberg study

The reader should not be left with the impression that Herzberg's research is not without serious weaknesses. For example, the stories, obtained as they were through interviews, are highly subjective accounts of job situations, and the chances are great for misclassifying the comments or even for developing the wrong categories to begin with. Thus, the zeal of the investigator concerning his own beliefs about job motivation may be reflected in the categorizations developed from such subjective information. Herzberg's results also suffer from the select nature of the sample of subjects participating in the study. If (as we might expect) engineers and accountants are more desirous than other employees (such as production workers or secretaries) of opportunities for achieving and for gaining a sense of recognition or esteem, then the results can be said to apply only to them, and other similar studies need to be conducted on other occupational groups before the results can be widely generalized. Finally, Herzberg's study relied solely on statements from the respondents. No observations or measurements of actual job behavior were made; thus, it is not really possible to draw conclusions about actual job behaviors occurring as consequences of the satisfying and dissatisfying job situations described by the respondents.

However, even though Herzberg's research can be regarded only as a bare beginning, it does constitute an important and provocative first step toward a better understanding of human motivation in industry. His studies have attracted much attention and have stimulated a growing number of other research studies. Beginning with his taxonomy of job situations, we may expect in the years ahead to witness the development and utilization of measurements of job motivation possessing the desirable features we outlined in the previous section.

PERFORMANCE = MOTIVATION × ABILITY

It should be apparent now that our present knowledge of human motivation in industry is indeed rather limited. We have said that motivation represents the *action* phase of behavior; yet, human motivation has *not* been adequately measured, and efforts to demonstrate relationships between human motives and actual job behaviors have often ended with essentially negative or, at best, inconsistent results. In fact, any industrial psychologist who seeks to describe and predict employee behavior by referring exclusively to motivational concepts is bound to be disappointed. Because our discussion here has been directed toward motivation, we have not mentioned ability, but the reader should be reminded that performance in industry depends not only on motivation but very obviously and very importantly also on ability. The highly motivated and inept person will fail to do an effective job just as surely as the highly able but apathetic employee. Future research in this complex area must then take full account of the multiplicative features of ability and motivation for describing and predicting employee behavior. As better measures of human motivation are developed, it will be important that they be studied along with measures of human abilities which already have been shown to be effective predictors of industrial behavior.

Suggested Additional Reading

Astin, A. W., and Nichols, R. C. Life goals and vocational choice. *J. appl. Psychol.*, 1964, **48**, 50-58.

Atkinson, J. W. Motivational determinants of risk-taking behavior. *Psychol. Rev.*, 1957, **64**, 359-372.

Cofer, C. N., and Appley, M. H. *Motivation: theory and research*. New York: Wiley, 1964.

Gellerman, S. W. *Motivation and productivity*. New York: American Management Association, 1963.

Glanzer, M. Curiosity, exploratory drive, and stimulus satiation. *Psychol. Bull.*, 1958, **55**, 302-315.

Herzberg, F., Mausner, B., and Snyderman, B. *The motivation to work*. New York: Wiley, 1959.

Katzell, R. A. Personal values, job satisfaction, and job behavior. In Borow, H. (Ed.), *Man in a world at work*. Boston: Houghton Mifflin, 1964.

Landsberger, H. A. *Hawthorne revisited, management and the worker, its critics and developments in human relations in industry*. Ithaca, N.Y.: New York State School of Industrial and Labor Relations, 1958.

Meyer, H. H., Walker, W. B., and Litwin, G. H. Motive patterns and risk preferences associated with entrepreneurship. *J. abnorm. soc. Psychol.*, 1961, **63**, 570-574.

Myers, M. S. Who are your motivated workers? *Harvard Business Review*, 1964, **42**, 73-88.

Seward, J. P. The structure of functional autonomy. *Amer. Psychologist*, 1963, **18**, 703-711.

Strong, E. K., Jr. *Vocational interests 18 years after college*. Minneapolis: The University of Minnesota Press, 1955.

Vroom, V. H. *Work and motivation*. New York: Wiley, 1964.

White, R. W. Motivation reconsidered: the concept of competence. *Psychol. Rev.*, 1959, **66**, 297-333.

7

ORGANIZATIONAL PSYCHOLOGY

THE SCOPE OF ORGANIZATIONAL PSYCHOLOGY

If you were asked to name a major difference between working for a large company and working for a small one, you would probably say something like this: "It's easier to know what's going on in a small company. Larger companies are too split up into departments and are very formal. As a result, it's harder to get to know people in a larger company." Such a comment reveals just one of many seemingly obvious differences between large and small companies and illustrates one of the possible effects of organizational size. It *is* harder to know people; communications become more difficult and interpersonal relationships are more complex in a large company.

Size alone, however, is not the only variable that affects the working relationships of people in companies. As we noted in the first chapter, Worthy (1950) contended that Sears was a more effective company because of its flat structure with relatively few levels of management. Does a flat, horizontal structure of organization have great advantages over a tall, vertical structure? As yet, there is no definitive answer to this query, but the question itself is illustrative of the kinds of questions asked by organizational psychologists.

Organizational size and structure then are examples of the kinds of things that are studied under the heading Organizational

Psychology. The organizational psychologist, in particular, is concerned about the effects of these variables upon people and the way they work in organizations. It is easy enough to say that organizational psychology is a study of organizations and their interactions with people. It is much more difficult to delineate the scope of what organizational psychology should cover. Organizations have been studied, as we shall see, by economists, sociologists, political scientists, and even mathematicians. All have their own thoughts, techniques, and tenets in this area.

Organizational psychology studies conflict

We shall define organizational psychology as the study of the organization, its processes, and its relationships with people within the organization. With this definition we are led rather forcefully to the study of areas of potential conflict between the personalities of individual employees and the demands of the organization on them. When we join an organization, we usually expect to give up some of our freedom in order to receive certain rewards for being a part of the organization. A good example of this is the everyday employment situation in which the individual employee gives up some freedom (e.g., coming and going as he pleases), and, in return, he receives monetary rewards to help sustain himself and his family or perhaps prestige or status rewards to help him gain recognition from his peers. The employee's own perception of what he gives up for what he receives can suggest conflict between him and his company. Different people will vary greatly in their response to this potential conflict. Whatever their responses may be are of great interest to the organizational psychologist.

Organizational psychology also has been defined simply as the study of the behavior of individuals in organizations. It should be apparent that this definition is subsumed under our more broad definition given above.

What is an organization?

Before we move on to discuss some of the studies performed by organizational psychologists, we should consider briefly just what an organization is. Guest (1962) has defined an *organization* as consisting of any large group of persons engaged in mutually dependent activities for some specific purpose. He states further that an organization is rationally structured in that:

1. The organization has been formed as a legal entity at some identifiable point in time and space.
2. Men and physical objects have been deliberately brought together to achieve a defined goal.
3. The manner in which the task is to be accomplished is based on calculation and reason, which distinguish it from spontaneous formation or actions.
4. The arrangement of men and material objects assumes the form generally recognized and agreed upon by the participants.

Guest's outline constitutes a good definition of an industrial organization. However, other definitions are common: some writers define the term simply to consist of activity groupings and authority relationships; others call organizations the sum total of human relationships in any group activity. Thus, there is no shortage of definitions for the word *organization,* and behavioral scientists may argue at length concerning the best definition. However, in our brief overview of organizational psychology, we will look upon organizations as being synonymous with industrial concerns set up along the lines outlined by Guest and devoted to the broad goal of realizing a profit from the production and marketing of goods and services.

One other point demands comment. There is no end to the things that organizational psychology might study. It is legitimately concerned with behavior on the job, relationships among individuals, relationships among groups, and with all the interrelations of these with the general structure and function of the organization in which the individuals work. As a result, it is impossible in this one chapter to encompass the whole of this rapidly burgeoning field. Our intent, instead, is simply to review some of what has already been learned, illustrate some present research, theory, and problems and speculate briefly about the future of the field.

CLASSIC ORGANIZATION THEORY

Although the field of organizational psychology is relatively new, thinking about organizations is quite old. In fact, modern organizational psychology stems directly from what might be labeled "classic organization theory." Let us examine these past influences and see how they have affected today's theories.

First, what is classic organization theory? There are differing viewpoints, but they all come down to three main themes:

1. The search for efficiency
2. The search for general principles
3. The search for a perfect organizational structure

The search for efficiency

As we saw in the last chapter, the scientific management movement was an early effort to understand organizations by studying the workplace with the ultimate goal being the greatest possible efficiency of production. As we have seen, Frederick Taylor became known as the Father of Scientific Management and is generally regarded as the first so-called efficiency expert. Using the methods of time and motion study and with pay as the primary incentive, Taylor was able, for a time, to bring about dramatic increases in productivity. His techniques were, of course, most successful in organizational settings involving very repetitive tasks and including many physical activities in production. Scientific management was production- and factory-oriented. It stressed the idea that men were inefficient compared with machines and that the major need was to make humans as much like machines as possible by standardizing their work activities. Each task had a standard way it should be done and this could be measured and converted into a standard operating procedure. However, such tasks as problem solving or decision making did not fit nicely into the scientific management framework because they could not usually be standardized or measured adequately.

For better or worse, Taylor's thinking and scientific management have enjoyed a central position in classic organization theory over the years. Even today, one often hears the need expressed in industry for an efficiency expert to come in to see what might be done to improve a particular organizational setup.

The search for general principles

Much time and effort in the past and even now have been spent searching for general principles of management and organization. Some of the more common principles are outlined below:

Principle	Explanation
1. Specialization	Each activity in an organization must be specialized (i.e., rigidly defined and limited in scope).
2. Span of Control	There is a limit to the number of persons one individual can direct and control.
3. Chain of Command	Progressively greater power is vested at successively higher positions in an organizational hierarchy.
4. Unity of Direction	People in control direct their own subordinates, not persons in other units.
5. Authority	A person in charge has power vested in him in some way (e.g., through outside influence or by reason of the power in the position itself).

Of these and the many others that have not been cited, the most "sticky" principle is that of authority. What is authority? Who should have it? How should it be delegated? These are still perplexing questions with varying answers. Basic, however, to classic theory is the idea that authority is the primary method of controlling other people's activities.

Actually, the search for general principles is extremely perplexing because these principles very rarely generalize. Take span of control as an example. Original thoughts on this were that one person could not supervise more than six to fifteen persons. In modern day retailing firms, however, any given supervisor may have as many as 70-80 subordinates. Span of control is just one illustration of the present sad state of inadequate knowledge concerning the validity of organizational principles. For every example supporting some so-called principle of organization, there seems to be another which refutes it. One of the major tasks, therefore, of modern organizational psychologists, is to submit these many and varied principles to experimental study and empirical test to see which should be retained as important and valid and which should be discarded as old wives' tales.

The search for the perfect organization structure

Implicit in the search for general principles of organization is the notion of a perfect organizational structure or format. It is not enough just to have general principles because principles alone still may not produce top efficiency of operation. What is needed, according to theorists in this area, is an ideal type of formal organization.

Perhaps the best illustration of this is the concept of "bureaucracy." Weber, whose name is associated with this concept speaks of bureaucracy as the form of administrative organization capable of attaining the highest degree of efficiency. Central to the bureaucratic approach are two main ideas:

1. Impersonality
2. Discipline

Impersonality is the idea that the power to direct action is not vested in any one individual as such but rather in the office or position which the individual occupies. Discipline implies that definite rules and regulations are to be followed in a very precise and orderly fashion. Bureaucracy involves such principles as specialization and division of activities and further stresses impersonal, formalized procedures.

From this brief description, then, it is not surprising that government employees at all levels in the United States today are commonly called bureaucrats, for highly formalized procedures mark our system of government and the office rather than the individual is considered most important.

Criticism of classic theory

An excellent critical summary of classic organization theory has been made by Haire (1962), a modern theorist. In his summary he outlines the classical theory as follows:

1. Classical organization theory is built on a combination of the accounting and industrial engineering model. This generally involves breaking the total job down rationally and assigning the parts to different employees. In general, each part has a certain defined amount of authority and responsibility.
2. Classic organization theory maximizes neatness and control. Haire suggests that by breaking up the job into little pieces, the impression is given that everyone knows exactly what ought to be done.
3. Classic organization theory puts special emphasis on error or the detection of error and its correction after an error has occurred. The standard organization is set up so that everyone has something he ought to do and the system is designed to find out if he does or does not do it.
4. Classic organization theory embodies the "extra pair of hands" concept. This implies that the total job is understood only at the top and that the job is broken up into pieces and an extra pair of hands recruited for each piece.
5. Classic organization theory assumes man to be relatively homogeneous and relatively unmodifiable. In other words, it does not matter too much what person is in the job. The assumption is that people are almost perfectly interchangeable from job to job.
6. Stability of employees is a goal. The organization is designed to "standardize" employees and to minimize any behavioral deviations from the standard model.
7. Classic organization theory is centralized.
8. The integration of the system is achieved through the authority and control of the central mechanism.

Rather obviously, then, according to this summary, classic organization theory stresses tight controls, very formal structure, tightly defined and definite policies and procedures, and essentially a rather nonhuman approach or a lack of concern about differences between people.

Errors and problems of classic organization theory

Let us now review some of the errors and problems that exist in this theory. First and foremost, it is quite clear that there appear to be many unfounded assumptions about human beings. For example, classic theory assumes that people are more or less necessary evils on the job and that they really don't enjoy working. McGregor (1960) has summarized these kinds of assumptions about human behavior in what he calls Theory X or the traditional view of direction and control as follows:

1. The average human being has an inherent dislike of work and will avoid it if he can.
2. Because of this human characteristic of dislike of work, most people must be coerced, controlled, directed, and threatened with punishment to get them to put forth adequate effort toward the achievement of organizational objectives.
3. The average human being prefers to be directed, wishes to avoid responsibilities, has relatively little ambition, and wants security above all.

It is obvious that these assumptions do not paint a flattering portrait of human behavior on the job. From our discussion of human motivation in the last chapter, it should also be clear that these assumptions are not based on research evidence. It may be that the classic assumptions about human beings on the job are valid for some persons and for some circumstances, but it is an obvious oversimplification to make such assumptions for *all* persons in *all* circumstances. This, then, is a major criticism of classic organization theory. It has made many assumptions about how human beings actually behave without testing the assumptions against research studies or scientific evidence.

There are other important criticisms. For example, many of the traditional organizational principles were derived primarily from the study of the wrong kind of model, such as military or church organizations, which probably differ in many important ways from modern industrial organizations. McGregor cites the example of unity of command, which probably is necessary on the battlefield, but which may be inappropriate for most other organizational situations. Principles of organizational behavior in military settings may differ greatly from those applicable to industrial organizations.

Another major criticism made by McGregor and which, in fact, may be his most important one is that one single incorrect assumption tends to pervade conventional organizational theory. This is the belief that authority is the central, indispensable means of managerial control. McGregor believes this is a wrong assumption because he views authority as just one of several ways of influencing or controlling people. Persuasion, for example, is another very effective method of getting people to do things or to influence their views. Instead of being absolute, McGregor more correctly points out that authority is only effective for controlling others when it is enforced through punishment. In the past, authority was enforced in industry by threatening employees with the loss of their jobs or other dire consequences. Today, however, threats are much less effective. Employees are better organized and can respond with countermeasures such as restricting output. McGregor wisely suggests that interdependence of persons upon one another at all levels in industry precludes relying solely on authority as the primary method of accomplishing organizational goals. Authority then as the central method of managerial control probably is an illusion rather than a reality.

Another criticism of classic theory is that it comes from the past and is based on political and social conditions that existed many years ago. Times have changed and the world today is much different than it was at the turn of the century. Concepts that seemed logical and useful then may not make sense today. Even the so-called natural laws of physics have changed greatly as we have learned more about the lawful behavior of matter. If this is true in the physical sciences, it is likely to be even more true in the much less well-defined areas of the behavioral sciences.

These, then, are some of the errors and problems of classic organization theory. Behind most of these incorrect assumptions and errors of reasoning was the failure of classic organization theory to consider the fundamental complexities of human beings. One of the best illustrations of this failure is Taylor's widely quoted comment: "One of the various first requirements for a man who is fit to handle pig iron is that he should be so stupid and so phlegmatic that he more nearly resembles the ox, than any other type; he must consequently be trained by a man more intelligent than himself."

March and Simon (1958), too, point out that classic organization theorists had a tendency to view the employee as an inert instrument simply performing a task assigned to him. One reason, of course, for this lack of concern with human beings as such is the fact that the people who outlined these theories were not generally behavioral scientists, such as psychologists and sociologists, but instead tended to be economists and industrial engineers. Since neither of these disciplines is oriented toward the study of human behavior, it is not surprising that these early theories adopted overly simplified views of man and his role in organizations.

A RECENT STUDY OF ORGANIZATIONAL CHANGE

Now that we have reviewed the difficulties and inadequacies of classic organization theory, it is well to turn to a recent example of a carefully conducted observation of organizational change. By reviewing this study in some detail, we will be able to set the background for our later discussion of the thinking of modern organizational theorists.

Index	Plant Standing 1953	Plant Standing 1956
Overall Efficiency	poorest	best
Quality	poorest	best or second best
Indirect Labor Costs	highest	tied for lowest
Safety Record	poorest	best
Labor Grievances	second highest number	lowest number
Absenteeism	highest	unknown but markedly decreased
Turnover	highest	unknown but markedly decreased

Using personal interviews as his major research method, Guest (1962) made careful observations of the overall operations of an auto assembly plant in 1953 and again in 1956. During the intervening three-year period, sweeping changes occurred in the overall efficiency and net effectiveness of the plant. The magnitude of these changes is evident in the table above in which the plant is compared with five similar plants on a number of production and cost indexes both before (1953) and after (1956) organizational changes were introduced. It is clear that this plant moved from dead last on nearly every index to just about the best on all of them. What happened to cause this? What changes occurred?

Very simply, the major change was the introduction of a new plant manager into this particular auto assembly plant. In 1953 when the new manager arrived, the plant, according to interviews conducted with all levels of personnel from subordinates to top management people, was under extreme pressure from central headquarters to produce. The old plant manager had received directive after directive on how to do things and he passed these directives along to his subordinates. In general, the whole atmosphere was one of fear and distrust. Departments were poorly integrated and unaware of each other's assignments; control groups, like inspectors, did not communicate or get along with the people on the production line. It was a perfect portrait of a sick organization.

Conveniently, for the purposes of experimental observation, other factors remained very nearly constant during the administration of the new manager. For example, top management above the plant manager remained the same. The plant itself retained essentially the same supervisory people. The formal structure of organization was not changed in any important way. The plant produced the same line of products and utilized the same general layout in technology. In addition, this plant was subject to the same car model changes and market changes that the other similar plants faced.

What then did happen? Did a dramatic change occur overnight because of the new manager or was it a gradual process of change? Had the old manager been so cordially hated by everyone that anyone could have come in and produced this organizational change? While the answers to these questions are not certain, it is clear that the changes were gradual ones. It also appeared that while the old manager was probably not the most popular person in the plant, he *was* respected for his extensive knowledge of the automobile business.

Managerial changes

The new manager began his term in office by telling everyone that he was *not* going to conduct a general "housecleaning" or get rid of people or "sweep out the dead wood." He said, in effect, that he believed the plant had good people in it and that they could work out their problems together. Second, and this may be a highly significant factor in what happened, he was given a relatively free hand by his top management. The number of directives coming down to him diminished considerably below the number that had gone to the previous manager; thus pressure from the top was greatly lessened. Third, the new manager introduced general meetings as a regular part of company procedure so that people could get together and communicate and talk about solving plant problems. Meetings in the past had been held more or less on an emergency basis. These meetings, however, were set up on a regular basis. Interestingly, these formal meetings tended to spread downward. Although originally they included only some of the higher plant officials, meetings soon began to be set up at all levels. Fourth, the new manager spent much of his time during the first few weeks simply listening to other people and observing overall plant operations. Finally, the new manager made some physical changes in the plant; he fixed up the cafeteria at a rather large cost to the company, and he fixed up the washrooms.

The net effect of all this was gradual but it did help to change both the general climate of fear and dislike and the attitudes and sentiments of people in the plant. Supervisory changes were also made, but these came much later. These changes did not involve a general housecleaning but instead involved many transfers of personnel within the plant. In general, foremen were encouraged to develop understudies for themselves. Technical changes in the actual assembly work were also made. These tended to come later, but, in contrast to the old situation where these changes were made somewhat arbitrarily and passed on to the people to carry out, nearly everybody concerned knew about anticipated changes and the reasons for them well ahead of the changeover.

In analyzing what happened, Guest suggests some of the following possibilities: first, where most communications or interactions between people had occurred downward from superior to subordinate in the past, these downward interactions decreased quite markedly over the three-year period. Thus, there came to be more a pattern of total communication, both up and down the supervisory ladder. Second, there was a marked shift in the sentiments of plant people toward increased job satisfaction. Third, and very important, the general focus in the plant had turned to solving *problems* rather than to singling out and blaming *individuals*. Interestingly, many members of the organization perceived what they believed to be actual changes in the personalities of their own superiors or subordinates.

Suggested organizational principles

In summarizing the results of his observations, Guest suggests the following hypotheses or principles of organizational change:

1. When the organization is a subordinate unit to a larger organization and when the patterns of internal relationships within the subordinate organization are similar to those linking it to the large, changes leading to more successful performance within the subordinate organization will only take place after there has been a change in the pattern of relationships (interactions and sentiments) linking the larger to the subordinate organization.
2. The length of time required for an organization to improve its performance is a function of the following:
   a. the size of the organization in terms of the number of individuals
   b. the number of levels in the hierarchy
   c. the number of specialized service, reporting and control groups
   d. the complexity of technical operations
   e. the degree of intensity of personal insecurity and of interpersonal hostility at the outset of the change process
3. For a complex organization to move from one pattern of behavior to another, it is not necesary that its formal structure be altered.
4. The process of successful change in a hierarchial organization will start and continue to the extent that the members perceive the behavior of superiors, peers, and subordinates to be more in keeping with the norms of behavior in the larger culture.

All of these hypotheses were, to one extent or another, tested and confirmed in Guest's study.

What does this study suggest for the student of organizational psychology? It provides rather dramatic evidence of the effect that individuals can have upon the effectiveness of an organization. Here was a situation where the organizational structure of the plant did not change especially. The people in the plant remained basically the same. The method of doing things remained basically the same. The only change introduced was a new manager who was thrown into what was considered a rather hopeless situation but was given a free hand to operate as he desired. His method of operation probably would be labeled democratic by persons who describe managerial behavior on an authoritarian-democratic continuum. The important thing to recognize, however, is that the new leader had to gain the confidence, respect, and trust of the people in the plant. His general behavior over the first few months was highly consistent. He tried to find out what was wrong and he tried to find out what people thought. He tried to do something about the problems.

As indicated, the actual changes in organizational efficiency did not occur overnight. It took some time for people to believe in the new manager. When this occurred, however, and when interpersonal communications began to increase and people began to discover and emphasize problems rather than individuals in the plant, the upward movement of the plant was evident. Of course, the positive changes had a reinforcing effect. The more good things that happened, the more people believed that these would continue to happen. From this study, therefore, it is clear that leadership is a crucial organizational variable. Because this is a case study of just one firm, it is impossible to use the results to formulate general rules or principles of organizational change. However, the results were dramatic and do suggest many of the major themes running through some of the modern organization theories which are presented and discussed below.

EXAMPLES OF MODERN ORGANIZATION THEORY

What constitutes modern organization theory? As has been implied, there is no single answer because modern organization theorists have many different emphases and approaches. We shall, however, review the general models or theories of two of the better known writers in the field: Chris Argyris (1960) and Rensis

Likert (1961). Their theories will serve to illustrate many elements of the newer approaches to the study of organizations.

Argyris' diagnostic approach

Argyris (1960) is one of the many organizational theorists who emphasize human behavior in organizations. He tends also to favor a more clinical, more diagnostic, and perhaps more anecdotal approach than most. Specifically, he suggests starting with two basic parts, the formal organization and the human being, determining what is known about each, and then predicting the effects of interactions between them. From these predictions evolves the framework of Argyris' view of organizational behavior. His formal model can be outlined as follows:

1. Human personality develops in certain ways. It can be assumed that human beings
   a. move from a passive state as infants to more active states as adults,
   b. develop from a state of dependence upon others as infants to a state of more or less independence as adults (This independence involves the ability to stand on one's own two feet and also the ability to acknowledge dependencies when they exist.),
   c. develop from behaving only in a limited number of ways as an infant to being capable of behaving in a wide variety of ways as an adult,
   d. tend to develop from having rather shallow and casual and quickly dropped interests as an infant to having more deep interests as an adult (The mature state, in fact, is characterized by facing many different challenges which, as we have seen in the last chapter, may motivate the mature individual through desires for competence, achievement, or both.),
   e. move from having a short-time perspective as an infant to having a much longer time perspective as an adult (The adult considers both the past and the future consequences of his own behavior.),
   f. develop from operating in a subordinate position in the family and society as an infant to attempting or aspiring to occupy equal or better than equal positions relative to their peers as adults,
   g. develop from a lack of awareness of self as an infant, to an awareness of and control over self as an adult. (This leads to the development of a sense of personal integrity or identity.)
2. Many human problems in organizations occur because people who

are more or less healthy or mature are asked to participate in work situations which make them operate as dependent and subordinate and submissive individuals and do not allow them to use more than a few of their, as Argyris puts it, "skin-surface" abilities.

3. Three major sets of variables cause dependence and subordination and these are: the formal organization-structure (including technology), directive leadership and managerial controls such as budgets, and time and motion studies.

4. The degree of dependence and subordination that are caused by these various variables increases as one goes down the chain of command and as one approaches mass production activities.

5. Healthy human beings find dependence and subordination frustrating and would prefer to be relatively independent, would like to use many of their latent abilities and aspire to positions higher or equal to their peers. This causes frustration which leads to behavior such as regression, aggression, and tension. In turn, these lead to conflict.

6. People will adapt to the frustration and conflict and failure by engaging in one or a combination of these kinds of activities:
   a. leave the situation (absenteeism)
   b. seek to move up the organizational ladder
   c. become defensive through such techniques as grievances, feelings of low sense of self-worth, daydreaming, etc.
   d. become apathetic and disinterested in the organization and what it is doing
   e. create informal groups to sanction (through affiliative behavior) the various defenses in (c) and (d)
   f. formalize such informal groups into forms such as trade unions
   g. de-emphasize such things as creativity and self-growth and emphasize monetary and material rewards
   h. accept these various ways of behavior as being proper for their life outside the organization

7. Management in turn will look at most of these informal activities as being detrimental to the formal organization. In turn they will resist the informal activities by tightening up the structure, exerting more directive leadership, and establishing additional managerial controls.

From these propositions, it is clear that Argyris' model involves the major theme that individuals in industry are often frustrated by the demands of the organization. This results in counteractions by the individuals leading to further organizational actions in the form of controls, and, thus, a vicious cycle of organizational constraints and employee counteractions is set off again. In his study of an organization and its processes, Argyris suggests investigating the following areas:

1. Demands made of the participant by the formal organization (includes job demands, policies and practices, rules, regulations, etc.)
2. Predispositions or needs that participants may wish to express while participating in the organization
3. Informal activities that employees may create to aid in their adaptation to the demands of the organization
4. The administration's reaction to these informal activities

In order to learn all these things, Argyris has developed rather thorough data-gathering methods involving intensive interviews with employees at all levels and the clinical assessment of the resulting information. His procedures are very similar to those used when a physician diagnoses a patient's ailment. There are rules to follow, important questions to ask, symptoms to look for, and certain behavioral manifestations that are presumed to be related to various organizational conditions. Thus, just as in medical practice, Argyris' approach to the diagnosis of organizational processes is characterized by a fairly substantial degree of subjective judgment and the artful application of scientific knowledge. Indeed, Argyris has been called an "organizational clinician" (Dunnette, 1961). In general, his theoretical model is a good beginning and it certainly serves as an excellent illustration of how modern theorists have come to emphasize the crucial roles of the individual in the organization and the effort to humanize their theories of organizational behavior.

Likert's theory of organization and management

Likert (1959, 1961), like Argyris and others, believes that a modified theory of organization and management is needed. Very simply, he believes that employee motivation is the key to overall organizational effectiveness and his theory strongly stresses techniques and methods which take better account of what people seek from their job and organizational environments.

Central to Likert's (1959, p. 191) theory are a variety of research results indicating that subordinates react favorably to experiences which are supportive to them and which help them increase their sense of importance and personal worth. From his analysis of these studies comes his general formula for applying his theory, namely:

The organizational structure and its manner of functioning must insure a maximum probability that in all interactions, each of the individuals involved will, in the light of his background, experience, and expectations, view the interactions as supportive and one which contributes to his sense of personal worth.

Using this formula, Likert proceeds to outline an organizational structure based on overlapping work groups rather than the traditional format of the organizational chart involving a man-to-man relationship. He espouses the "linking pin" principle which means that individuals hold membership in overlapping work groups at different hierarchical levels. One individual, then, can be a link between his own general group and the one above. Crucial to this concept is the idea that the manager or supervisor can only perform his supervisory functions effectively if he is able to exert influence upward. Likert is not suggesting any dramatic changes in the structure of organizations, but by emphasizing the linking pin concept, he is forcefully calling attention to the fact that any supervisor is a member of two groups, and he (Likert) is emphasizing the importance of the supervisor's playing significant roles in both groups.

Likert, then, ends up with an "interaction system" combining the following characteristics:

1. *Structure.* Emphasis should be placed on the overlapping membership of groups in the organization.
2. *Atmosphere.* A supportive, ego-building atmosphere in which people feel respected is required. The key word here is *supportive.*
3. *Personnel.* People in the organization should have the appropriate aptitudes and training to perform the functions for which they are responsible, but they should also have adequate interpersonal skills.
4. *Established relationships.* Organizational members should know other members of other work groups and units of which they are a part well enough so that there is confidence, trust, and a good flow of

information. In addition, an effective flow of influence should be established. Likert further indicates that rapid turnover and shifts in personnel would not be good.

5. *Measurements.* Members of the organizations should have available to them accurate and current measurements which indicate such things as the internal state of the organization and its present performance. These measurements should be made available to all persons whose decisions affect any of these particular variables.

It is obvious from the above characteristics that Likert has advanced a system where effective communication and supportive interpersonal relationships are crucial. Additionally, he recognizes the need for accurate information through measurement of what is going on within the organization so that well-informed and more accurate decisions can be made.

What would happen if this kind of organization were to be set up? Likert indicates that a number of outcomes would be likely:

First of all, he suggests that there would be a full and complete flow of communication among members of the organization. People would trust one another and it is likely, therefore, that they would not withhold information from other individuals.

Second, he indicates that a flow of influence comparable to the flow of information would occur. This implies that people at all levels would feel that they do have some influence on others and their decisions.

Third, decision making would be easier. Each decision would be made at the lowest possible level of the organization and the theory would strongly imply that decentralization would be involved. All this would occur because the flow of communication and the flow of influence would be highly efficient throughout the organization.

Fourth, individuals and groups in the organization would have high ego-involvement which would in turn produce a very high level of effective motivation. The goals of the individuals would have been established through participation in them and through mutual influence on one another. Likert feels that the individuals' personal needs would be strongly integrated with the organization's objectives.

Likert's theory, like Argyris', stresses the human being. His emphasis, however, is upon motivation of human beings through more effective structuring of group relationships and places greater emphasis upon behavior that makes people feel important and valuable to the organization. These then are typical of new approaches in studying organizations. The human being has become a central and crucial focal point. Instead of being a necessary evil, he has become vital to proper organizational functioning.

AN ORGANIZATIONAL VARIABLE: TECHNOLOGY

Organizational psychologists while placing this great emphasis upon human behavior in the organizational area also are investigating the effect of organizational variables upon the behavior of people. While many of the newer theories suggest that the individual is all important and has great effect upon the organization, it should not be forgotten that the organization itself can have major effects on how people function and behave.

For example, one major organizational variable is that of the technology of the plant. This includes plant layout, its work flow, and the like. Evidence is increasing that the technology of a firm can determine to a large degree the kind of work behavior occurring in the plant. Sayles (1958) has demonstrated this in a rather involved and lengthy study of about 300 work units in over 30 different firms. In his study, Sayles interviewed workers and supervisors at various levels concerning their jobs, their job behavior, satisfaction with the firm and with each other. He sampled such various industries as automobile, office equipment, breakfast food, and fiber cartons, thus suggesting some generality for his findings.

His basic conclusion was that the technology of the modern plant and factory tends to mold the type of work units that evolve within the plant. His further conclusion is that, from analyses of work unit records, it is possible to predict which unit will challenge the actions of both management and union and which will accept their conditions of work. In addition, the methods used by these units to achieve their goals will be predictable.

How did he arrive at these conclusions? In the first place, he identified four basic types of work units, depending upon the nature of their methods of dealing with or negotiating with management. The four types were found in all of the industrial groupings studied; the four, and the labels he gave them are:

Apathetic Units
Erratic Units
Strategic Units
Conservative Units

In general, the names of the units reflect the general mode of behavior that they exhibited on the job, particularly in terms of grievance and pressure tactics. The apathetic units, for example, were made up of people on jobs requiring relatively low skill and which were low paying. These persons produced relatively few grievances and little pressure on management. They did not have any clearly identifiable leadership. They were not particularly content but they didn't do much about it. They were, as the label indicates, apathetic.

The erratic units, on the other hand, were featured by tendencies toward erratic behavior. There did not seem to be any relation between the objective seriousness of their grievances and the intensity of their protests. These were the units more likely to go out on wild-cat strikes, and both unions and management felt that they did not know exactly what to expect from them in any given situation. Sayles suggests that erratic work units were made up primarily of people on jobs in which everybody had identical tasks.

The strategic group was well named. Its members used pressure tactics when the occasion demanded and would turn them on or off as needed. They were generally on jobs that were individual operations but not technologically independent. Their jobs were better and usually more interesting than those found in the apathetic and erratic groups.

The conservative units were probably the most stable of all. These were people who worked on very high-level skilled jobs and who tended to be conservative in the grievance activities, primarily because they were dealing from strength.

Sayles indicates that the quality of pressure exerted by these units was affected by the internal organization of the work, as determined primarily by the work flow and the division of labor. For example, he concluded that interdependent jobs in the work process were associated with the more spontaneous and sporadic outbursts, while the sustained pressure activities, carried out with care and forethought, were more likely to be associated with independent jobs involving more individual operations. From his observations, Sayles concluded that rather accurate predictions about the behavior of work units may be made from such items as the organization chart, the pattern of work flow, and the nature of the division of labor.

A similar series of observations was made by Woodward (1958) in England. She studied 100 industrial firms and found that meaningful comparisons could be made by grouping the firms according to the type of production system used. Using an index of industrial relations effectiveness (including such factors as number of grievances processed) as a criterion, she showed that labor discontent was lower in firms utilizing either small batch production or rather complex automatic flow production processes than it was in firms utilizing assembly line, mass production systems. In fact, it appeared that the pressure increased at all levels of work in the mass production industries. Woodward also concluded that mass production type activities involve highly interdependent type jobs, whereas unit or small batch production and process production would be more associated with independent and individual operations. As in Sayles' study, then, the technology of the firm seemed related to industrial relations behavior. Thus, in spite of the great difficulty of gaining full experimental control over all potential variables, the Sayles and Woodward studies result in essentially very similar conclusions. In broad terms, at least, the behavior of work groups in both England and the United States seems to be predictable from a knowledge of the technology and organizational structures within which they are working.

In addition to this gratifying similarity in conclusions, the two studies are important because they confirm the folly of expecting to find any one ideal organizational setup. The Woodward study, in particular, suggests strongly that different types of firms differ greatly in the kind of organization which may be expected to result in optimal employee efficiency and satisfaction and overall industrial relations effectiveness. These two studies, though important, are mere starting points in the effort to relate technology and organizational structure to organizational effectiveness; studies utilizing more careful controls and more objective measures must now be undertaken.

In this vein, a quasi-experimental study was undertaken in England by Trist and Bamforth (1951). Their purpose was to study the effects of introducing a technological (or organizational) change into a coal mining operation. Before the change, the mining activities were carried out by a small group of men working together on one shift. Each of the men was responsible for his own individual work; yet, they worked together in the same general area and seemed to form a rather friendly and close-knit group. The changeover involved the introduction of mechanized techniques for handling the coal, and, since the mechanized procedures required fewer men to be working at any one time, the group was split into three subgroups which were placed on a three-shift, 24-hour-per-day operation. It was no great surprise to observe that the workmen were quite dissatisfied with the new setup; they ignored or resisted opportunities to put forth additional effort, and they even began to blame their former co-workers on the other shifts for any work problems which might arise. The change in organizational structure from a closely knit group to a more impersonal, mechanized, assembly line operation was probably the major factor producing the change in attitudes and work behaviors. It will be the job of the organizational psychologist in firms of the future to learn how such changes can be introduced without the disruptive effects on individuals observed by Trist and Bamforth.

OTHER ORGANIZATIONAL VARIABLES

Technology, of course, is not the only organizational variable that could have an effect upon employee behavior. Let us review briefly some of the other organizational variables that have been investigated by organizational psychologists in an effort to discover the effects that they might have upon human behavior within organizations.

Shape

Most, if not all, American organizations are pyramid shaped; there are many people at lower levels and relatively few at the top. Leavitt (1962) suggests that the narrowing at the top, coupled with the strong desire of people to get to the top of the heap, creates a general atmosphere of competition for advancement. Without question, our society is based on competition. However, it is possible that interpersonal competition may not be the most effective means of accomplishing organizational objectives. Cutthroat competition can result in anxiety and withdrawal for the losers and perhaps in feelings of guilt for the winners. Thus, some writers have suggested that the pyramidal shape of modern American firms may be much less effective than other shapes, such as, for example, the flat structure advocated by Worthy (1950).

Porter and Lawler (1964) studied the job satisfaction of over 1900 managers employed at various levels in firms throughout the United States. They found a moderate tendency for managers in "flat" organizations to feel more self-actualized (i.e., they felt greater opportunities for full use of their abilities and for self-development) than managers in more traditionally organized, "tall" organizations. In general, however, relationships between organizational shape and managerial satisfactions were small or nonexistent; Porter and Lawler suggest that future research should be done to study the relative advantages of "tall" and "flat" structures in firms of different size and type (i.e., retail trade, manufacturing, insurance, banking, etc.).

Line versus staff

Some firms favor strong line organizations with few staff advisors or experts; others favor large numbers of staff advisors to a relatively few topflight line administrators. Woodward found large differences in the line-staff compositions of the organizations she studied. Thirty-five firms utilized a strong line or military type structure and about half (50) utilized varying degrees of staff guidance to the line organization. That this can be an important variable, too, is shown in Porter's study (1963a) which suggests that staff managers find less challenge in their jobs and greater necessity for "organization-man" behavior than line managers do. Perhaps staff type jobs are inherently more frustrating.

Authority

Leavitt (1962) has discussed our old friend, authority, as a probable source of problems in organizations. Why is this so? He suggests that the distribution of authority follows the general pyramidal shape of the organization; thus, people at the top have more authority and the people at the bottom less, with the result that persons at the lower levels feel more dependent. This dependency, in turn, may strongly affect organizational behavior. This is, of course, the major theme suggested by Argyris, who, with Leavitt, believes that organizational effectiveness could be greatly improved by changing the pattern of authority relationships in modern day firms, thereby reducing employees' dependency reactions and eliciting more mature and more personally productive behavior from them.

Size

Size is, of course, an obvious organizational variable which already has been discussed briefly at the beginning of this chapter. In addition to the more obvious concomitants of size such as greater complexity of communications and less closeness of interpersonal relationships, the very process of increasing size or growth may be accompanied by changes in organizational effectiveness. For example, Haire (1959) compares the effects of growth in organizations with the pattern of biological growth in animals. It is a well-known fact that increase in the size of organisms is limited by the nature of their structure and shape. For example, humans could not triple their height without an accompanying massive increase in the strength and bulk of their lower extremities to accommodate their greatly increased overall weight; their shape or form would need to be changed drastically to allow survival of the species. Haire suggests that the survival of organizations, as they increase in size, may also be dependent upon the flexibility with which they are able to change their organizational forms to accommodate the new requirements of their constituent parts. Thus, developmental or longitudinal studies of the growth of organizations and the changes accompanying such growth constitute a much needed type of research information; Haire already has made such studies of a small number of firms in order to illustrate the inferences mentioned above.

ORGANIZATIONS AND PROBLEMS

Because organizational psychology is so new, our discussion probably has seemed rather disjointed and somewhat poorly organized. This is, however, a fairly accurate reflection of the current diversity of research and thinking in this infant area. In spite of the diversity, it is possible to list, in summary fashion, some of the major problems of organizational psychology needing study. These are:

1. What can be done about the potential conflict existing between the personality of the individual and the demands of the organization?
2. What can be done to reduce feelings of frustration of people on the job?
3. What changes in organizational variables such as size, shape, and structure are most apt to be effective in the firm of the future?

Is there one general theme running through these problems? Leavitt suggests there is. He believes that organizational factors such as authority are tending to force management people toward very subjective and short-term kinds of behavior but that the changing business environment today demands more objective and long-term kinds of activities and decisions. The problem becomes one of modifying the organization so that it makes long-term, more objective behavior more possible and more likely.

How can organizations be changed to solve this problem and the others listed above? This is the challenge for the organizational psychologist. Right now, there are no general principles to apply to solve all organizational problems. There are, however, some clues for directing future actions; Leavitt (1958) has listed four needed steps as follows:

1. Change the organization structure so that it conflicts less with human needs. As an example, companies might become more decentralized or set up more committees to handle company affairs.
2. Change people on the jobs and fill the jobs with people who are psychologically better able to deal with the conflicting forces that arise because of the organizational structure. This implies selection of people, who, for example, are more problem oriented and indicates a need for selection procedures to focus not only on selecting people to meet specific job demands but also in terms of their abilities to cope with organizational requirements.
3. Change the climate or atmosphere of the organization so that organizational pressures may be eased. Rules and regulations could be decreased; competition might be lessened.
4. Simplify the organization by programming some jobs like middle-management so that this, in effect, eliminates decision making on the part of these employees. Computers would take over the "sticky" problem areas and routinize these kinds of jobs.

In general, these appear to be fair solutions to the general problems that exist. How these solutions might actually be applied is, of course, a problem to be studied by research now and in the future. Regardless of solutions, it becomes apparent that theorists, classic or modern, really are after the same things. Both want to improve efficiency, discover general principles of operation, and discover the best organizational structure to meet the needs of each new set of organizational requirements.

There is one other major problem, however, in this field. Researchers, depending upon their own motivations, place different emphases on what should be studied. There is a central core of knowledge, but there is not a central theory that encompasses all the various viewpoints of writers such as Likert, Haire, Argyris, March, Simon, and the rest. It may be that a global theory encompassing all of the research conducted today and all of the projected solutions is not possible. In order to realize definite progress in this area, however, a greater interlocking and coordination of future research in the field is needed.

THE FIELD OF THE FUTURE

This chapter has presented an overview of the past and the present; it seems clear that the organization and the individual are intertwined in a complex set of interactions. The "untangling of the vines" of these intertwined relationships is the subject matter of organizational psychology. As the behavioral sciences become more sophisticated in research techniques and as more and more researchers focus on the problems of organizations (even without agreement as to what should receive central attention) it is easy to agree with Leavitt (1961) who sees organizational psychology as the "field of the future."

Suggested Additional Reading

Adams, R. N., and Preiss, J. J. (Eds.) *Human organization research.* Homewood, Ill.: Dorsey, 1960.

Argyris, C. *Integrating the individual and the organization.* New York: Wiley, 1964.

Bakke, E. W. *The individual and the organization.* New Haven: Yale Univ., Labor and Management Center, 1951.

Blau, P., and Scott, R. W. *Formal organizations.* San Francisco: Chandler, 1962.

Brayfield, A. H., and Crockett, W. H. Employee attitudes and employee performance. *Psych. Bull.,* 1955, **52**, 396-424.

Brown, A. Some reflections on organizations: truths, half-truths, and delusions. *Personnel,* 1954, **31**, 31-42.

Gouldner, A. W. Organizational analysis. In Merton, R. K., Broom, L., and Cottrell, L. S., Jr. (Eds.), *Sociology today. Problems and prospects.* New York: Basic Books, 1959.

Kasl, S., and French, J. R. P., Jr. The effects of occupational status on physical and mental health. *J. Social Issues,* 1962, **18**, 67-89.

Katzell, R. Contrasting systems of work organization. *Amer. Psychol.,* 1962, **17**, 102-108.

Leavitt, H. J., and Bass, B. M. Organizational psychology. *Annual Review of Psychology,* 1964, **15**, 371-398.

Likert, R. *New patterns of management.* New York: McGraw-Hill, 1961.

Maier, N. R. F., and Hoffman, L. R. Organization and creative problem solving. *J. appl. Psychol.,* 1961, **45**, 277-280.

Marriott, R. Size of working group and output. *Occup. Psychol.,* 1949, **23**, 47-57.

Mechanic, D. Sources of power of lower participants in complex organizations. *Admins. Science Quart.*, 1962, **7**, 349-364.

Porter, L. W. Job attitudes in management: IV. perceived deficiencies in need fulfillment as a function of size of company. *J. appl. Psychol.*, 1963b, **47**, 386-387.

Runan, W. W. Work group attributes and grievance activity. *J. appl. Psychol.*, 1963, **47**, 38-41.

Terrien, F. W., and Mills, D. L. The effect of changing size upon the internal structure of organizations. *Amer. Sociol. Rev.*, 1955, **20**, 11-13.

8

THE PSYCHOLOGY OF LABOR-MANAGEMENT RELATIONS

OVERVIEW

Every day in innumerable conference rooms in the United States representatives of labor and management sit down at a bargaining table to attempt a resolution of their differences. This process, known as "collective bargaining," has been called the keystone of management-labor relations. As knights of old, these union and management representatives joust on economic battle grounds, not with lances, but with psychological weapons, such as the threat of the shutdown of the plant by either side.

No lengthy detailing of the importance of collective bargaining to the American economy is needed. As Stagner (1963) has pointed out, however, few aspects of modern industry show so much irrationality on both sides as does the collective bargaining process. It is obvious that human behavior is involved to a large extent and it is here, of course, that the psychologist has a major interest.

Where does the psychologist fit into labor-management relations, negotiations, solution of grievances, and the like? He is not usually a bargainer nor a mediator, but instead his influence to date has been that of a researcher, an investigator, and, in some cases, an innovator. It is rare for a psychologist actually to sit in on a collective bargaining session between union and management representatives. The psychologist, even though he may be recognized as an expert on human behavior, has not been summoned by either management or union people to operate in such settings.

Actually, the psychologist in industry has been employed most often by business firms. On only a few occasions have psychologists been employed directly by labor unions. As a result, the union view of a psychologist, if not one of suspicion, is at least one of general apprehension. The union's feeling, as expressed by many writers, is that the psychologist is a representative of management. Since he is paid by management, he must, in the view of unions, also share the goals and values of management. In discussing labor-management relations, let us, therefore, be realistic. We are dealing in an area in which industrial psychologists generally function as researchers rather than as participants; often the psychologist is considered as part of the management team rather than as a union representative. With this much said, our intent in this brief chapter is to look at some of the research that has been done and to suggest the ultimate roles for psychology and psychologists in the labor-management relations of the future.

COLLECTIVE BARGAINING TRENDS

First, let us review the general process of collective bargaining. Harbison and Coleman (1951) list a number of recent trends in the development of collective bargaining:

1. Strikes have become more peaceful.
2. Employers have come to use less emotional tactics in dealing with unions.
3. Workers look to unions for "policing" management practices and for rendering services to them (the workers) much more now than ever before.
4. Decision-making power within unions has gravitated from rank and file members to full-time union functionaires.

Thus, it appears that collective bargaining is becoming a more sedate, less emotional, and more formal process for both labor and management. In a sense, collective bargaining has become a highly ritualistic and highly formalized procedure. This does not mean that conflict has been eliminated from collective bargaining. Processes involving conflict have become more predictable, however.

Another trend occurring over the past few years is a strong tendency for governmental intervention of one kind or another into the collective bargaining process. This is particularly true of strikes involving the public welfare. Extreme pressures have been brought to bear on both union and management representatives by government to solve their differences.

Not all writers are highly praiseful of collective bargaining. Jacobs (1963), for example, speaks of collective bargaining as looking "old before its time at twenty-eight" (collective bargaining became official public policy under the Wagner Act of 1935). He also feels collective bargaining has been unable to deal effectively with automation and large-scale unemployment problems. He suggests a great need for a new kind of collective bargaining system.

Conway (1963) feels, however, that collective bargaining will still be important in the future and this is likely to be the case. Changes and innovations may occur but both management and unions seem committed to the free exercise of collective bargaining. Problems inherent in the collective bargaining process now will probably exist also in the future. We examine some of these problems later in this chapter.

Definition and aims

For our purposes, the best definition of collective bargaining is given by Harbison and Coleman (1951). They define collective bargaining as a treaty-making and treaty-enforcing process undertaken by the chosen representatives of management and labor. The important point of this definition is that collective bargaining is not *just* interrelationships between people. It is a definite, specified activity involving the relative power of both labor and management. As we shall see later, people and their personalities are entwined in collective bargaining; it is never a one-man affair. More often, it is similar to a contest of power between two teams in a sports spectacle.

What do the representatives involved in collective bargaining hope to accomplish in negotiations? Peters (1955), a long-time mediator, states that there are three main objectives in negotiations:

1. The parties attempt to influence each other, the employees, and public opinion by advocating the merits of their respective positions.
2. They indicate their strength to one another.
3. They seek to learn each team's maximum and minimum expectations with a view toward avoiding, if possible, an economic contest (e.g., a strike) which is damaging to both sides.

Collective bargaining, then, always involves a show of strength by both sides, various tactics designed to influence one another and other persons, and a genuine exploration of what each side wants and what it will take.

In addition to these aims, management and union representatives each have certain individual objectives. Harbison and Coleman (1951) list the following five management objectives:

1. *Preservation and strengthening of the business enterprise.* This refers to keeping the firm financially solvent and having a good organization of local employees.
2. *Retention of effective control over the enterprise.* This refers to management's striving to maintain its authority to direct its own activities.
3. *Stable and businesslike relations.* This refers to the effort to set up a straightforward process of handling grievances and complaints and to make the union responsible for the acts of their people.
4. *Broad social and economic goals.* This refers to management's desire to defend the free enterprise system as it sees it.
5. *Pursuit of personal goals and ambitions.* This refers to the particular needs and desires of individual management negotiators who seek to "look good" and to gain respect from colleagues in their firms.

In turn, Harbison and Coleman list these five similar objectives for unions:

1. *Preservation and strengthening of the union as an institution.* Like management representatives, union leaders also want to build the union as an institution and promote its security and stability.
2. *Promotion of the economic welfare of the members.* This refers to

getting more wages, better fringe benefits, better working conditions and the like.

3. *The acquisition of control over jobs.* This involves such things as setting up seniority rules and limiting the employer's right to hire and to fire.

4. *Promotion of broad social and economic goals.* Again, like management representatives, labor leaders too, have broad social and economic goals as they see them.

5. *Pursuit of personal goals and ambitions.* Not too surprisingly, labor officials also want to advance their own personal goals and ambitions. In many cases, this means getting reelected to office.

When these rather similar but opposing objectives of companies and unions are joined across the bargaining table, it is obvious that conflict is a natural and usual outcome. For example, if both management and union representatives are seeking more control over job rules and regulations, conflict is bound to result. Inevitably, conflict also occurs when personal goals and ambitions clash. In fact, the list of possible areas of conflict in collective bargaining is endless.

PROBLEMS OF COLLECTIVE BARGAINING

With collective bargaining involving power struggles and conflict of interests, it is obvious that many problems exist that merit the attention of the industrial psychologist. Let us examine some of these in light of psychological research results.

Communications barriers

One major problem area in the field of union-management relations is the lack of good communications between many management and labor representatives. Even without getting into differences in background and personality that we will touch upon in a later section, there are obvious communication barriers that exist. For example, in listening, most persons can gain information more rapidly than it can be transmitted. As a result, there is a tendency in most conversations for the listener's mind to wander around while the other person is speaking. Generally, this results in a gap in communications because the listener often has not heard everything that the speaker has intended him to hear. It is apparent that in the emotionally-charged atmosphere of collective bargaining negotiations, this tendency toward inefficient listening is probably very prevalent. Here the negotiator all too often is only waiting for a chance to jump in and is not, in fact, listening. He is really making up a speech of his own while supposedly listening to the other individual.

Another communications barrier usually present in labor-management negotiations is the tendency to evaluate or to approve or disapprove of what is communicated rather than to seek the factual content of what is said. This tendency occurs primarily because of emotionally-keyed words. For example, in politics, the words *Democrat* and *Republican* bring pleasant or unpleasant thoughts to mind, depending upon one's political point of view. Likewise, in labor-management bargaining, key words or phrases may be all that is heard by either side who then immediately evaluate or judge rather than listen. These tendencies to judge and to criticize can result in a very abrupt blocking of communications. Another form of this occurs between people who dislike one another and, therefore, have great difficulties communicating because of the overriding and persistent tendencies toward interpersonal evaluation.

Furthermore, most of us assume that because we hear something a certain way, everyone has heard it the same way. We know from studies of listening behavior that if two or three people are listening to the same speaker, they do not necessarily hear the same words and, in many cases, do not even hear the speaker at all. Just because we hear a statement made does not mean that someone else has heard it or interpreted it in the same way.

Another basis for poor communications among individuals is the need on the part of some to maintain authority by not communicating properly. In other words, they attempt to maintain an air of mystery or secrecy about what is going on. Sometimes in labor-management negotiations this is good strategy for it is not necessarily an advantage to put all of one's cards on the table. On the other hand, holding back vital information or miscommunicating because of personal needs for authority can lead to extremely faulty transmission of information.

There is evidence, too, that a common reason for faulty communications between union and management representatives, is the reading difficulty of most labor contracts. Tiffin and Walsh (1951) applied the well-known Flesch readability formula to 59 union-management agreements. They found that the mean *reading ease* of these agreements was a level requiring high school or some college education (96% of the agreements required a reading ability equivalent to a high school education while almost one-third required ability equivalent to a college education). It was also shown that the mean reading ease of grievance clauses was at a level requiring the equivalent of a college education. The trend was for reading ease scores to become more difficult as the number of members covered by the agreement increased; that is, the larger the union, the more likely was the agreement to be extremely difficult to read. Thus, it is likely that many union and management representatives, particularly first-level foremen and union stewards, just do not understand what the union agreement says. There may be good reasons why the language in these contracts has to be spelled out in rather legalistic terms, but steps need to be taken to assure that simplified versions are prepared so that average union members and front-line foremen can understand what the labor contract says.

Another problem in communications involves semantics. Thompson and Davis (1956), in a study of essays written by workers in the General Motor's "My Job and Why I Like It" contest, suggested that "security" in the essays usually meant assurance of continued work and income. Security was also used, however, to refer to financial safeguards in times of emergencies. Some even identified security with physical safety. From this rather simple example, it can be seen that the term *security* suggested different things to different people. It is not surprising that negotiations on the general question of union security might cause similar problems and lead to misunderstanding.

Gateways to effective communication

What can be done in labor-management problems to improve communication? Several techniques have been suggested that are not too difficult to undertake. First, representatives of both management and unions must learn to listen with understanding to the other side. This means that they must be receptive to the content of what is being expressed rather than the conditions or manner of its expression. This can be learned rather simply. For example, if you are listening to someone talking, a friend or co-worker, and if you force yourself to delay speaking until you have first restated for yourself the information, attitudes, or feelings that the other person has just transmitted, you will learn to be a much more accurate listener. Why is this so? Because it forces the feedback that is crucial to effective communicating. Representatives of management and labor would do well to practice this simple method during their collective bargaining sessions.

Another technique is to tailor the information to fit the way the recipients have organized the situation. Information should always be presented in such a way as to elicit interest on the part of the recipient. For example, the management representative ought to present his views in a framework familiar to the union representative and vice versa.

Information, too, should be transmitted in small units. The old saying, "One picture is worth ten thousand words," is not inappropriate. One small unit of information is much easier to comprehend than a large mass of many information units. This is particularly true in labor-management negotiations when large tables of statistical data may be brought into play in order to prove such facts as wages being low, high, or average. Careful foreplanning and arranging of such material into relatively small logical information units can help to assure that they will be effectively conveyed to other persons.

Still another way to destroy barriers to good communications is to get firmly in mind what is to be communicated. Both sides ought to outline their objectives clearly and indicate what they want to accomplish and how they hope to accomplish the objectives. These rules will not always assure complete accuracy in labor-management communications, but they are a needed step in this direction.

As an indication of this, Peters (1955), in summarizing a large number of cases in which he acted as a labor mediator, stresses very strongly the importance of being able to pick up communications clues. For example, how union or management representatives word their statements, how they make physical gestures, and how they seem to react to proposals that are made provide vital clues in negotiations. It appears from his analysis that those people who are more alert get better results in collective bargaining. This, in fact, would seem to be one test of individuals for collective bargaining work. Are they good communicators? Can they respond effectively to the other person? Can they put themselves in the other person's shoes in order to understand what the other person is attempting to do? Naturally, the industrial psychologist has strong interest in the problem of communication and this is one of the areas in which more research is necessary.

Faulty perception

Perhaps the biggest problem by far in collective bargaining relationships is faulty perception on the part of both union and management representatives. This faulty perception occurs in many ways. It occurs through misperceiving the motives and the desires of the other side; it involves the misperception of the total situation; it involves the misperception of the facts as they are actually presented. An interesting example of this is cited by Peters (1955). He describes a management negotiator who attempted to get a settlement on a wage rate which actually was below the existing wage rate in the area. This was an impossible goal and, according to Peters, illustrates an instance of extremely faulty perception of what the union desired. The outcome was a strike, which was deeply injurious to both labor and management.

It is obvious that people see the same thing in different ways. A heavy rainstorm may produce smiles and expressions of joy from an amateur gardener while the same rainstorm could cause the owner of a baseball team to be extremely annoyed. In union-management relationships the psychologist is concerned with how each side sees a given situation and how facts are perceived. Many factors can affect such perceptions. Stagner (1948) has listed four:

1. *Biological quality of the organism.* He cites the case of a color-blind man who, of course, does not enjoy technicolor movies in the same way that persons with normal vision do. Naturally, biological differences do not normally play an important role in labor-management relationships.

2. *The past history of the organism.* As we shall see later, there are substantial differences in the background of labor and management executives which can lead to differences in perception and disagreements about facts.

3. *The purposes of the organism.* A prime purpose of management, for example, is to make a profit and cost figure seem highly important. To the union official, this purpose is not as important as high wages.

4. *Attitudes.* Differing feelings, beliefs, and opinions between union members and management obviously affect the way different things are perceived.

Of the four factors listed above, attitudes, purposes, and past experiences can differ markedly for industrial managers and union representatives. In this vein, studies reported by Stagner (1948) are enlightening. In one study he interviewed several union and management representatives asking their opinions on such things as attitudes toward present union-management relations, union leadership, attitudes toward labor legislation, personal feelings after a negotiation meeting, and other factors. He found that the major characteristic among union officials was a feeling of distrust and suspicion of management's statements. This was expressed in several ways but, all in all, it boiled down to an unfavorable attitude toward management and a strong suspicion of management's motives in negotiations. Similarly, interviews with company managers also showed feelings of suspicion toward labor. Managers expressed hostility toward union representatives and toward union principles. Stagner suggests that the emotional coloring of facts in the minds of workers and executives tended to play an important role in their perceptions of one another. He suggests that men from plants with poor labor relations records had more emotionally-toned perceptions than others.

In a second study, Stagner used a checklist of 20 adjectives. Subjects (college students) were asked to check those adjectives they believed to be characteristic of factory workers and of business executives and to indicate the relative desirability of each of the adjectives. In addition, they also checked the ones they felt applied to themselves and rated themselves on a scale designed to measure the extent of their pro-labor feelings. To no great surprise, the subjects who considered themselves strongly pro-labor viewed the typical worker more favorably than the typical executive. Antilabor students showed the reverse trend. These results confirm the fact that persons who are markedly prolabor or antilabor will have strong and differing feelings about persons on the other side of the fence.

In a parallel set of studies, Remmers and Remmers (1949) and Miller and Remmers (1950) also found differences in perception between union and management personnel. Managers were asked to estimate the responses of labor leaders on a widely used test of supervisory attitudes (How Supervise?), and labor leaders were asked to estimate the answers of managers. The managers overestimated the labor leaders' scores and the labor leaders greatly underestimated the managers' scores. The estimates by labor leaders were much lower than the scores they obtained when filling it out for themselves. In other words, they attributed much less favorable supervisory practice scores to management persons than they themselves held and, in turn, managers attributed much more favorable supervisory attitudes to union leaders than they actually had. These studies simply confirm the differing perceptions that each group has of the others' attitudes.

From the above, it is clear that union and management representatives must recognize and accept as natural the fact that their motives and desires will very likely be viewed with suspicion by persons on the other side of the bargaining table. Thus, they both need to take steps to try to see the other's points of view more clearly and more accurately. Stagner (1948) suggests that executives should take great pains to give full information to the union on all changes affecting workers and to be scrupulously honest in standing behind even seemingly trivial promises. Moreover, he urges the use of extreme patience in listening to all grievances or complaints. Stagner feels that such an approach will, in the long run, lead to a lessening of the suspicions felt by union people. The same tactics of fair play and scrupulous attention to commitments must also, of course, be employed by union leaders in order to reduce suspicion and misperceptions on the part of managers and company representatives. Needless to say, the task of getting management and labor to avoid misunderstandings and suspicions remains an extremely difficult one. However, psychologists can help simply by pointing up the natural difficulties of accurate interpersonal perception and by continuing to collect information and to design and to conduct research on the ways of overcoming the communication barriers between labor and management.

Personality

From the preceding discussion of faulty perception, we can recognize the potential effects of personality differences on perception. For example, Bogard (1960) compared the answers to a number of personality tests, occupational rating scales, and biographical questionnaires made by 40 enrollees in a union leadership institute with the answers made by 40 management trainees working for a steamship line. The management trainees were better educated, on the average, and the union trainees tended to identify with somewhat lower socioeconomic classes. On a measure of values (Allport-Vernon-Lindzey Scale of Values) the union group scored higher on the social scale and lower on the economic scale than the management trainees. Other personality differences showed the union members to be more altruistic, less concerned with practical matters, and perhaps less socially mature. Biographical data suggested that during the formative years, management trainees had apparently been more successful in peer group interactions and that they had been reared by parents who were more conforming to social pressures.

Another study bearing on personality differences was done by Rosen and Rosen (1957). They interviewed and tested 21 union-business agents belonging to the same international union. They discovered that the job of the business agent was about the same from one local union group to another. All had heavy demands made upon their time and energy and this tended to isolate them from their family, friends, and home. They were constantly faced with the problems of others, and they were under almost constant tension. Yet, they were expected to keep their tempers and to be diplomatic; thus, they had to be cautious and skeptical in their dealings with both management and with their own union members.

These pressures and tensions were reflected in their replies and scores on tests of personality. They scored high on scales indicative of psychosomatic illnesses and they exhibited an undue concern about their physical well-being. They also scored high on measures of activity level and ego-strength, suggesting a general tendency to bounce back quickly from tough problems or losses. A further comparison was made between agents rated high and low in overall effectiveness. The higher rated group was less depressed, tended to show stronger ego-strength, higher self-confidence, and a somewhat greater degree of sensitivity to other people than the lower rated group. All of these differences, of course, tie in with the requirements of the job as outlined by Rosen and Rosen.

Personality studies have also been made of labor mediators, the neutral third party whose job it is to act as a "go-between" among management and labor negotiators to aid them in arriving at solutions to problems. In an early study, Wechsler (1950) obtained effectiveness ratings of 146 different mediators, plus biographical data and test information. He compared the good and bad mediators on such factors as intelligence, personality variables, and attitude items. Although only a few differences between good and poor mediators were discovered, the good mediators tended to be middle-aged rather than extremely young or extremely old and they tended to score high on a measure of general mental ability, suggesting that good mediators probably were "sharper."

In a later study of the behavior and personality of labor mediators, Landsberger (1960) investigated mediators in two different cities, New York and Detroit. In each city, a large number of raters from both union and management were obtained to assess the effectiveness of the particular mediators involved. Several rating dimensions were used. In general, Landsberger found that regardless of which side was doing the rating, there was general agreement as to who were the best mediators. Partiality toward one side then was not necessarily a prerequisite for winning the esteem of a particular group. In investigating behavior dimensions, Landsberger found that the most important aspect of behavior, at least in the minds of the persons doing the rating, was that of intellectual skills such as IQ, knowledge, and originality. These were ranked high as important behavior dimensions and, in fact, intelligence was rated highest. So-called soft human relations variables such as humor and unobtrusiveness were the least important of the behavior dimensions. Landsberger also conducted a factor analysis of the behavior ratings and found a strong general factor, heavily loaded with intellectual ratings. As a result he concluded that at this level of general professional competence, intellectual skills were of more importance to the mediator than a "good" personality.

It seems obvious from these studies then that personal characteristics are of great importance in union-management relations. Through studies such as these, industrial psychologists have been making important contributions toward a better understanding and definition of the personal attributes contributing to successful union-management relationships in collective bargaining.

OTHER PROBLEMS IN COLLECTIVE BARGAINING

The factors of poor communication, faulty perception, and differences in personality are all important in union-management relationships and particularly in collective bargaining. In addition to these, other problems reveal that:

1. Collective bargaining can be too formal and overly structured. As a result both management and union representatives can get caught in a ritualistic straitjacket, tending to make innovation and new approaches to the collective bargaining process nearly impossible. In fact, critics of collective bargaining suggest that one of the main problems of collective bargaining is that both union and management representatives are too set in their ways and too concerned about carrying out collective bargaining in the way that has always been followed. In other words, they

are not open to new ideas or to changes. It is typical, for example, in collective bargaining negotiations for the union to begin with an extremely high set of demands. Management may, or may not, counter at this time with an extremely low estimate of what it will yield. Both sides, however, know that their positions are going to change. Much time is usually wasted by starting from positions that are untenable to both sides. This is the way collective bargaining usually has been done and is usually the procedure still followed. It is well-known, however, in problem-solving experiments that persons who have strong perceptual "sets" have difficulty solving problems that require new approaches and innovation. While most people tend to approach new problems with old solutions and old methods, the most successful problem-solvers are those who can change their set or approach. Overformalized approaches to collective bargaining probably result in severe constraints on producing new and different solutions to problems.

2. Collective bargaining often becomes embroiled in political contests which may be irrelevant to the issues being negotiated. This is particularly true for the union representative. Why is this so? Simply because many union members, as indicated earlier, have to be voted into office. As a result, collective bargaining often involves problems of saving face for the union representatives involved in the process. Problems may arise simply because demands are made that are related to political needs rather than to actual employee needs. This further complicates the communications picture for, in most cases, the union negotiator cannot openly bring up the question of obtaining concessions designed solely to make him look good to his membership. He must try to communicate this indirectly and to persons who may not be listening for it. While the labor relations negotiator for management is not voted into office, it is obvious that he, too, faces political problems in an effort to look good to top management. Certainly both sides in collective bargaining would do well to recognize this need and to cast it in its proper perspective.

3. Proper support for both sides of the collective bargaining relationship is often lacking. For example, the union membership may not always ratify the agreement their representatives have labored long to achieve. Likewise, top executives of many com-

panies have pulled the rug from under their labor relations executives by rejecting the result of the negotiated settlement. McFarland (1954), in discussing the dilemma of the industrial relations man, says that today's industrial relations man finds it hard to establish and maintain effective channels of communications with other executives, particularly his own superiors. He argues for better understanding from top management concerning industrial relations persons within a company. In the same vein, one of the trends in today's management-labor relations is for union representatives to become full-time bargainers, rather than part-time. In some cases, this has resulted in the full-time union representative actually being closer to management than to the union membership. It has been shown, for example, that as union-representatives deal more in negotiations they come to appreciate more of management's problems. This is commendable but it can, at the same time, result in their becoming alienated from their own membership, and they may eventually be voted out of office. The lack of proper support seems to be a perennial problem for both sides of the union-management ledger.

Many other problems in collective bargaining could be mentioned. However, the major problems listed earlier and those immediately above give the general tone of the kinds of problems faced. They are illustrative of the complexities faced by the industrial psychologist concerned with studying labor-management relationships.

WHAT DO UNION MEMBERS WANT?

Let us turn now from the problems of collective bargaining and research done on them to another area which industrial psychologists have worked on. Specifically, this involves two closely related questions: Why do people join unions, and what do union members want? An understanding of union members' desires and what they seek from union membership should aid in improving collective bargaining practices as well as contributing to better relationships between unions and management.

A common belief is that individuals join unions because they are generally dissatisfied with poor working conditions, low wages, lack of benefits, and the like. This belief is based in turn on the principle that people, when faced with stressful circumstances, will join together not only to commiserate with one another but also to gain added strength and power with which to bargain for improved conditions of employment and a consequent increase in job satisfaction. Research evidence does, in fact, show that union membership and job satisfaction go hand in hand. For example, Stagner (1958), in studying Communist and non-Communist union members in Italy, discovered that Communist union members were much more dissatisfied with their jobs. His data suggest that persons who were extremely dissatisfied with their jobs and their working conditions developed strongly aggressive tendencies which achieved expression by following the more militant and action-oriented doctrine and leadership of Communism. Thus, in this study at least, marked dissatisfaction was associated with more extreme action groups, thus confirming indirectly the belief stated above.

In another culture, India, Sinha, and Sarma (1962) reported a negative correlation between attitudes toward the union and job satisfaction for a sample of 100 workers in a light engineering factory; that is, the greater the degree of dissatisfaction with the job, the greater the degree of favorableness toward the union. This finding fits the belief that the union serves as a channel for the expression of employees' needs and demands. It suggests, too, that satisfied workers probably feel less eager to join unions.

Speroff (1959), in studying small unorganized plants in the United States, found a high negative correlation between job satisfaction and the number of job-related interview sessions that workers had. Since these interviews consisted mostly of sessions devoted to an airing of employee complaints, these results are in agreement with the other studies mentioned above.

It seems clear then that dissatisfied individuals on the job are more ready for union membership than are the more satisfied individuals. These various studies also suggest that the greater the dissatisfaction, the more extreme may be the tendency to join action groups.

Dual allegiance

It does not necessarily follow from the above that union members automatically dislike or are disloyal toward their particular company. To the contrary, there is strong evidence of dual allegiance toward both the company and the union. Purcell (1954), in a widely-known study, interviewed 385 packinghouse workers and found 73% favorable to both the company and the union. Purcell suggests that the labor and management leaders should recognize that employees are strongly in favor of peaceful coexistence between the union and the firm and that this should help to eliminate some of the areas of misunderstanding between them. Apparently, employees want *both* a good union and a good company.

The importance of wages

Related to the question of what union members want are results of a study conducted by Thompson (1953), who studied human relations in collective bargaining. He interviewed management and union persons from the tractor industry. He reports that wages are the prime element influencing employee satisfaction in unionized industry. He says that psychological rewards, no matter how desirable, cannot serve as substitutes for collective wage agreements. In fact, he states that the ultimate aim of collective negotiation should be to arrive at wages and other terms of employment acceptable to both parties for a given contract period. Stagner (1950), however, argues strongly that wages are *not* the most important motivator for persons in industry. He argues convincingly that ego-satisfaction is far more crucial to workers and cites evidence showing that ego-motivation rather than economic motivation is predominant. His argument is reminiscent of the results of Herzberg's study discussed in Chapter 6, for he feels that factors such as prestige, recognition, and achievement are far more important to most employees than dollars and cents.

It is likely that both Thompson and Stagner are correct. Wages do play an important role in collective bargaining and usually are a primary issue in negotiations. At the same time, however, demands for increased wages may often really reflect a demand for status, prestige, and recognition instead of dollars and cents per se. Stagner feels that workers want more of whatever is needed to maintain status at a particular time. For example, if they are approaching old age, they want security; when prices are higher, they want higher pay.

Related to this hypothesis are results of a recent study by Nealey (1964) in which he sought to learn what workers prefer in the form of extra benefits. He obtained questionnaires from over 1,000 union members of the International Brotherhood of Electrical Workers in which he asked them to state their preferences from among a pay raise, a longer vacation, a shorter work week, complete hospital insurance, a pension increase, or a union shop. Surprisingly, hospital insurance was by far the most preferred. Less surprising is the finding that pensions were viewed as more important by older persons. Ranking far down the scale, for all ages, was a shorter work week. Even though this study is limited to just one industrial union, the results do suggest that research can be helpful in determining employee preferences for different kinds of benefits. With this kind of research information, both unions and management would be better informed for the bargaining process, and the outcome would more likely be based on solid evidence rather than on argumentation, threat, and coercion, as so often occurs now. The study is important then in showing how psychological research can yield objective and significant results which may have immediate utility in helping to settle areas of potential conflict between labor and management.

THE ROLE OF THE PSYCHOLOGIST

From the foregoing research and speculation, what can we say now about the proper role of the industrial psychologist in studying labor-management relations? There are at least four different roles that he may be called upon to play. These are:

1. *Clinician.* Stagner (1963) sees the psychologist's role as one of helping to eliminate the childish and irrational components in the labor-management conflict. The major aim of the psychologist, in his role as a clinician, is to help parties in the conflict to

achieve better understanding of themselves and of others. The psychologist's activities in selection, training, and policy planning can, of course, contribute to better understanding indirectly, but Stagner calls for a more direct approach focused on eliminating the misperceptions and personality problems detrimental to successful collective bargaining. Viewed in this way, the psychologist becomes primarily a communications link between labor and management, helping to interpret the union to management and vice versa.

2. *Experimentalist.* Barkin (1961), in discussing the generally negative view of psychology held by union members, sees the experimental or engineering psychologist as most capable of improving psychologists' image among union members. Anything done to make jobs safer and healthier is of obvious value; thus, the engineering psychologist's concern with the effects of equipment design and factors in the physical environment (heat, lighting, noise, etc.) on human endeavor fits him well for contributing to improved relations between labor and management. Barkin states that the findings of experimental and engineering psychologists need to be more broadly recognized and popularized.

3. *Professional expert.* Levenstein (1961) sees the psychologist in union-management relations as a professional expert, following in the footsteps of the industrial engineer and the lawyer who have preceded him. He points to a parallel between management's use of their services and those of psychologists. At first, unions distrusted both industrial engineers and lawyers, but soon they, too, began to seek aid from them in negotiations, handling of grievances, and arbitrations. Levenstein believes that the psychologist is in a similar position and that he is gaining more and more acceptance on both sides of the labor-management conflict. He believes that the industrial psychologist should be used as a professional expert, called in to gather facts from which the negotiations may proceed. In other words, the role of the psychologist can be one of providing information to aid in reducing the areas of uncertainty between the two sides.

4. *Social scientist.* Shepard (1961) feels that the role of the psychologist in union-management relations should be to investigate experimentally the conditions under which real conflicts of

interests are perceived and the manner in which they may be most easily resolved. In this role, the psychologist is primarily a researcher and a problem-solving strategist. In promoting a problem-solving point of view, the psychologist would, therefore, help to dissipate the win-lose attitude so common now in collective bargaining, and he would help to create the conditions in which both sides would use their creative abilities in a joint effort to advance the interests of both.

Here then are four views of the psychologist involved in labor-management relations: clinician, social scientist, experimental psychologist, and professional expert. At present, unfortunately, it is rare for psychologists to have formally assigned responsibilities directly involving labor-management relations; however, it should be apparent from the above that the significance and diversity of his potential contributions are great. In fact, a psychologist, simply by working in the industrial setting, can have a strong impact on the nature of union-management relations even if he is given no formal responsibility for them. Feinberg (1961) has pointed out that the industrial psychologist's concern with human behavior in industry automatically affects the fate of both union members and of the management team. The kinds of things the psychologist works with—employee selection, personnel training, human motivation, organizational form and structure—all have profound and presumably beneficial effects on the nature of employment relationships in industry. Thus, it is abundantly clear that the psychologist is in a central position from which to effect improved and more sensible labor-management relationships in the years ahead.

Suggested Additional Reading

Christian, R. W. Status and future of industrial relations. *Factory,* 1963, **121,** 80-83.

Cole, D. L. *The quest for industrial peace.* New York: McGraw-Hill, 1963.

Cook, Alice H. *Union democracy: practice and ideal, an analysis of four large local unions.* Ithaca, N.Y.: Cornell Studies in Industrial and Labor Relations, 1963, **60.**

Dent, J. K., and De La Paz, R. Union security and management attitudes. *Personnel Psychol.*, 1961, **14**, 167-181.

Derber, M., Chalmers, W. E., and Stagner, R. The labor contract: provision and practice. *Personnel*, 1958, **34**, 19-30.

Derber, M., Chalmers, W. E., Stagner, R., and Edelman, M. *The local union-management relationship.* Urbana, Ill.: Institute of Labor and Industrial Relations, The University of Illinois Press, 1960.

Fleishman, E. A., and Harris, E. F. Patterns of leadership behavior related to employee grievances and turnover. *Personnel*, 1962, **15**, 43-56.

Jackson, J. M. The organization and its communications problem. *Adv. Mgt.*, 1959, **24**, 17-20.

Kornhauser, A., Dubin, R., and Ross, A. M. (Eds.) *Industrial conflict.* New York: McGraw-Hill, 1954.

Maier, N. R. F., and Hoffman, L. R. Seniority in work groups: a right or an honor? *J. appl. Psychol.*, 1963, **47**, 173-176.

McKersie, R. B., and Brown, M. Nonprofessional hospital workers and a union organizing drive. *Quart. J. Econ.*, 1963, **77**, 372-404.

McMurray, R. War and peace in labor relations. *Harv. Bus. Rev.*, 1955, **33**, 48-60.

Muench, G. A. A clinical psychologist's treatment of labor-management conflicts. *Personnel Psychol.*, 1960, **13**, 165-172.

Parker, G. M. The union role in decision-making in small plants. *Labor Law Journ.*, 1963, **14**, 532-541.

Peterson, Florence. *American Labor unions: what they are and how they work* (2nd rev. ed.). New York: Harper & Row, 1963.

Purcell, T. V. *The worker speaks his mind on company and union.* Cambridge: Harvard, 1953.

Seidman, J., London, J., Karsh, B., and Tagliacozzo, Daisy L. *The worker views his union.* Chicago: The University of Chicago Press, 1958.

Speroff, B. J. Group psychotherapy in labor relations: a case study. *Personnel Journ.*, 1960, **39**, 14-17.

Stagner, R. *The psychology of industrial conflict.* New York: Wiley, 1956.

Ways, M. Labor unions are worth the price. *Fortune*, 1963, **67**, 108-113 ff.

Weber, A. R. The craft-industrial issue revisited: a study of union government. *Indust. Labor Relat. Rev.*, 1963, **16**, 381-404.

9

SURVEY RESEARCH

The opinions of potential consumers about a firm's products or services can mean the difference between success and failure for the firm. A firm's marketing decisions relative to product innovation, product modification, advertising strategies, and the development of new or improved services can be aided substantially by knowing ahead of time the reactions to be expected from the consumer. However, in order for the decisions to be better than mere guesses, they must obviously be based on an accurate assessment of the mood and predispositions of the consumer. This is where the psychologist, acting as a specialist in survey research, comes in. Over the years, psychologists have developed sophisticated methods for the sampling and measuring of opinions and attitudes; as a result, they have come to play an increasingly prominent role in survey and consumer research activities.

THE QUESTION OF ACCURACY

As suggested above, the key problem in consumer research is to obtain an *accurate* estimate of what the consuming public will do in response to a new product or service. The question of accuracy is, therefore, paramount, and the survey research psychologist is primarily concerned with developing a survey of consumer opinion or behavior which minimizes all possible sources of error. What are some of the sources of error in survey and consumer research? Unfortunately, there are many. They include:

1. *Conceptual Errors.* Many survey research studies never get off the ground because they are undertaken without sufficient

care in thinking through the overall purpose of the survey. The problems for which the survey is to provide information must be carefully specified. It is not enough simply to say that the survey is designed to learn about the company's image or how well a new product will be received by consumers. The purpose must be reduced to operational terms. Exactly what kinds of information will be taken as defining the image of a company? What kinds of information concerning the new product will prove useful for making subsequent marketing decisions? In other words, exactly what kinds of responses will be taken as indicating either favorable or unfavorable reception of the product by the public? Finally, what groups of persons shall be defined as consumers—housewives, teenagers, business executives? It seems obvious that the population to be surveyed must be specified during the very early stages of a survey study; yet, a surprisingly large number of surveys are conducted without giving sufficient attention to *what* is to be asked of *whom*. This results in rather grievous conceptual difficulties in interpreting the results; thus, survey conclusions can only be as good as the care and planning going into the initial design of the study.

2. *Instrument Errors.* Instrument errors refer to errors arising from poorly designed questionnaires or attitude measures developed to elicit responses from survey respondents. The design of questionnaires used in a survey is, to a large degree, an artful process. Questions must be worded with great care so that their meanings are clear and to assure that they do not "lead" the respondent to give certain answers. There is no substitute for actual experience in learning how to write good questionnaires, but fortunately there are some general guidelines (presented in a later section) which can be helpful even to the novice. In contrast, the development of attitude measures is less of an artful process and utilizes agreed upon psychometric methods similar to procedures employed in selecting items for psychological tests. Even so, attempts to shortcut or ignore these necessary steps are not uncommon, with the result that poorly developed attitude scales abound and are often a major source of serious instrument errors.

3. *Sampling Errors.* In the absence of unlimited time and financial resources, a survey study obviously cannot secure re-

sponses from all members of a population of consumers. It is necessary, therefore, to select a *sample* of persons from the population and to use responses from these persons to derive inferences about the results to be expected if all persons in the population could be questioned. Ideally, each person in the population should have an equal (or at least a known) chance of appearing in the sample. Such a sample is called "random," and it assures that the characteristics of persons in the population will be accurately portrayed by persons in the sample. Any departure from random sampling procedures introduces varying degrees of error into the conclusions derived from the sample results. Sometimes, the magnitude of such errors may be estimated; more often, they cannot be. Various sampling methods and the kinds of errors involved in each of them are discussed in a later section.

4. *Interviewer Errors.* The face-to-face interchange between an interviewer and his respondent can lead to serious distortions unless special pains are taken to avoid them. Interviewers must be selected with care; they must be well trained, and they must be motivated to do a thorough and conscientious job. Most important perhaps, they need to be protected from themselves; that is, evidence is clear-cut that an interviewer's own opinions or attitudes about an issue can result in his unconsciously causing the respondent to alter or color his replies to survey questions. Thus, the interviewing instrument must be carefully standardized so that the interviewer's behavior also is standardized. He should merely be the agent for presenting questions to the respondent and recording replies from the respondent; the *less* of the interviewer (his opinions, predispositions, and personality) that is allowed to emerge in the interviewing situation, the better. Yet, the interviewer must, of course, also be friendly, warm, gracious, and courteous in order to gain and maintain cooperation and close rapport with the respondent. Clearly, good interviewers are rare. They are a critical link in the chain connecting the original inception of a study to the final reporting of results. We shall have a good deal more to say about the "care and feeding" of interviewers in a later section.

5. *Interpretation or Analysis Errors.* It is during the analysis of the data from a survey that it is well to review again the origi-

nal intent or purpose of the survey. The interpretation and reporting of results should ordinarily be directed only at fulfilling the original purpose. The most common error made at this stage is to go beyond the data or to extrapolate results from it which the survey was never designed to uncover. Thus, it may seem proper to infer future buying behavior from results showing that most consumers react enthusiastically to the advertisement planned for introducing a new product. However, nothing of the sort can or should be inferred; in fact, it has been shown that many consumers do not even follow through on their stated intentions (obtained during surveys) to purchase or not to purchase various types and brands of products. If the purpose of the survey is to predict the actual buying behavior of consumers, this should be specified and designed into the research study from the very beginning, not brought in the back door during the analysis of results designed for some other purpose. Such auxiliary inferences or hypotheses may, of course, form the basis for initiating another research study designed to fulfill purposes suggested by results from the first.

The survey director who can remove or at least minimize the sources of error discussed above will have solved the problem of accuracy. Results reported to the sponsor of the research will accurately portray the opinions, attitudes, or behavioral predispositions of a defined population of consumers. The consumer psychologist's major job, therefore, is to minimize each of these errors; because of their prime importance in consumer research, each is further amplified and discussed in greater detail in the following sections.

PLANNING THE SURVEY

Without careful advance planning, there is grave danger that a survey study will go in the wrong direction—asking the wrong questions of the wrong people at the wrong time and for the wrong purposes. Investment of time at this stage is relatively cheap, and it will reap large dividends in the form of greatly increased efficiency during the later, more expensive, stages of the survey study.

Even a short discussion of the purpose of the proposed survey with the sponsor of the research can do much to avoid false starts and misdirected efforts. Recently a large surveying organization was approached by the manager of a teenage charm school. He claimed he wanted to survey female teenagers to learn which problems of personal grooming, appearance, and interpersonal effectiveness concerned them most—certainly a legitimate area of research among the potential consumers of his school's services. However, during the preliminary planning stages, it soon developed that the sponsor wanted to supply the survey firm's interviewers with brochures advertising the charms of his charm school, and he also wanted to train the interviewers to give a sales pitch to the respondents. In other words, his real intent was to use the interviewers as a ready-made sales force of his firm's services. By insisting on a clear definition of the purpose of the study, the director of the survey firm was able to avoid a great deal of wasted effort and time. As it was, of course, the manager of the charm school was told to find his salesmen elsewhere—that the surveying organization was in business to gather information, not to disseminate promotional information about products or services.

The discussion and planning sessions will usually clarify the survey objectives and define the population to be surveyed; however, before actually designing the survey instruments it may be desirable, if he is not already working for the firm, for the survey director to become much more familiar with the sponsor's organization. Thus, he may choose to spend some time (a week or two) working for the sponsor's firm in order to become intimately aware of the nature of the problem and to suggest leads for the content of the questionnaires or attitude measures to be developed.

One further safeguard to assure that the sponsor and the survey director see eye-to-eye is the presurvey report. This is simply a dummy report showing the various tables and statistical breakdowns that will be prepared after the study is completed. The sponsor, in going through such a report, will quickly recognize areas about which he may want either more or less information. In a sense, such a report serves as a summary of the planning discussions; it reflects the purposes of the survey, the population surveyed, and the anticipated results to be derived from the survey instruments. In presenting the sponsor with a presurvey report, the survey director is, in effect, saying, "This is what we hope to give you after conducting the survey. Is it what you had in mind? If so, fine; if not, what changes should we make now *before* we get under way?"

We cannot emphasize too strongly the importance of these preliminary planning and initial developmental sessions to the eventual success of a survey study. Everything coming later rests on the foundation that has been established during the first stage.

DESIGNING THE SURVEY INSTRUMENT

Two major techniques are in common use for gathering information from respondents. Perhaps the most usual is the use of a questionnaire consisting of a set of standardized questions designed to elicit information decided upon as necessary during the planning stage of the survey. The second method involves the scaling of responses to yield a stable measurement of consumer attitudes in the area of study. Both techniques demand careful attention to the design of the instruments to be used in order to be certain that they are accurately eliciting the kind of information desired.

Questionnaires

Developing a good questionnaire is not easy. Attention must be paid to a careful writing of the specific questions to be used, to the format or organization of the various questions in the questionnaire, and to specifying clearly the directions to the interviewers so that they will know *exactly* how to handle each interview.

The following checklist summarizes some of the more important pitfalls to be avoided in writing questions for a survey:

1. Avoid complex or technical words and abstract concepts which may obscure the meaning of the question. For example, one would *not* ask, "Do you like the polyhedral, interwoven, underslung coil construction of your new Tangent Mattress?" Instead, one might simply ask, "What features of your new Tangent Mattress do you especially like or dislike?"

2. Use open-end questions sparingly and with caution. Open-end questions do not offer the respondent a set of structured alter-

natives from which to choose a response. "What do you think of the car you are now driving?" is an open-end question. Such questions are useful and often necessary during the early or exploratory phases of a consumer study—before the survey director knows very much about the range or type of responses to be expected. They also probably provide deeper insights into a respondent's motivations. At the same time, however, they tend to allow the interviewer more leeway and to place a greater burden on him than may be desirable. He must either try to copy the responses verbatim or to abstract from them the essence of what the respondent is saying, resulting usually in the loss or inadvertent distortion of the respondent's reply. Finally, the open-end question is difficult to handle because of respondent differences in their desires or abilities to verbalize their opinions; some are "impossible to turn off"; others hem and haw and never really get started. Thus, the open-end question is best reserved for exploratory studies to form the basis for writing structured questions on the same material or for simply gaining some knowledge of the flavor of consumer opinion to be used in supplementing or rounding out information from the structured questions designed to tap the same opinions or reactions.

3. Avoid loading the question or leading the respondent to give a particular answer. A query may be weighted in a variety of ways: by

- appealing to the *status quo*
- using the prestige of important people to direct a response
- using emotion-laden or stereotypic words
- personalizing the question

An example of a horrible question using all the above loading techniques is: "As you know, nearly all the famous movie actors (prestige) have been using Cut Throat Razor Blades to increase their sex appeal (stereotype) for years now (status quo). Don't you think it's about time for you (personalized) to begin using these blades?" The foregoing is so blatant that most respondents would probably be repulsed and answer, "No!" However, much more subtle forms of question loading are possible; obviously, such tactics must be scrupulously avoided.

4. Don't imply alternative responses; actually spell them out. Instead of asking, "Do you have a generally favorable overall impression of the Fine and Upright Company?" ask, "Is your overall impression of the Fine and Upright Company generally favorable or generally unfavorable?"

5. Place various alternative responses in different orders on different questionnaires. Some persons may have a preference for choosing the alternative in the first position, or in the last position, or some other form of response bias. By placing the alternatives in different sequences on different questionnaires, any such response set biases will be equated across the respondents.

6. Avoid double-barrelled questions. Each question should allow the respondent to consider a single issue and respond accordingly. Payne (1951) gives the following example of a double-barrelled and obviously untenable question: "Do you prefer girls who are short and dark or tall and blonde?"

Once the questions have been written, they must be combined into the actual questionnaire. Common sense and good judgment are most helpful at this stage. The questions should be arranged in a logical order; simple, easy-to-answer questions should be early in the questionnaire, more difficult questions, later. Questions related to similar topics should be grouped together. Personal questions involving such things as age, income, marital status, etc., should perhaps be embedded in the middle or toward the end to assure that good rapport has been established before they are asked. It is also important, of course, to work out a pleasing format for the questionnaire. The typing should not be crowded; plenty of room should be left for interviewer directions and to allow for incidental notes and marginal notations.

Finally, great care must be taken in writing directions telling the interviewer exactly how to proceed as he conducts the interview. It is common to enclose all such directions in boxes or, perhaps, to print them in different-colored ink. Arrows are usually employed to link the various parts of the interview together and to assure that no questions are missed. A typical page from a questionnaire illustrating the questions and directions to the interviewer is shown in Figure 9.1.

C1 RECORD SEX OF RESPONDENT

1. ___ Male
2. ___ Female

C2 ESTIMATE RESPONDENT'S AGE

1. ___ 15–20
2. ___ 21–35
3. ___ 36–50
4. ___ 51–65
5. ___ Over 65

C3 Did you attend any of the Minnesota Twins' baseball games last year?

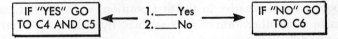

| IF "YES" GO TO C4 AND C5 | ← | 1. ___ Yes 2. ___ No | → | IF "NO" GO TO C6 |

C4 How many times did you attend games last season?

1. ___ 1–3
2. ___ 4–10
3. ___ 11–20
4. ___ Over 20

C6 Would you say you like or dislike baseball?

1. ___ Like
2. ___ Dislike

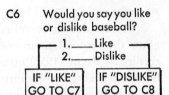

| IF "LIKE" GO TO C7 | IF "DISLIKE" GO TO C8 |

C5 What about baseball do you especially like?

1. ___ Relaxing
2. ___ Like the competition
3. ___ Never over until the last out.
4. ___ Other_____

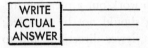

WRITE ACTUAL ANSWER _____

C7 What was it, then, that kept you from going to any of the games last year?

1. ___ Stadium too far away
2. ___ Rather see it on TV
3. ___ Don't like crowds
4. ___ Other_____

WRITE ACTUAL ANSWER _____

C8 What is it that you dislike about baseball?

1. ___ Boring
2. ___ Too slow
3. ___ Don't understand
4. ___ Too long
5. ___ Other_____

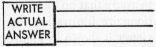

WRITE ACTUAL ANSWER _____

Fig. 9.1. Excerpt from Questionnaire Concerning Opinions about Baseball.

The crucial part of any questionnaire design is the pretest. After a preliminary form of the questionnaire has been developed, a small number of interviewers may try it among a group of respondents. In this way weaknesses in the questionnaire (such as poor and ambiguous questions, unclear directions, etc.) are detected and corrected before the actual survey is conducted. There is no substitute for a pretest of a new questionnaire. This is an absolute must, which, surprisingly, is a forgotten step in more than a few survey research studies.

Attitude measures

Standardized questions yield classifications of respondents into a number of rather broad categories. In many instances the categories may be too broad. In fact, we know that most beliefs and attitudes should more appropriately be expressed along a continuum rather than in a number of discrete categories. Consequently, in many consumer studies, it is desirable to develop attitude measures or scales so that respondents may be scored and assigned to different places along the continuum. Such measures require much more developmental work and more careful pretesting than the usual questionnaire.

An *attitude* may be defined as a relatively stable or enduring syndrome of consistent responses made by an individual with respect to some psychological object—any symbol, slogan, product, institution, person, group, or issue—with which he may be confronted. Certainly, we could infer persons' underlying attitudes toward various objects by observing their behavior over a lengthy period of time, but such observations would be hard to standardize, time consuming, and costly. In lieu of direct observations, the next best bet is to obtain verbal responses to a set of standardized statements carefully selected and pretested to reflect the attitude being measured.

Thus, the first step in developing an attitude scale is to write a series of statements about which people may differ in their degree of endorsement. For example, in measuring persons' attitudes toward watching baseball, the following statements might be useful:

- Watching a baseball game is one of the most enjoyable things a person can do.
- Baseball is a boring game to watch.
- There is nothing exciting about a baseball game.
- About the most relaxing and enjoyable way to spend a summer evening is to go to a baseball game.
- If there isn't much else to do, watching a baseball game is all right.
- Baseball is about the best of all spectator sports.
- It's hard to understand how such an uninteresting game as baseball continues to attract spectators.

These statements are merely illustrative of the many that could be written; actually, the preliminary pool of statements for an attitude scale might number as many as 200-300. It is important that the number be large to assure that the total range and content of attitudes has been sampled. Having written a large pool of statements, three things are necessary to form the final attitude measure:

1. The number of statements must be reduced to manageable size (15-25) so that responses can be obtained in a survey without an undue expenditure of time from each respondent.

2. Each statement should be scored (scaled) so that a respondent's answers (degree of agreement or disagreement) may be used to place him at a particular point on the attitude continuum. Note in the baseball statements that the statements differ in the degree of favorableness they reflect. It is necessary to estimate the amount by which they differ and to give each a *scale value*.

3. Estimates should be made of how well each statement actually is measuring the intended attitude; thus, estimates or measures of item ambiguity, relevance (to the attitude being measured), understandability, etc., are necessary.

The two methods most commonly used to achieve the above goals are the Method of Equal Appearing Intervals (Thurstone and Chave, 1929) and the Method of Summated Ratings (Likert, 1932).

Equal appearing intervals

In this method, a group of persons (numbering 50-100) is asked to estimate the relative favorableness of each of the statements by judging them against an eleven (or nine) interval scale such as the following:

1	2	3	4	5	6	7	8	9	10	11

Most unfavorable statement that could be made   Most favorable statement that could be made

The judges are told to imagine that the intervals are psychologically equal to one another, that is, that a statement placed in 10 is as much more favorable than one in 9, as a statement in 8 is than one in 7, and so on. The outcome of this judging procedure is a series of frequency distributions for all the statements in the initial pool of items. Two such distributions and the items on which they are based are shown below.

1. Baseball is a boring game to watch.

Judgment	Interval	Number of Persons	
1	(.5–1.5)	20	$Q_1 = 1.67$
2	(1.5–2.5)	30	$Q_2 = 2.50$
3	(2.5–3.5)	40	$Q_3 = 3.13$
4	(3.5–4.5)	10	
	TOTAL	100	$Q_3 - Q_1 = 1.46$

2. Baseball is about the best of all spectator sports.

Judgment	Interval	Number of Persons	
6	(5.5–6.5)	5	
7	(6.5–7.5)	10	$Q_1 = 8.0$
8	(7.5–8.5)	20	$Q_2 = 9.1$
9	(8.5–9.5)	25	$Q_3 = 10.0$
10	(9.5–10.5	30	
11	(10.5–11.5)	10	$Q_3 - Q_1 = 2.0$
	TOTAL	100	

A study of the two distributions shows some interesting contrasts. Item 1 is judged to be generally unfavorable and the judges appear to agree with one another. The other item is judged as generally favorable, but the judges agree less than on the first item; apparently the second item is more ambiguous and possibly irrelevant (since it involves a comparison among different sports rather than reflecting solely an attitude toward baseball per se). Calculation of the quartiles (Q_1, Q_2, Q_3) is useful, for the median (Q_2) can be taken as the scale value of the statement, and the difference between the third (Q_3) and first (Q_1) quartiles affords an index of how well the judges agreed in estimating the overall favorableness of the statement. These simple statistics may then be used to select the statements for the final form of the attitude scale. Usually, about 20-25 items are selected which are representative of all points along the continuum (1 to 11) and which have the lowest indices of item ambiguity ($Q_3 - Q_1$). If possible, it is wise to develop two forms of each scale so that the overall stability of respondents' attitudes may be estimated by comparing their scores on the two different forms. In the actual survey, the set of statements gathered and analyzed in this manner is presented to each respondent, and he is asked to check those items which he endorses. His attitude score is simply the average (mean or median) of the scale values for the items he selects.

Summated ratings

In this method, no single index or scale value is determined for each statement. Instead of simply endorsing or not endorsing a statement, each respondent is asked to indicate his *degree* of agreement or disagreement by choosing one of five alternative responses, such as:

Baseball is a boring game to watch.

Strongly Disagree	Disagree	Undecided	Agree	Strongly Agree
(4)	(3)	(2)	(1)	(0)

The respondent's choice is scored according to the numbers in the parentheses; a person responding Strongly Agree to the above statement is presumably reflecting the least favorable attitude toward baseball, and he receives a score of zero. A person responding Strongly Disagree is presumably reflecting the most favorable attitude toward baseball, and he receives a score of four. A person's total score on all the statements consists, then, of the sum of the scores on the individual items; thus, the name of the method—"Summated Ratings."

However, this arbitrary scoring device provides no basis for discarding unsuitable items. This is accomplished by an *item analysis,* carried out as follows: If care has been taken in the writing and editing of the original pool of statements, it is probably safe to assume that persons with high total scores (say the highest 25%) possess generally much more favorable attitudes than persons with low total scores (say the lowest 25%). Responses of these two groups to each one of the items may be studied or analyzed to see how well responses to each statement reflect the total scores on all the statements. The usual method of analysis is simply to compare the mean item score for the favorable persons with the mean item score for the unfavorable persons; the difference between these means for any given item is called the Scale Value Difference (SVD) for that item. A low SVD suggests that the statement is, for some reason (ambiguity, irrelevancy, obscurity, etc.) unsuitable; a high SVD suggests that the item is suitable because it *does* discriminate between persons identified as favorable and unfavorable by their summed scores on *all* the items. Consider the following two statements:

1. Baseball is a boring game to watch.

Responses of 50 Favorable Persons
(Total Scores among the *highest* 25%)

Strongly Disagree	Disagree	Undecided	Agree	Strongly Agree	
(4)	(3)	(2)	(1)	(0)	
20	20	10	0	0	$M_f = 3.2$

Responses of 50 Unfavorable Persons
(Total Scores among the *lowest* 25%)

Strongly Disagree	Disagree	Undecided	Agree	Strongly Agree	
(4)	(3)	(2)	(1)	(0)	
0	5	5	30	10	$M_u = 1.1$

$$SVD = M_f - M_u = 3.2 - 1.1 = 2.1$$

2. Baseball is about the best of all spectator sports.

Responses of 50 Favorable Persons
(Total Scores among the *highest* 25%)

Strongly Disagree (0)	Disagree (1)	Undecided (2)	Agree (3)	Strongly Agree (4)	
0	5	30	15	0	$M_f = 2.2$

Responses of 50 Unfavorable Persons
(Total Scores among the *lowest* 25%)

Strongly Disagree (0)	Disagree (1)	Undecided (2)	Agree (3)	Strongly Agree (4)	
0	15	30	5	0	$M_u = 1.8$

$$SVD = M_f - M_u = 2.2 - 1.8 = 0.4$$

The first statement is obviously a highly discriminating statement; favorable and unfavorable people differ greatly in the way they answered it. The second item, however, is a poor one; most people, both favorable and unfavorable, are undecided about baseball being the best spectator sport, and the responses of the two groups differ only slightly.

Since the SVD index is an effective measure of item suitability, the 20-25 statements with the highest SVD's are selected for the final form of the attitude scale; here, too, it is wise to develop two forms so that the relative stability of respondent's attitudes may be estimated. Subsequent respondents will be scored only on these final forms, and the survey director, if he has done a careful job of item analysis, will be assured that the responses reflect quite accurately the total range of attitudes shown by responses to the total pool of original items.

Other methods of scaling

We have chosen to discuss the above two methods because they are perhaps the most widely used and versatile of the methods available. However, other scaling methods abound—ranging from simple ranking methods or graphic rating scales to more complicated scales involving complex multidimensional mathematical models. The interested reader may wish to refer to Edwards (1957) or Torgerson (1958) for much more comprehensive discussions of the many methods available. Whatever the scaling procedure that is chosen, the major goal is, of course, the development of a carefully standardized and thoroughly pretested survey instrument which will yield accurate and reliable estimates of the opinions and attitudes of the respondents.

CHOOSING RESPONDENTS

Defining the population of respondents

One of the most important steps in any survey is to decide who is to be surveyed. During the initial planning discussions careful attention should have been given to defining the specific population of potential consumers from whom the research sponsor desires information. In the example discussed earlier, the manager of the charm school was interested in surveying adolescent (teenage) girls. Had the survey gone beyond the preliminary discussions, the population of respondents would perhaps have been defined as all teenage girls living in a certain geographic area (e.g., within a certain radius of the school's location). Other surveys would, of course, be directed toward different populations, such as: all registered voters in the State of Minnesota, all housewives in Minneapolis, St. Paul and suburbs, or all students attending the University of Minnesota; conceivably, the number of different populations can be as great as the number of surveys conducted. The important point is that the population of respondents must be specified *ahead of time,* during the planning stages of the survey. If this is not done, the question (considered in the next section) of how to sample respondents from the population is obviously meaningless and unanswerable.

The questions, "who?" and "how?"

As we have said, limitations of time and money preclude getting responses from each member of the population; thus, it is necessary to select a sample of persons. Ideally, we want respondents whose answers will accurately portray the responses of all members of the population. How shall the respondents for the survey be selected to achieve this aim? A number of methods are in common use. Let us first consider and dispense with a couple of the less desirable ones:

The least costly method is to allow the interviewers to make their selection of respondents with no restrictions or directions of any kind. Thus, an interviewer could simply stand on a well-traveled street corner and ask passersby to answer his survey questions; such a choice of respondents is purely *accidental*. Responses from respondents in such a sample could by no stretch of the imagination be said to portray or be representative of *any* population. The popular use of straw ballots by radio and TV stations and by some newspapers in which listeners, viewers, and readers are asked to express an opinion by writing or calling is an example of accidental selection procedures. The results of such ballots are worthless. No one knows from what population the respondents may have been drawn. Yet, a surprising number of survey studies utilize just such accidental selection procedures. If you are ever stopped on the street by an interviewer who wants to ask you some questions, it will be a good opportunity for you to deliver a short lecture on the uselessness of what he or she is doing and to refuse to waste either your or his time with such foolishness.

A second, somewhat more systematic approach, is to assign *quotas* to interviewers. Thus, an interviewer's assignment may be to secure interviews with persons of certain specified characteristics (for example, a certain number of men and of women of various specified ages, and of certain income and socioeconomic characteristics). The quotas are set ahead of time by the survey director and are usually based on census information; the assumption is that if the respondents are representative of the population on certain selected variables (such as age, sex, socioeconomic status, education, etc.), they will be representative of the population on the survey responses, too. Although this assumption is appealing, there is little evidence to support its validity. A major problem is that it is impossible to identify ahead of time exactly those variables which are highly correlated with and relevant to the opinions and attitudes comprising the subject matter of the survey. Equally serious is the difficulty of measuring many of the variables which might be relevant. For example, socioeconomic status, occupation, income, and education may all seem to be important in a consumer research study and might be desirable quota control variables; yet, classification schemes for the first two are poorly defined, and it also is impossible, unfortunately, to estimate a respondent's status on most such variables without first asking him. Since most potential respondents do not welcome being asked a series of personal questions about age, income, level of education, occupation, etc., it is quite understandable that most interviewers, in perfectly human fashion, endeavor to fill their quotas in the easiest manner possible. Therefore, they may concentrate their efforts in neighborhoods most familiar to them or go to locations where they have learned it is most easy to locate cooperative respondents. Thus, the people ending up in the typical quota sample are not truly representative of the intended population, and, what is even worse, it is impossible even to estimate accurately the nature of the biases possibly present.

It should be apparent that the accidental and quota selection methods have little to recommend them other than convenience and economy; certainly no claim can be made that such samples accurately portray characteristics of the intended population. Unfortunately, the appealing advantages of convenience and economy have been and continue to be foremost considerations for many firms and surveying organizations, and accidental and quota procedures continue to be widely used; no one can tell how inaccurate the results produced by such surveys may be.

Preferred methods

Under examination, the major weakness in both accidental and quota procedures is that the interviewers are responsible for choosing respondents instead of members of the central staff of the survey organization. Preferred sampling methods relieve the interviewers of most of this responsibility, thereby making possible more careful planning and reducing the possibility of arbitrary decisions in choosing respondents. These preferred methods include "random," "stratified random," and "area" sampling. These methods are discussed in some detail below:

A *simple random* sample is one in which each member of the population has an equal chance of being selected. In order to select a random sample the members of the population must be completely enumerated. If such an enumeration is possible, a table of random numbers [1] may be used to select the sample. This is done by blindly choosing an initial number from the table; the member of the population with that number is selected as the first member of the sample. Subsequent numbers are chosen in the order that they appear in the table until a sufficient number of persons has been chosen. Note that this method of sample selection demands the definition and enumeration of population members ahead of time and the use of random numbers rules out the use of the arbitrary and accidental procedures common to the two methods discussed previously. The fact that each member of the population has an equal chance of being selected assures that the sample characteristics are representative of the population characteristics. It is true, of course, that the sample results will never be identical to those which would have been obtained from the total population, but the rules of statistical inference are applicable to samples selected randomly and may be used to estimate precisely the degree of error due to the sampling procedure and to estimate the characteristics of the population from which the sample was drawn.

The magnitude of the error for any given opinion or attitude is related directly to the amount of variation (the degree of heterogeneity) on that opinion shown by members of the population. At the one extreme, if everyone in the population shares identical attitudes, a sample of just one person would be sufficient to describe the attitudes of all population members. However, as the

[1] Tables of random numbers may be found in most statistics textbooks. These are sets of numbers which have been generated by random means (such as by a computer) and which show no evidence of any systematic ordering. It is necessary to use such a table in order to guard against the possibility of some unrecognized systematic bias which could otherwise influence the selection of sample members.

population heterogeneity increases, larger samples will be required to reveal with equal accuracy the population characteristics. Very generally, then, we can state that random sampling error for any opinion is *directly* proportional to the heterogeneity (usually measured by the variance) of opinion in the population and *inversely* proportional to the size (number of persons, *N*) of the sample. It is possible to use this knowledge to maximize the efficiency of our sampling. If we suspect or know that different population subgroups differ in the heterogeneity of their opinions, we should select smaller samples from the more homogeneous groups and larger samples from the more heterogeneous ones. For example, in measuring attitudes toward baseball, we might expect men to be more homogeneous (more uniformly favorable) than women. Thus, in selecting our sample, we would first divide the population into two strata (groups) based on sex and randomly select respondents from each, relatively more women and relatively fewer men. This approach is called *stratified random sampling*. As has been suggested, it is used when we wish to allocate our survey resources most efficiently to capitalize on prior knowledge or expectations about differing degrees of heterogeneity in various population subgroups.

An obvious practical difficulty or roadblock to selecting a random sample is the near impossibility, usually, of securing an up-to-date and accurate enumeration of all population members. Rarely in most consumer studies would a complete listing of the intended population members (e.g., all teenage girls) be available. Even if a complete list were available, the potential respondents, selected randomly, would be widely dispersed geographically, and, as a result, very costly to contact; the cost might very quickly exceed the budgeted resources for the project. Thus, although the random sample is to be hoped for as an ideal, it is rarely realized in actual practice. What, then, shall be the sampling plan? What is needed is a method which avoids the arbitrariness of the quota or accidental selection procedures but which also avoids the practical disadvantages of the simple random sample.

A solution to the problem is suggested by the method used when a medical technician makes a blood count. She takes a drop of blood from the finger of a patient and smears it in a thin film across a specially prepared glass slide which is marked off in a grid of small squares. She counts the blood cells located in the four corner squares and in the center square, and multiplies the result by a constant to give the blood count. The sampling plan illustrated by this technique is called *area sampling*. Note that it is not necessary to count all the cells in the drop of blood nor even to sample cells directly from an enumeration of all the cells. The units of sampling are the small standard size squares (areas) marked off on the surface of the slide.

A similar method has been used with great success in survey research. Instead of sampling people directly, the sampling units are geographic areas or specific locations such as city blocks or dwelling units. It is much easier, working from up-to-date maps of national, state, county, or metropolitan areas to make a complete enumeration of area units than it is to prepare a listing of people. The population of areas (city blocks, voting precincts, and the like) may then be sampled randomly to yield the sample of locations in which interviews are to be carried out. The result of area sampling is to select the actual sites where interviews are to be conducted. Each interviewer is directed to go to specified dwelling units and to interview persons living there. The actual selection of which persons from the dwelling to interview depends on the purpose of the survey; in the study contemplated by the charm school, interviews would be with any teenage girls living in the selected dwelling units; in a survey of voting preferences, interviewees would be either all eligible voters in the dwellings or a random selection of them. Thus, in this method, the interviewer does not have the option of deciding whom to interview. He goes to the specified dwelling and selects the interviewee by a specified procedure. If no one is home, he goes back again and again until he gets the interview, or, if the respondent refuses to cooperate (which, incidentally, is rare in a properly handled survey), the interviewer may either go to an immediately adjacent dwelling or he may be directed by the survey director to go to another dwelling selected from a replacement sample. An excellent step-by-step account of procedures for selecting an area sample from a large metropolitan area is given by Backstrom and Hursh (1963).

A carefully developed area sample fulfills the requirement that each member of the population have an equal probability of being included in the sample. Moreover, after the sample is selected, the cost of contacting respondents is much less than for a simple random sample, because the interviewing sites are clustered within specified areas rather than being spread all over as in a random sample. Finally, the area sample is extremely versatile. The sampling plan can be used to collect information from respondents representing many different populations—teenage girls, eligible voters, working mothers, persons of certain income, etc.—all such biographical information can be collected during the interview and various groups of respondents can be used or not used according to the specific demands and purposes of any given survey study.

THE SELECTION, TRAINING, AND CARE OF INTERVIEWERS

Only rarely does an industrial firm maintain its own permanent staff of interviewers. Usually a consumer survey is carried out by contracting for the services of a private surveying organization. However, it is a well-known fact that even the most carefully conceived survey, supported by an excellent questionnaire and utilizing a sophisticated sampling design, will fail miserably if the interviewers do their jobs poorly. Thus, it is well to consider some of the problems involved in building an effective interviewing team, so that the quality of interviewers and administrative procedures used by any surveying organization may be judged.

Selecting interviewers

Experience has shown that women make the best interviewers. They can approach a home and be invited in more easily than men can; women are not as likely to be viewed with suspicion and there is less expectation that they might be selling something than with men. Moreover, more women than men are available for part-time work; this is a particular advantage because most surveying organizations value the flexibility of having interviewers who can be called on when needed rather than being on the payroll full-time. Beyond being a woman, the following qualifications are desirable in an interviewer:

- should be mature in appearance and behavior (probably should be at *least* 21 or older)
- should like people (One study showed that better interviewers were those who scored high on personal contact interests on the Strong Vocational Interest Blank.)
- should not be opinionated; that is, should be neutral or middle-of-the-road on controversial issues, willing to *listen* rather than expostulate
- should be reasonably intelligent, able and willing to follow directions, probably wise to select from among women with some college training
- should have permanent residence and be fairly familiar with area in which interviewing is to be done

In recruiting such persons, it is well to ask local professional people, civic leaders, churchmen, and school officials to suggest candidates; usually women suggested by such people will be solid citizens—stable members of the community who possess many of the qualifications outlined above.

Training interviewers

It is important to brief all new interviewers thoroughly before they do any interviewing. This should be done in a series of formal training sessions in which the importance of objectivity, courtesy, impartiality, and friendliness are emphasized. Training sessions should make liberal use of demonstration interviews to illustrate proper interviewing tactics, and each trainee should try out one or more practice interviews on friends; this should increase her confidence and also highlight problems and suggest questions to be discussed in later training sessions. An excellent set of checklists of points to be covered in training interviewers is given by Backstrom and Hursh (1963); this set of checklists is reproduced at the end of this chapter. Since many studies have shown that interviewers can influence the nature of responses they obtain from respondents, a most important feature of training is to show the trainees exactly how to be completely objective and impartial in their interviews. Another central objective of the training is to instill confidence in the trainees by teaching them exactly what is expected of them and spelling out what they should do in any contingency that may arise. The importance of interviewer training cannot be overemphasized. It is critically important that the interviewer learn to behave as a neutral agent assuring the most accurate and complete transmittal possible of the respondents' opinions and attitudes to the central office of the surveying organization.

Maintaining interviewer morale

Since most interviewers are part-time employees and since many of them have only mail contact with the home office, maintaining their morale often presents special problems. Yet, it is obviously very important to keep their morale high so that they will continue to exert themselves seriously and conscientiously in their jobs. No single set of rules can cover all circumstances, but the following points suggest some of the problems that may arise and the steps which may be taken to overcome them:

1. One of the most demoralizing influences is a poorly developed, ambiguous, or overlong questionnaire. The best way to avoid this problem, obviously, is to be certain that a questionnaire is pretested before asking interviewers to use it. The interviewers should also be encouraged to take an active role in the design of questionnaires by forwarding their suggestions for improvement to the central office, and any such suggestions should be acknowledged gratefully and action taken on them.

2. A point closely related to the above is that the total interviewing assignment should be as clear and as free from ambiguity as is possible.

3. Efforts should be made to give interviewers a feeling of close contact with the central office. Many organizations publish a periodic newsletter with "newsy" items about things going on in the organization—upcoming surveys, the results of previous ones, etc. If possible, it is wise to bring all the interviewers together periodically so that they may meet each other, members of the

central office staff, and thereby come to feel more a part of the organization.

4. Obviously, any delays in being paid can be extremely demoralizing. The checks for a survey should be sent out immediately upon receiving the questionnaires from the interviewer—even before checking them over for accuracy, completeness, etc.

5. Finally, methods should be employed to impress the interviewers with the importance of doing a quality job. If interviewers are allowed to feel they can get by with a poor job, this in itself is demoralizing. One way of impressing them with the importance of high quality is to pay them on an hourly basis rather than on a per questionnaire basis. Other methods are considered in the next section.

The question of cheating

Even with the best methods of selection, training, and central office administration, an occasional bad apple may come into the organization. Because of this, it is wise to spot-check the respondents to verify the information shown on the questionnaires. This must be done immediately, before the respondents forget they were interviewed. The checking is most easily done by telephoning a sample of the respondents to be sure they were actually interviewed and to confirm that the interviewer asked all the questions. Actually, the instances of "fireside research"—the practice of falsifying questionnaires—are extremely rare. The practice of verifying the questionnaires, although useful in detecting cheating, should be viewed more positively as a means of rating the overall performance of the interviewers and as one further managerial tool for recognizing and rewarding individual merit.

ANALYSIS AND INTERPRETATION

The analysis of the responses to the survey instrument is the logical climax (or, perhaps, anticlimax) of every survey research study. This step is either the easiest of all or the most difficult, depending upon the care taken in each of the previous steps. If the purpose has been rigidly specified, if the instrument has been shrewdly designed and well pretested, if the population has been defined and sampled by sophisticated methods, if the interviewers have been selected with care and well trained, and if good personnel policies have been developed and maintained with the interviewing staff, the results and interpretations will flow almost automatically from the completed questionnaires. Presumably, the survey director and the sponsor of the study will have decided long before what they wish to learn from the data. Ideally, the empty tables, based on the desired cross-tabulations, will already have been prepared, awaiting only the tallying and accumulation of results from the survey instruments. Only in those cases where prior planning and survey design have been haphazard or nonexistent will the analyses seem difficult. Unfortunately, many organizations do collect data without careful forethought; many erstwhile survey experts can testify to the feeling of dismay which sweeps over a person when he suddenly finds himself confronted with great piles of completed questionnaires, and he begins to wonder what to do with the data. In such circumstances, about the only recourse is to conduct a postmortem examination on the body of survey information in a belated effort to learn when the study died and of what cause.

As we have said, the initial purpose of the survey should be paramount in determining direction of analyses and nature of interpretations undertaken. This is no time for the survey director to forget his role as a scientist; thus, he must maintain his stance of objectivity, avoiding unwarranted extrapolations, miscellaneous conclusions, and extensions of his data based on after-the-fact analyses. First, and most important, then, the analyses should serve the initial survey purposes by answering the questions posed during the planning stages. Only secondly should the analyses be used to suggest new leads, new hypotheses, or further questions to be investigated in subsequent research studies.

THE ACCOMPLISHMENTS OF SURVEY RESEARCH

The accomplishments of survey research procedures are many and varied, ranging from measuring advertising effectiveness

(Lucas and Britt, 1963) to forecasting election outcomes (Fenton, 1960) and helping to settle legal questions in courts of law (Barksdale, 1957). In nearly all instances, our major interest is simply to learn how a group of respondents feel about something, what their opinions or preferences may be, or what they say they will do if confronted with certain circumstances. Thus, the measurement of advertising effectiveness is devoted mostly to learning how many people saw or heard a given advertisement, what they can recall about it, and how their perceptions or opinions about the advertised product may have been affected by the ad. Or, in assessing the preferences of voters for different political candidates, the political pollster simply asks each respondent which candidate he would vote for if the election were being held tomorrow. In recent years, the high incidence of success of survey research procedures in forecasting the actual outcome of most national and many state elections is strong evidence in favor of the potentially high accuracy of well-conducted studies. It is also good evidence that persons are able to estimate their own future behavior (in this case, voting behavior) and that careful survey design and interviewing can make them willing to share their estimates openly with others. We must emphasize, however, that survey research is no magical method allowing us to remove all guesswork from our predictions of consumer behavior. It is simply a way of obtaining more information about presumably relevant reactions, opinions, stated preferences, etc., from which we may make more informed and hopefully more accurate "guesses." Thus, we are best off, and survey research is accomplishing the most for us when we can interpret the respondents' replies directly, without finding it necessary to infer other behaviors from the results obtained. Below is a description of a study in which the respondents' replies are directly interpretable with no further behavioral inferences necessary for satisfying the purpose of the survey.

A SURVEY RESEARCH STUDY

In 1955, the Robin Hood Popcorn Company sought to register the term ROBIN HOOD as a trademark for their buttered popcorn. The registration was opposed by the International Milling Company because they had for some years previously been registrants for the trademark ROBIN HOOD, which they used for marketing farina, rolled oats, oat meal, and wheat flour. They sought, through court action (International Milling Co. vs. Robin Hood Popcorn Co., 1950), to prevent the use of the trademark by the popcorn company because they did not want the other company to capitalize freely on the years of advertising which had gone into the building of the Robin Hood name as a brand label for International Milling Company products. Thus, it became necessary to convince the court that potential buyers of Robin Hood buttered popcorn would associate the product in some way with the milling firm or with products marketed by it. In order to obtain relevant information, a sample of 512 dwellings in the city of Minneapolis was chosen randomly, and two interviewers were employed to obtain responses from the cross section of Minneapolis householders. The interviewers were never told that their actual employer was International Milling Company nor were they informed in any way of the purpose or intent of the survey.

The questionnaire was simple, but the four brief questions were focused directly at discovering any consumer confusion between Robin Hood Popcorn and Robin Hood Flour. First, the interviewer showed the respondent six brand labels (with the name of the manufacturers removed)—Carnation Milk, Ivory Soap, Robin Hood Popcorn, Baker's Chocolate, Log Cabin Syrup, and Monarch Green Beans. The first question was "What is the name of the company that makes this product?" When answering this question with reference to the Robin Hood label, 384 persons said "Don't Know"; 91 named a milling or flour company; 31 said "Robin Hood Company"; and 6 mentioned various other miscellaneous companies. The second and third questions asked whether any family member had ever purchased the product, and, if so, who in the family had made the purchase. These questions were used primarily to disguise the true purpose of the survey from the interviewers. The key question was the fourth: "If you can think of any other products put out by the producer of Robin Hood popcorn, please name them." To this, 179 responded "None"; 302 responded "flour"; 13 responded "Robin Hood Flour"; and the remaining respondents mentioned various products such as pancake flour, cake mix, cereals, etc. Thus, a large number of the respondents associated the Robin Hood name with a milling firm, and over 60% of them associated the name with one or more of the products marketed by the International Milling Company. Faced with this evidence of confusion between Robin Hood Popcorn and the flour products of International Milling Company, the court's decision was to refuse the application of the Robin Hood Popcorn Company for use of the Robin Hood brand name. In the words of the court:

> The record here requires a conclusion that "Robin Hood" used on buttered popcorn has resulted and will continue to result in confusion of the type contemplated by the statute; and such confusion will result in damage to opposer (International Milling Company). The decision of the Examiner of Interferences is reversed and registration is refused.

In this survey study, it was necessary only to show the confusion in the consumer's mind between the brand labels; the respondents' replies were interpreted directly, and no further inferences about other kinds of behavior were necessary. This is an example of survey research at its best, illustrating the usefulness of survey information for making decisions of many types—in this instance, a legal judgment having important implications for the future profitability of a firm's product.

SURVEY RESEARCH METHODOLOGY

This chapter has been primarily a presentation of the methods of survey research; in a sense, it has been a how-to-do-it statement of survey research methodology. In spite of this, the reader should be cautioned against feeling that this brief overview will in any way be sufficient to make an expert survey researcher of him. This has not been our hope nor our intention. Instead, we chose to discuss the methods of survey research because we believe this to be the most efficient means of describing exactly what the industrial psychologist should be concerned with when called upon to answer questions about marketing decisions and the consuming public. Most important, we have intended, through this chapter, to inform the reader of the complexities and difficulties involved in carrying out a good survey research study. Our major aim has been, therefore, to make you sufficiently aware of the various sources of error in survey research and sufficiently aware of methodology for overcoming them so that you will be able to judge the relative adequacy of survey research studies when you see them conducted. Thus, in the years ahead, when and if you have opportunities to use the results of survey research or to buy the services of survey research organizations, you should be able more effectively, we hope, to judge the quality of the product you are getting.

Suggested Additional Reading

Anastasi, Anne. Scope and methods of consumer psychology. In Anastasi, Anne, *Fields of applied psychology*. New York: McGraw-Hill, 1964. Ch. 10.

Backstrom, C. H., and Hursh, G. D. *Survey research*. Evanston, Ill.: Northwestern, 1963.

Barksdale, H. C. *The use of survey research findings as legal evidence*. New York: Advertising Research Foundation, 1957.

Edwards, A. L. *Techniques of attitude scale construction*. New York: Appleton-Century-Crofts, 1957.

Lucas, D. B., and Britt, S. H. *Measuring advertising effectiveness*. New York: McGraw-Hill, 1963.

Parten, M. *Surveys, polls, and samples*. New York: Harper & Row, 1950.

Payne, S. L. *The art of asking questions*. Princeton, N.J.: Princeton, 1951.

Selltiz, C., Jahoda, M., Deutsch, M., and Cook, S. W. *Research methods in social relations, revised*. New York: Holt, Rinehart and Winston, 1961.

Torgerson, W. S. *Theory and methods of scaling*. New York: Wiley, 1958.

CHECKLISTS OF FUNDAMENTAL POINTS TO BE EMPHASIZED IN INTERVIEWER TRAINING

CHECKLIST 9: INTERVIEWER'S CODE

You must be:

1. Completely honest in your work.
2. Reliable and conscientious.
3. Utterly objective in your manner of asking questions.
4. Faithful and neutral in recording answers.
5. Willing to write answers fully and legibly.
6. Interested in people; understanding.
7. Able to inspire people's confidence and put them at ease.
8. Inconspicuously, but neatly dressed.

Be sure to:

1. Study all questions until you know what they mean and are familiar enough with them so you can really ask the questions instead of blindly reading them.
2. Interview yourself by answering each question thoughtfully. Then interview someone else, for practice. Of course, these interviews are not counted as part of the assigned interviews you turn in.
3. Plan to interview at various times of day between 9 A.M. and 9 P.M.,

SOURCE: Backstrom, C. H. and Hursh, G. D. *Survey Research*. Evanston, Ill.: Northwestern University Press, 1963. (Checklists 9, 10, 11, and 13; pages 134-144)

since different kinds of people (workingmen, housewives, executives) are home at different hours.

4. Reread your instructions between interviews—you may pick up points you missed before or correct errors you have begun to make.

Your attitude should be:

1. NEUTRAL

As an interviewer you merely soak up information like a sponge without giving any of it back. Your job is to record that information, regardless whether you think it good, bad, indifferent, boring, or exciting.

Don't—by word, action, or gesture—indicate surprise, pleasure, or disapproval at any answer. Even a slight grimace or gasp will cue a respondent that you have reacted to his answer.

Don't attempt to influence responses in any way. The truth is all that really counts—what the person *really* thinks or feels about the subject. Thus:

a. Never suggest an answer. And don't give your own opinions. This is a survey of respondents' feelings, not yours.

b. For the same reason—so the response will not be influenced in any way—you must ask the question exactly as they are worded and in the same order every time. Each interview must be done the same way to assure uniform and reliable results.

c. If the respondent doesn't understand a question, repeat it exactly as written rather than explain it. Otherwise you're sure to give away yourself or the answer you may be expecting. Repeat the question only twice, then go on if the person still does not understand it.

2. IMPARTIAL

Whatever you may think of an individual or his opinion, keep it to yourself. Each interview you are asked to get, and therefore each person you speak to, is equally important.

You should be adaptable to anyone and gracious to all. Each person you approach poses different problems requiring different techniques. The important thing is to inspire the confidence of every respondent regardless of sex, age, residence, income, political affiliation or whatever.

3. CASUAL

You are not a spy out on a secret mission. If you pursue your assignment too earnestly, too grimly, the respondent is forced to be on the defensive. He won't tell you what he honestly thinks.

You are not subjecting the individual to the third degree. This is not in any sense a quiz or intelligence test. He'll tell nothing if he thinks you're watching for errors or conducting an examination. Don't make him think it's a matter of life and death. Take it easy. Approach the interview pleasurably and let the respondent enjoy it, too. Assume that he wants to express his opinion and wants to be interviewed. You merely are giving him the chance to express himself on matters that may be important to him.

4. CONVERSATIONAL

Use an informal manner of speaking, natural to you, and aimed at putting the individual at ease. Know the questions so well that you never sound as though you're reading them formally.

Although you are conversational, never lose control of the interview. From the moment the correct respondent appears at the door, talk him through the introduction and right into the body of the questionnaire before he reacts negatively.

Be ready with stock answers (see Checklist 13) to handle interruptions or objections. Give these answers in an offhand tone of voice as though you've heard the objection a hundred times, and proceed with the questions.

5. FRIENDLY

A major objective is to put the respondent at ease. If he isn't relaxed, you can't make him talk. The burden of ignorance has to be lifted from the respondent's shoulders—that is, he must not be made to feel ashamed of his lack of information. Your attitude, therefore, must be sympathetic and understanding. Emphasize that there are no correct answers. Rather, he must be made to realize that what he thinks really is what counts.

If the respondent is forced to answer, "I don't know," to a series of information questions, he may become embarrassed and start grasping for any other answers. Good question wording will provide alternatives like ". . . or haven't you had a chance to read about that?" A sympathetic interviewer will make these alternatives seem like natural parts of the question instead of making them sound like, "You don't know that either?" or something equally demoralizing.

Again, if the individual seems confused by a question, even after repetition, record whatever answer is given. Or if the respondent objects to a question, you are allowed to side with him only to the extent that you say with a smile, "I don't know why, but that's the way my office has the question worded."

Remember: the object of the survey is to get the honest, uninfluenced opinion of each individual interviewed. You are merely the medium through which the opinion is conveyed. Nothing of *you* should be in the interview results.

CHECKLIST 10: INTERVIEWING TACTICS

1. Usually the first meaningful reaction to a question is the important or true one. Don't record any changes in an answer to a past question if you already have gone on to other items. Note at the point he wishes to go back that the respondent now indicates he would say something else.

2. But don't record a "don't know" answer too quickly. People say, "I don't know" when stalling for time to arrange their thoughts. The phrase merely may be an introduction to a meaningful comment, so give the respondent a little time to think.

3. When straight "Yes" and "No" answers are accompanied by qualifications such as "Yes, if . . ." or "Yes, but not . . . ," record the comments, regardless of whether space has been provided for them. Later they may reveal something important about the question which was not anticipated.

4. Record comments or remarks just as they are given. The exact words people use to describe their feelings are important. Include the flavor of language used, rather than summarize the comments in your own words. Of course, if the comment is lengthy and you cannot write down every word, make notes that give the sense and the style of the comment. Use abbreviations that are understandable, so in checking over the interview you can fill in the content of the answer.

5. Get specific comments, not vague, meaningless generalities like, "I like it because it's good" or "because it's interesting" or "It's okay." Ask "Why?" in such cases.

6. Keep talking as you write. Ask the second question as you record the response to the first. Start the respondent thinking about a question. If you let a silence grow, he has more opportunities to become distracted, bored, resentful, or may even change his mind. Keep the pencil and notebook as inconspicuous as possible. Keep eye contact with the respondent, and do the writing unobtrusively. This is one key to the informal atmosphere essential to successful interviews.

7. Focus the respondent's attention on the questions. If he wants to talk about his new car or the New Frontier, politely but firmly steer him back to the questions. Smile and say, "That's interesting . . . now what would you say about this question?"

8. Record all the answers yourself; never allow the respondent to do so. Under no circumstances should he see the questions, for if he knows what is coming he is already contriving an answer. Exception: Sometimes there is a separate section in the questionnaire that the respondent is asked to fill out.

9. Get all the information you are asked to get. That means, ask every question and record every answer—in the correct place. A questionnaire with serious omissions or errors may have to be discarded. The ordinary analyst cannot guess answers. Therefore, check over the questionnaire at the end of each interview *before you leave the respondent's presence.* You can't supply answers after you leave. Say, "Now, let's see if we've got everything," to allow you to look over each question to see that it is answered and the answer recorded correctly. This applies to the demographic data as well.

CHECKLIST 11: INTERVIEWING CAUTIONS

Never do any of the following:

1. Never interview more than one person in the same family or the same housing unit. Members of one family are likely to share the same opinions on many subjects, and the sample calls for the diverse opinions of the community.

2. Never interview your friends. Strangers are preferred—because you'll find it easier to be objective and impartial with them.

3. Never interview by telephone. It is impossible to convey the subtleties of questions intended for a personal interview. Too, respondents find it easier to hang up than to refuse the interviewer at the door.

4. Never take a friend or anyone else along when you do interviewing. Go alone. Respondents will be more inhibited in the presence of "extra" interviewers.

5. Never allow anyone other than the designated respondent to answer your questions. Seek privacy. If others must be present and they start talking, or if the respondent asks for their opinions, tell him only his opinions are important. Gently but firmly instruct family members not to interrupt.

6. Never let someone else do the work for you. Substitutes are worthless, since you are the trained interviewer. If you cannot complete the work yourself, notify the study director at once.

7. Never reveal the details of your job or of specific interviews to others. The information you obtain is confidential and you must respect this.

8. Never correct errors on someone else's advice. Instead, tell the director about your difficulties.

9. Never falsify interviews. All work is carefully examined and methods of detecting false information have been devised. It isn't worth the trouble to do the job poorly or wrong.

Always do each of the following:

1. Always follow instructions carefully.
2. Always study the questionnaire until you are familiar with all the questions.
3. Always use the brief introductory approach written into the questionnaire.
4. Always be completely neutral, informal, conscientious.
5. Always read questions just as they are written.
6. Always ask all of the questions.
7. Always ask questions in the order they appear.
8. Always record comments accurately.
9. Always interview only the proper person at the housing unit designated by your procedure.
10. Always check each questionnaire to make sure you have completed every item.
11. Always interview people you don't know, and interview them alone.

CHECKLIST 13: STOCK ANSWERS TO RESPONDENTS

WHAT YOU SHOULD SAY . . .

1. IF RESPONDENT ASKS: "Who is doing this survey?"

"This survey is being conducted by the Research Division of Model State University. We are trying to get some idea about what people think about current issues in Model City."

2. IF RESPONDENT PRESSES FOR A BETTER ANSWER ON AUSPICES:

"Well . . . I'm a professional interviewer. The people in charge of this survey are at the Research Division at Model State University. They'd be glad to explain the survey to you. Would you like their phone number so you could call them?" (If "Yes," give trouble number.)

3. IF RESPONDENT WONDERS WHY HE IS BEING INTERVIEWED, OR SUGGESTS INTERVIEWING SOMEONE ELSE:

"You were selected completely *by chance* according to procedures worked out by my office: So *your* opinions are important and interviewing someone else wouldn't be as good."

4. IF RESPONDENT SAYS HE DOESN'T HAVE TIME TO BE INTERVIEWED:

"The questions won't take long. You can go right on with your work and I'll just run through these items." (Begin questioning immediately.)

5. IF RESPONDENT INSISTS HE IS TOO BUSY:

"What would be a better time soon for me to come back? I'll note down an appointment that would be more convenient for you."

6. IF RESPONDENT SAYS HE DOESN'T KNOW ENOUGH TO GIVE GOOD ANSWERS:

"In this survey, it's *not* what you know that counts. Rather, it's what you happen to think about various topics that is important."

7. IF RESPONDENT IS AFRAID TO ANSWER SOME QUESTION OR ASKS: "What are you going to do with these answers?" or "Why do you want to know that?"

"Well . . . many people are being asked these same questions, of course, and what you say is confidential. We are interested in these questions only to see what a *lot* of people in Model City generally are thinking about."

8. IF RESPONDENT RESENTS QUESTIONS THAT TALK DOWN TO HIM:

"The people in my office made up these questions, and we are instructed to read each one just as it is written."

9. IF RESPONDENT IS ANNOYED AND JUST PLAIN REFUSES TO ANSWER A QUESTION:

"Of course, you don't have to answer any question you'd prefer not to. I'm only trying to get your opinion because our study is more accurate that way." Then if respondent still refuses, don't comment, just go on quickly to the next question. Mark the item "Refused."

REFERENCES

Adams, R. N., and Preiss, J. J. (Eds.) *Human organization research.* Homewood, Ill.: Dorsey, 1960.

Albright, L. E., Glennon, J. R., and Smith, W. J. *The use of psychological tests in industry.* Cleveland: Howard Allen, Inc., 1963.

Allison, R. B. *Learning parameters and human abilities.* Princeton, N.J.: Educational Testing Service, 1960.

Anastasi, Anne. Scope and methods of consumer psychology. In Anastasi, Anne, *Fields of applied psychology.* New York: McGraw-Hill, 1964. Pp. 251-285.

Argyris, C. *Integrating the individual and the organization.* New York: Wiley, 1964.

Argyris, C. *Understanding organizational behavior.* Homewood, Ill.: Dorsey, 1960.

Atkinson, J. W. (Ed.) *Motives in fantasy, action, and society.* Princeton, N.J.: VanNostrand, 1958.

Backstrom, C. H., and Hursh, G. D. *Survey research.* Evanston, Northwestern, 1963.

Baker, C. A., and Grether, W. F. *Visual presentation of information.* Technical Report 54-160. Wright Patterson Air Force Base, Wright Air Development Center, 1954.

Bakke, E. W. *The individual and the organization.* New Haven: Yale University Labor and Management Center, 1951.

Barkin, S. Psychology as seen by a trade-unionist. *Pers. Psychol.,* 1961, 14, 259-270.

Barksdale, H. C. *The use of survey research findings as legal evidence.* New York: Advertising Research Foundation, 1957.

Barry, Ruth and Wolf, Beverly. *An epitaph for vocational guidance.* New York: Bureau of Publications, Teachers College, Columbia University, 1962.

Bellows, R. *Psychology of personnel in business and industry* (3rd ed.). Englewood Cliffs, N.J.: Prentice-Hall, 1961. Pp. 89-90.

Bennett, E., Degan, J., and Spiegel, J. (Eds.) *Human factors in technology.* New York: McGraw-Hill, 1963.

Birren, J. E., Butler, R. N., Greenhouse, S. W., Sokoloff, L., and Yarrow, Marian R. (Eds.) *Human aging.* Bethesda, Md.: U.S. Dept. of Health, Education and Welfare, National Institutes of Health, 1963.

Black, J. D. *Some principles and techniques of employee counseling.* Stanford: Stanford, 1955.

Blau, P., and Scott, R. W. *Formal organizations.* San Francisco: Chandler, 1962.

Blum, M. L., and Balinsky, B. *Counseling and psychology.* Englewood Cliffs, N.J.: Prentice-Hall, 1951.

Bogard, H. M. Union and management trainees—a comparative study of personality and occupational choice. *J. appl. Psychol.,* 1960, **44,** 56-63.

Borow, H. (Ed.) *Man in a world at work.* Boston: Houghton Mifflin, 1964.

Brayfield, A. H. Vocational counseling today. In *Vocational counseling: a reappraisal in honor of Donald G. Paterson.* Minnesota Studies in Student Personnel Work, No. 11. Minneapolis: The University of Minnesota Press, 1961. Pp. 22-58.

Brayfield, A. H., and Crockett, W. H. Employee attitudes and employee performance. *Psychol. Bull.,* 1955, **52,** 396-424.

Brown, A. Some reflections on organizations: truths, half-truths, and delusions. *Personnel,* 1954, **31,** 31-42.

Campbell, J. P., and Wernimont, P. F. *Some recent developments in management training.* Unpublished paper, University of Minnesota, 1962.

Carlson, H. C., Lawrie, J. W., Rosensteel, R. K., and Crissey, O. L. *Gyro assemblymen and their motivation to work.* Flint, Mich.: Personnel Evaluation Services, General Motors Institute, 1963.

Chapanis, A. *Research techniques in human engineering.* Baltimore: Johns Hopkins, 1959.

Chapanis, A., Garner, W. R., and Morgan, C. T. *Applied experimental psychology, human factors in engineering design.* New York: Wiley, 1949.

Christian, R. W. Status and future of industrial relations. *Factory,* 1963, **121,** 80-83.

Coakley, J. D. *Human influence on the product of automatic machines.* New York: The Psychological Corporation. Research Report, 1942.

Cole, D. L. *The quest for industrial peace.* New York: McGraw-Hill, 1963.

Committee on Undersea Warfare. *A survey report of human factors in undersea warfare.* Washington, D.C.: National Research Council, 1949.

Conway, J. T. *Ideological obsolescence in collective bargaining.* Berkeley, Calif.: Institute of Industrial Relations, University of California Press, 1963.

Cook, Alice H. *Union democracy: practice and ideal, an analysis of four large local unions.* Ithaca, N.Y.: Cornell Studies in Industrial and Labor Relations, **60**, 1963.

Cook, D. W. Psychology challenges in industry. *Personnel Series No. 107.* New York: American Management Association, 1947.

Covner, B. J. Course outlines and lesson plans. In National Defense Research Committee, *Human factors in military efficiency training and equipment.* Washington, D.C., 1946. Summary Technical Report, **2**.

Crawford, M. P. Concepts of training. In Gagne, R. M. (Ed.), *Psychological principles in system development.* New York: Holt, Rinehart and Winston, 1962. Ch. 9.

Crook, G. H., and Heintein, M. *The older worker in industry.* Berkeley, Calif.: Univ. of Calif. Institute of Industrial Relations, 1958.

Crowder, N. A. Automatic tutoring by means of intrinsic programing. In Galanter, E. (Ed.), *Automated teaching: the state of the art.* New York: Wiley, 1959.

Cureton, E. E. Validity, reliability, and baloney. *Educ. psychol. Measmt.,* 1950, **10**, 94-96.

Dent, J. K., and DeLaPaz, R. Union security and management attitudes. *Pers. Psychol.,* 1961, **14**, 167-181.

Derber, M., Chalmers, W. E., and Stagner, R. The labor contract: provision and practice. *Personnel,* 1958, **34**, 19-30.

Derber, M., Chalmers, W. E., Stagner, R., and Edelman, M. *The local union-management relationship.* Urbana, Ill.: Institute of Labor and Industrial Relations, University of Illinois, 1960.

Deterline, W. A. *An introduction to programed instruction.* Englewood Cliffs, N.J.: Prentice-Hall, 1962.

Dickson, W. J. Understanding and training employees. *Personnel Series No. 35,* American Management Association, 1936. Pp. 4-18.

Division 14, American Psychological Association. *The psychologist in industry.* New York: Research Institute of America, 1959.

Dunnette, M. D. A note on *the* criterion. *J. appl. Psychol.*, 1963, **47**, 251-254(a).

Dunnette, M. D. A modified model for test validation and selection research. *J. appl. Psychol.*, 1963, **47**, 317-323(b).

Dunnette, M. D. Personnel Management. *Annual Review of Psychology*, 1962, **13**, 285-314.

Dunnette, M. D., and England, G. W. A checklist for differentiating engineering jobs. *Personnel Psychol.*, 1957, **10**, 191-198.

Dunnette, M. D., and Kirchner, W. K. A checklist for differentiating different kinds of sales jobs. *Personnel Psychol.*, 1959, **12**, 421-429.

Dunnette, M. D., and Kirchner, W. K. Validities, vectors and verities. *J. appl. Psychol.*, 1962, **46**, 296-299.

Edgerton, H. A. *Should theory precede or follow "how to do it" phase of training?* Contract Nonr 1722(00). New York: Richardson, Bellows and Henry Co., 1956.

Edgerton, H. A. *The relationship of method of instruction to trainee aptitude pattern.* Contract Nonr 2313(00). New York: Richardson, Bellows and Henry Co., 1958.

Edwards, A. L. *Techniques of attitude scale construction.* New York: Appleton-Century-Crofts, 1957.

Feinberg, M. R. Introduction to a symposium on implications of psychology in labor-management relations. *Pers. Psychol.*, 1961, **14**, 239-241.

Fenton, J. M. *In your opinion.* Boston: Little, Brown, 1960.

Fine, S. A. Matching job requirements and worker qualifications. *Personnel*, 1958, **34**, 52-58.

Fine, S. A., and Heinz, C. A. The estimates of worker trait requirements for 4000 jobs. *Person. guid. J.*, 1957, **36**, 168-174.

Fitts, P. M., and Jones, R. E. *Psychological aspects of instrument display: analysis of 270 "pilot error" experiences in reading and interpreting aircraft instruments.* Report No. TSEAA-694-12A. USAF Air Matériel Command, Aero Medical Laboratory, 1947.

Fitts, P. M., and Jones, R. E. Analysis of factors contributing to 460 "pilot error" experiences in operating aircraft controls. In Sinaiko, H. W. (Ed.), *Selected papers on human factors in the design and use of control systems,* New York: Dover, 1961.

Flanagan, J. C. The critical incident technique. *Psychol. Bull.*, 1954, **51**, 327-358.

Fleishman, E. A. The description and prediction of perceptual-motor skill learning. In Glaser, R., *Training research and education.* Pittsburgh: The University of Pittsburgh Press, 1962.

Fleishman, E. A., and Fruchter, B. Factor structure and predictability of successive stages of learning Morse code. *J. appl. Psychol.,* 1960, 44, 97-101.

Fleishman, E. A., and Harris, E. P. Patterns of leadership behavior related to employee grievances and turnover. *Pers. Psychol.,* 1962, 15, 43-56.

Fraser, R. The incidence of neurosis among factory workers. London: H. M. Stationery Office, Ind. Health Res. Board, No. 90, 1947.

Freeman, G. L. A high-level interest values preference test for counseling pre-retirants. *J. Psychol.,* 1958, 46, 121-139.

Gagne, R. M. (Ed.) *Psychological principles in system development.* New York: Holt, Rinehart, and Winston, 1962.

Gellerman, S. W. Personnel testing: what the critics overlook. *Personnel,* 1963, 40, 18-26 (a).

Gellerman, S. W. *Motivation and productivity.* New York: American Management Association, 1963 (b).

Ghiselli, E. E. Dimensional problems of criteria. *J. appl. Psychol.,* 1956, 40, 1-4.

Ghiselli, E. E., and Haire, M. The validation of selection tests in the light of the dynamic character of criteria. *Personnel Psychol.,* 1960, 13, 225-231.

Glanzer, M. Curiosity, exploratory drive, and stimulus satiation. *Psychol. Bull.,* 1958, 55, 302-315.

Glaser, R. Training in industry. In Gilmer, V. von H. (Ed.), *Industrial Psychology.* New York: McGraw-Hill, 1961.

Glennon, J. R., Owens, W. A., Smith, W. J., and Albright, L. E. New dimension in morale. *Harv. Bus. Rev.,* 1960, 38, 106-107.

Gouldner, A. W. Organizational analysis. In Merton, R. K., Broov, L., and Cottrell, L. S. (Eds.), *Sociology today.* New York: Basic Books, 1959.

Grether, W. F. *Analysis of types of errors in reading of the conventional three pointer altimeter.* Report No. MCREXD-694-14A. USAF Air Matériel Command, Aero Medical Laboratory, 1948.

Guest, R. H. *Organizational change: the effect of successful leadership.* Homewood, Ill.: Dorsey and Richard D. Irwin, 1962.

Hahn, M. E., and MacLean, M. S. *Counseling psychology* (2nd ed.). New York: McGraw-Hill, 1955.

Haire, M. Biological models and empirical histories of the growth of organizations. In Haire, M. (Ed.), *Modern organization theory.* New York: Wiley, 1959.

Haire, M. (Ed.) *Modern organization theory.* New York: Wiley, 1959.

Haire, M. Psychology and the study of business: joint behavioral sciences. In Dahl, R. A., Haire, M., and Lazarsfeld, P. F., *Social science research on business: product and potential.* New York: Columbia, 1959.

Haire, M. The concept of power and the concept of man. In *Social science approaches to business behavior.* Homewood, Ill.: Dorsey, 1962. Pp. 163-183.

Harbison, F. H., and Coleman, J. R. *Goals and strategy in collective bargaining.* New York: Harper & Row, 1951.

Heller, F. A. Studies in organization: the effect of structure on industrial relations. *J. indust. Relat.* (Australia), 1960, **2**, 1-19.

Hemphill, J. K. *Dimensions of executive positions: a study of the basic characteristics of the positions of ninety-three business executives.* Bureau of Business Research Monograph No. 98. Columbus, Ohio: Ohio State, 1960.

Herzberg, F., Mausner, B., and Snyderman, B. *The motivation to work* (2nd ed.). New York: Wiley, 1959.

Hollingworth, H. L. *Vocational psychology and character analysis.* New York: Appleton-Century-Crofts, 1929. Pp. 115-119.

Hoslett, S. D. Listening to the troubled or dissatisfied employee. *Personnel,* 1945, **22**, 52-57.

Hughes, J. L. *Programed instruction for school and industry.* Chicago: Science Research Associates, 1962.

International Milling Co. v. Robin Hood Popcorn Co. 110 U.S.P.Q. 368 (Comm'r. Pats. 1950).

Jackson, J. M. The organization and its communications problem. *Adv. Mgt.,* 1959, **24**, 17-20.

Jacobs, P. *The state of the unions.* New York: Athenaeum, 1963.

Kasl, S., and French, J. R. P., Jr. The effects of occupational status on physical and mental health. *J. social Issues,* 1962, **18**, 67-89.

Katzell, R. Contrasting systems of work organization. *Amer. Psychol.,* 1962, **17**, 102-108.

Katzell, R. A. Psychologists in industry. In Webb, W. B. (Ed.), *The professions of psychology.* New York: Holt, Rinehart and Winston, 1962. Pp. 180-211.

Kirchner, W. K., and Dunnette, M. D. Identifying the critical factors in successful salesmanship. *Personnel,* 1957, **34**, 54-59.

Kirkpatrick, D. L. Techniques for evaluating training programs: Part 1, Reaction; Part 2, Learning. *J. Amer. Soc. Training Directors,* 1959, **13**.

Kirkpatrick, D. L. Techniques for evaluating training programs: Part 3, Behavior; Part 4, Results. *J. Amer. Soc. Training Directors,* 1960, **14**.

Kleitman, N. The sleep-wakefulness cycle of submarine personnel. In Committee on Undersea Warfare, *A survey report of human factors in undersea warfare*, Washington, D.C.: National Research Council, 1949.

Kornhauser, A. Observations on the psychological study of labor-management relations. *Pers. Psychol.*, 1961, 14, 241-249.

Kornhauser, A., Dubin, R., and Ross, A. M. (Eds.) *Industrial conflict*. New York: McGraw-Hill, 1954.

Krug, R. E. Personnel selection. In Gilmer, B. von H., *Industrial psychology*. New York: McGraw-Hill, 1961. Ch. 6.

Landsberger, H. A. The behavior and personality of the labor mediator: the parties' perception of mediator behavior. *Pers. Psychol.*, 1960, 13, 329-347.

Landsberger, H. A. *Hawthorne revisited, management and the worker, its critics and developments in human relations in industry*. Ithaca, N.Y.: New York State School of Industrial and Labor Relations, 1958.

Laurent, H. *Early identification of management potential*. Social Science Research Report. New York: Standard Oil Co. (N.J.), 1961.

Laurent, H. *The identification of management potential*. Paper delivered at American Psychological Assn. Annual Convention, St. Louis, Mo., 1962.

Leavitt, H. J. *Managerial psychology*. Chicago: The University of Chicago Press, 1958.

Leavitt, H. J. *Toward organizational psychology*. For Walter V. Bingham Day, March 23, 1961. Carnegie Institute of Technology Graduate School of Industrial Administration. 1961.

Leavitt, H. J. Unhuman organization. *Harv. Bus. Rev.*, 1962, 40, 90-98.

Leavitt, H. J., and Bass, B. M. Organizational psychology. *Annual Review of Psychology*, 1964, 15, 371-398.

Levenstein, A. The psychologist joins the labor conflict. *Pers. Psychol.*, 1961, 14, 250-258.

Likert, R. A motivational approach to a modified theory of organization and management. In Haire, M. (Ed.), *Modern organization theory*. New York: Wiley, 1959.

Likert, R. *New patterns of management*. New York: McGraw-Hill, 1961.

Likert, R. A. A technique for the measurement of attitudes. *Arch. Psychol.*, 1932, No. 140.

Link, H. C. *Employment psychology*. New York: Macmillan, 1919.

Lucas, D. B., and Britt, S. H. *Measuring advertising effectiveness*. New York: McGraw-Hill, 1963.

Lumsdaine, A. A., and Glaser, R. (Eds.) *Teaching machines and pro-*

gramed learning: a source book. Washington, D.C.: National Education Association, 1960.

MacKinney, A. C. Progressive levels in the evaluation of training programs. *Personnel,* 1957, **34**, 72-77.

McClelland, D. C. *The achieving society.* Princeton, N.J.: Van Nostrand, 1961.

McClelland, D. C., Atkinson, J. W., Clark, R. A., and Lowell, E. L. *The achievement motive.* New York: Appleton-Century-Crofts, 1953.

McCormick, E. J. *Human engineering* (2nd ed.). New York: McGraw-Hill, 1964.

McFarland, D. E. Dilemma of the industrial relations director. *Harv. Bus. Rev.,* 1954, **32**, 123-132.

McFarland, R. A. *Human factors in air transportation.* New York: McGraw-Hill, 1953.

McGehee, W., and Thayer, P. W. *Training in business and industry.* New York: Wiley, 1961.

McGregor, D. *The human side of enterprise.* New York: McGraw-Hill, 1960.

McKersie, R. B., and Brown, M. Nonprofessional hospital workers and a union organizing drive. *Quart. J. Econ.,* 1963, **77**, 372-404.

McKinney, F. *Psychology of personal adjustment.* New York: Wiley, 1960.

McLean, A. A., and Taylor, G. C. *Mental health in industry.* New York: McGraw-Hill, 1958.

McMurray, R. N. Mental illness in industry. *Harv. Bus. Rev.,* 1959, **37**, 79-86.

McMurray, R. N. War and peace in labor relations. *Harv. Bus. Rev.,* 1955, **33**, 48-60.

Maier, N. R. F., and Hoffman, L. R. Organization and creative problem solving. *J. appl. Psychol.,* 1961, **45**, 277-280.

Maier, N. R. F., and Hoffman, L. R. Seniority in work groups: a right or an honor? *J. appl. Psychol.,* 1963, **47**, 173-176.

March, J. G., and Simon, H. A. *Organizations.* New York: Wiley, 1958.

Marriott, R. Size of working group and output. *Occup. Psychol.,* 1949, **23**, 47-57.

Mayo, E. *The social problems of an industrial civilization.* Boston: Harvard Business School, 1945.

Mechanic, D. Sources of power of lower participants in complex organizations. *Admin. Science Quart.,* 1962, **7**, 349-364.

Miller, F. G., and Remmers, H. H. Studies in industrial empathy: II.

Management's attitudes toward industrial supervision and their estimates of labor attitudes. *Pers. Psychol.,* 1950, **3**, 33-40.

Miller, R. B. Analysis and specification of behavior for training. In Glaser, R. (Ed.), *Training research and education.* Pittsburgh: The University of Pittsburgh Press, 1962. Ch. 2.

Morgan, C. T. *Introduction to psychology* (2nd ed.). New York: McGraw-Hill, 1961.

Morgan, C. T., Cook, J. S. III, Chapanis, A., and Lund, M. W. (Eds.) *Human engineering guide to equipment design.* New York: McGraw-Hill, 1963.

Muench, G. A. A clinical psychologist's treatment of labor-management conflicts. *Pers. Psychol.,* 1960, **13**, 165-172.

Murphy, J. R., and Goldberg, I. A. Strategies for using programmed instruction. *Harv. Bus. Rev.,* 1964, **42**, 115-132.

Myers, M. S. Who are your motivated workers? *Harv. Bus. Rev.,* 1964, **42**, 73-88.

Nagle, B. F. Criterion development. *Personnel Psychol.,* 1953, **6**, 271-289.

Nealey, S. M. Determining worker preferences among employee benefit programs. *J. appl. Psychol.,* 1964, **48**, 7-12.

Newton, R. *An investigation of certain personality factors in relation to industrial absenteeism.* Unpublished thesis, Pennsylvania State University, 1950.

Ohmann, O. A. Executive appraisal and counseling. *Mich. Bus. Rev.,* 1957, **9**, 18-25.

Parker, G. M. The union role in decision-making in small plants. *Labor Law Journ.,* 1963, **14**, 532-541.

Parten, M. *Surveys, polls, and samples.* New York: Harper & Row, 1950.

Payne, S. L. *The art of asking questions.* Princeton, N.J.: Princeton, 1951.

Peters, E. *Strategy and tactics in labor negotiations.* New London, Conn.: National Foremen's Institute, 1955.

Peterson, Florence. *American labor unions: what they are and how they work* (2nd rev. ed.). New York: Harper & Row, 1964.

Planty, E. G., McCord, W. S., and Efferson, C. A. *Training employees and managers.* New York: Ronald, 1948.

Plummer, N., and Hinkle, L. Life stress and industrial absenteeism; concentration of illness and absenteeism in one segment of a working population: New York Telephone Company. *Indust. Med.,* 1952, **22**, 363-375.

Porter, L. W. Job attitudes in management: III. Perceived deficiencies in need fulfillment as a function of line versus staff type of job. *J. appl. Psychol.*, 1963, **47**, 267-275 (a).

Porter, L. W. Job attitudes in management: IV. Perceived deficiencies in need fulfillment as a function of size of company. *J. appl. Psychol.*, 1963, **47**, 386-387 (b).

Porter, L. W. A study of perceived need satisfactions in bottom and middle management jobs. *J. appl. Psychol.*, 1961, **45**, 1-10.

Porter, L. W., and Lawler, E. E. III. The effects of "tall" vs. "flat" organization structures on managerial job satisfactions. *Personnel Psychol.*, 1964, **17**, 135-148.

Purcell, T. V. Dual allegiance to company and union-packinghouse workers. A Swift-UPWA study in a crisis situation, 1949-1952. *Pers. Psychol.*, 1954, **7**, 48-58.

Purcell, T. V. S. J. *The worker speaks his mind on company and union.* Cambridge, Mass.: Harvard, 1953.

Remmers, Lois J., and Remmers, H. H. Studies in industrial empathy: I. Labor leaders' attitudes toward industrial supervision and their estimate of management's attitudes. *Pers. Psychol.*, 1949, **2**, 427-436.

Rosen, H., and Rosen, R. A. H. Personality variables and role in a union business agent group. *J. appl. Psychol.*, 1957, **41**, 131-136.

Rosen, R. A. H., and Rosen, H. A suggested modification in job satisfaction surveys, *Pers. Psychol.*, 1955, **8**, 303-314.

Runan, W. W. Work group attributes and grievance activity. *J. appl. Psychol.*, 1963, **47**, 38-41.

Sadler, L. E. The counseling psychologist in business and industry. *Voc. Guid. Quart.*, 1960, **8**, 123-125.

Sayles, L. R. *Behavior of industrial work groups.* New York: Wiley, 1958.

Schachter, S. *The psychology of affiliation.* Stanford, Calif.: Stanford, 1959.

Schulzinger, M. S. *The accident syndrome.* Springfield, Ill.: Chas. C. Thomas, 1956.

Seidman, J., London, J., Karsh, B., and Tagliacozzo, Daisy L. *The worker views his union.* Chicago: The University of Chicago Press, 1958.

Sells, S. B., and Berry, C. A. (Eds.) *Human factors in jet and space travel: a medical-psychological analysis.* New York: Ronald, 1961.

Selltiz, C., Johoda, M., Deutsch, M., and Cook, S. W. *Research methods in social relations, revised.* New York: Holt, Rinehart and Winston, 1961.

Shackel, B. Ergonomics in the design of a large digital computer console. *Ergonomics*, 1962, **5**, 229-241.

Shannon, R. E., and Burgett, R. R. *Characteristics of the accident prone.* AC Sparkplug Personnel Research Report #45, 1960.

Shannon, T. E., and Burgett, R. R. *Characteristics of the female frequent insurance claimant.* AC Sparkplug Personnel Research Report #46, 1959.

Shepard, H. A. The psychologist's role in union-management relations. *Pers. Psychol.*, 1961, **14**, 270-278.

Shipley, T. E., Jr., and Veroff, J. A projective measure of need for affiliation. *J. exper. Psychol.*, 1952, **43**, 349-356.

Sinaiko, H. W. (Ed.) *Selected papers on human factors in the design and use of control systems.* New York: Dover, 1961.

Sinaiko, H. W., and Buckley, E. P. Human factors in the design of systems. In Sinaiko, H. W. (Ed.), *Selected papers on human factors in the design and use of control systems.* New York: Dover, 1961. Ch. 1.

Sinha, C., and Sarma, K. C. Union attitude and job satisfaction in Indian Workers. *J. appl. Psychol.*, 1962, **40**, 247-251.

Skinner, B. F. *Science and human behavior.* New York: Macmillan, 1953.

Skinner, B. F. The science of learning and the art of teaching. *Harv. Educ. Rev.*, 1954, **24**, 86-97.

Skinner, B. F. Teaching machines. *Science*, 1958, **128**, No. 3330. Pp. 969-977.

Speroff, B. J. Group psychotherapy in labor relations: a case study. *Pers. Journ.*, 1960, **39**, 14-17.

Speroff, B. J. Job satisfaction study of two small unorganized plants. *J. appl. Psychol.*, 1959, **43**, 315.

Stagner, R. A note on communist attitudes and job satisfaction. *Pers. Psychol.*, 1958, **11**, 509-513.

Stagner, R. Psychological aspects of industrial conflict: I. Perception. *Pers. Psychol.*, 1948, **1**, 131-143.

Stagner, R. Psychological aspects of industrial conflict: II. Motivation. *Pers. Psychol.*, 1950, **3**, 1-15.

Stagner, R. The psychologist's function in union-management relations. *Pers. Adminis.*, 1963, **26**, 24-29.

Stagner, R. *The psychology of industrial conflict.* New York: Wiley, 1956.

Stagner, R., Chalmers, W. E., and Derber, M. Guttman-type scales for union and management attitudes toward each other. *J. appl. Psychol.*, 1958, **42**, 293-300.

Stone, C. H., and Kendall, W. E. *Effective personnel selection procedures*. Englewood Cliffs, N.J.: Prentice-Hall, 1956.

Strong, E. K., Jr. *Vocational interests of men and women*. Stanford, Calif.: Stanford, 1943.

Strong, E. K., Jr. *Vocational interests 18 years after college*. Minneapolis: The University of Minnesota Press, 1955.

Stryker, P. How to retire executives. *Fortune*, 1952, 45, 110 ff.

Super, D. C., and Crites, J. O. *Appraising vocational fitness*. New York: Harper & Row, 1962.

Terrien, F. W., and Mills, D. L. The effect of changing size upon the internal structure of organizations. *Amer. Sociol. Rev.*, 1955, 20, 11-13.

Thompson, A. S., and Davis, J. A. What workers mean by security. *Pers. Psychol.*, 1956, 9, 229-241.

Thompson, K. M. Human relations in collective bargaining. *Harv. Bus. Rev.*, 1953, 31, 116-126.

Thorndike, R. L. *Personnel selection: test and measurement techniques*. New York: Wiley, 1949.

Thorndike, R. L., Hagen, E. P., Orr, D. B., and Rosner, B. *An empirical approach to the determination of air force job families*. AFPTRC-TR-57-5, Air Research and Development Command, Lackland Air Force Base, Texas, 1957.

Thorne, F. C. Directive counseling and psychotherapy. *Amer. Psychol.*, 1948, 3, 160-165.

Thurstone, L. L., and Chave, E. J. *The measurement of attitude*. Chicago: The University of Chicago Press, 1929.

Tiffin, J., and Walsh, F. X. Readability of union-management agreements. *Pers. Psychol.*, 1951, 4, 327-337.

Tilton, J. W. The measurement of overlapping. *J. educ. Psychol.*, 1937, 28, 656-662.

Torgerson, W. S. *Theory and methods of scaling*. New York: Wiley, 1958.

Trist, E. L., and Bamforth, K. W. Some social and psychological consequences of the longwall method of coal-getting. *Human Relations*, 1951, 4, 3-38.

Tupes, E. C., and Christal, R. E. *Recurrent personality factors based on trait ratings*. Tech. Report ASD-TR—61-97. Personnel Laboratory, United States Air Force, Lackland Air Force Base, 1961.

Ways, M. Labor unions are worth the price. *Fortune*, 1963, 67, 108-113 ff.

Weber, A. R. The craft-industrial issue revisited: a study of union government. *Indust. and Labor Relat. Rev.*, 1963, 16, 381-404.

Weiss, D. J., Dawis, R. V., England, G. W., and Lofquist, L. H. *The measurement of vocational needs.* Minnesota Studies in Vocational Rehabilitation, Bulletin 39. Minneapolis: Minnesota Center for Vocational Rehabilitation, 1964.

Weschler, I. R. The personal factor in labor mediation. *Pers. Psychol.,* 1950, **3,** 113-143.

Wherry, R. J. Criteria and validity. In Fryer, D. H., and Henry, E. R., *Handbook of applied psychology,* Vol. 1. New York: Holt, Rinehart and Winston, 1950. Ch. 4, section 27.

White, R. W. Motivation reconsidered: the concept of competence. *Psychol. Rev.,* 1959, **66,** 297-333.

Wilson, J. W. Toward better use of psychological testing. *Personnel,* 1962, **39,** 55-62.

Woodson, W. E. *Human engineering guide for equipment designers.* Berkeley: University of California Press, 1956.

Woodward, J. Management and technology. Problems of progress in industry, No. 3. Dept. of Scientific and Technical Research. Her Majesty's Stationery Office, 1958.

Worthy, J. C. Organizational Structure and Employee Morale. *Amer. Sociol Rev.,* 1950, **15,** 169-179.

Wulfeck, J. W., and Zeitlin, L. R. Human capabilities and limitations. In Gagne, R. M. (Ed.), *Psychological principles in system development.* New York: Holt, Rinehart and Winston, 1962.

INDEX

257